A Century
Cricket Quotations

Also by David Hopps
and published by Robson Books

Free As A Bird:
The Life and Times of Harold 'Dickie' Bird

We're Right Behind You, Captain!

A Century of Cricket Quotations

David Hopps

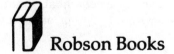 Robson Books

This edition published in Great Britain in 2000 by Robson
Books, 10 Blenheim Court, Brewery Road, London N7 9NT

First published in 1998 by Robson Books Ltd.

A member of the Chrysalis Group plc

British Library Cataloguing in Publication Data
A catalogue record for this title is available from the British
Library

ISBN 1 86105 346 0

Printed by Butler & Tanner Ltd, Frome, Somerset.

Contents

Foreword

By Frank Keating

Other than Sugar Ray Cain threatening: 'I'll moider de bum' before history's first-ever title defence, against Ted Kid Abel — or Francis Drake muttering something similar in the plural as the Spanish were sighted off Plymouth Hoe — I suppose the first enduring sporting quotation was Charles Kortright's in June 1898 at Leyton.

Playing for Essex against Gloucestershire, in two successive and snorting deliveries, the distinctly nippy fast bowler first had WG Grace transparently lbw, then palpably caught at the wicket. Both times the timorous umpire, under the batsman's famously beady stare, gave our bearded wonder the benefit of the doubt. Third ball, Kortright's vindictive yorker savagely spreadeagled both the Doc's middle and off stumps, and as the great batsman unbelievingly surveyed the wreckage of his castle, Korty, following through down the pitch, was unable to resist the immortal:

Surely you're not going, Doctor — why, there's one stump still standing?

That quotation had it all; it encapsulates the character of both great cricketers, and it sets them in their period and place. That's the knack in collecting them.

Sporting quotations come in all shapes and sizes. Some blaze across the sky, pointed and pithy for only a week or a day, but for collectors even then they have admirably served their purpose. Others stand the, test of time and, to be sure, can even grow in stature. In the same year as Kortright's dismissive sarcasm — 'On yer way, Doc' — exactly a century ago, so Arthur Shrewsbury explained his batting philosophy to Derbyshire's Levi Wright at Trent Bridge:

My experience, Levi, is that during a summer, the decisions given in your favour when you ought to be out are just about exactly balanced by those given against you when you ought to be in, so that, all in all, personally I don't bother me head about umpires' decisions, I just do what they suggest I should.

If only some English Test batsmen of precisely a hundred summers later could live by Arthur's wised-up tenets. '*Darrell, you're messing around with my career*,' said the surly Master Ramprakash to umpire Hair at Lord's in 1998 when the Australian official sent him on his way

I hope David Hopps has been able to include that latecomer as Stop Press to this sumptuous collection. If anything sums up the intensity and selfishness of a batsman it is those seven little words. Enough said. Now if Ramprakash had said to Hair, '*Darrell, you're messing with my team's chances of victory*' we'd have known Master R to be a very different kettle of calibre.

As you are about to find out, dear reader, here is the definitive bedside book, an indipper in the Curtly class — quick, pithy, pertinent; sometimes spot-on and inch-perfect accurate, sometimes overpitched and ravishingly OTT.

The 'Sporting Quotation' is a newish phenomenon. When Bobby Locke won the Open golf championship at St Andrews in 1957 he was uniquely brought into the press tent afterwards to 'talk them through it'. At which the *Daily Telegraph*'s doyen, Leonard Crawley, led out his confreres from *The Times* and *Manchester Guardian*, Messrs Ryde and Ward-Thomas — all three in a blazing huff — because, scoffed Crawley, 'our readers want to know what WE think of Locke's winning round, not what the damn fellow thinks of it himself'

It was about a dozen years later that (I like to claim after a convivial and bibulous late-night session) I was the British founder of what has become, in such diligent collectors of inspired trivia as Hopps, Phil Shaw, and their sometime and lamented collaborator, good Peter Ball, a thriving cottage industry.

In the 1960s, in *The Observer* each Sunday there were printed two or three 'Quotes of the Week', that is, passing one-liner spouts of guff by some politician or other. At the time, between stints for The Guardian, I was working for ITV and had occasion regularly to travel to the United States. One time, killing time, I came across a slim list of snippety-quotations from Hollywood figures down the century — from De Mille to Bogart. So I began, for fun, a similar collection of quips and quotes, readings and writings and sound-bites from the world of sport. At Christmas 1970, John Samuel printed a page of them in The Guardian — and by 1978 Andre Deutsch, bless them, had printed 1,000 or more in a book, *Caught By Keating*.

Mining these gems, truffling for these trouv6s, was richly reward-ing in those early days. You couldn't listen to a footer match on the radio without pencil and a back of an envelope at hand to log com-mentators' slips of the tongue – 'The audience is literally electrified as well as literally glued to their seats' (whispering Ted Lowe at snooker) remains just about my favourite – or read something in the dentist's waiting-room without surreptitiously ripping out the cru-cial page. I can still remember that glorious frisson I had when browsing through a dog-eared Church Times at a girl-friend's com-mon-room in Oxford and came across:

SITS. VAC: Old fashioned vicar (Thactarian) seeks colleague; fine church; good musical tradition. Parish residential & farm-ing. Good golf handicap an asset but not essential. Left-handed fast bowler preferred. Apply Box HV521.

Or when I snipped out this 'Letter to the Editor' from The Guardian after a Test match at The Oval:

Dear Sir, on Friday I watched JM Brearley very carefully as he directed his fieldsmen. He then looked up at the sun and made a gesture which seemed to indicate that it should move a little squarer. Who is this man? Yours sincerely, SA Nicholas, Longlevens, Glos.

Classic stuff. I could go on and on. And so YOU can — in the com-pany of Hopps's treasured trove. Hooray for Hoppsy He loves his cricket with a passion; he loves its goodness, and its infinite humours. Enjoy.

Frank Keating is a sportswriter on *The Guardian*.

Dedication

I was feeling my way as cricket correspondent of the *Yorkshire Post*, in the mid-1980s, when Peter Ball, then a football and cricket writer on *The Times*, first offered me the opportunity to co-edit a volume of cricket quotations. It was a chaotic and inspirational period. Books were skimmed, magazines searched, newspapers trawled. When it came to ordering the quotes into some sort of order, the Ball kitchen table was lost under a confused sea of glued-up paper. Fuelled by considerable quantities of red wine, many conversations idled into the early hours before the work was finally completed. Peter died of leukaema, aged 54. Before his illness, we had wondered about researching a new and more ambitious book of cricket quotes, one designed to mark the end of the century. I suppose, to a large extent, this is that book. At least, I hope it is. It is dedicated to Peter Ball.

Acknowledgements

Recognition for the structure of this book goes largely to Tom Jordan, who had the imagination and wit to organize more than 2,000 quotes into a coherent whole. Without his involvement, I would have still been labouring now. Tom gained an MA in English at Leeds University, and is currently working at Waterstones book-shop in Piccadilly, which should guarantee one good display! He is also a skilful club cricketer, not that he ever proved as much during a brief foray a few seasons ago, for my own village club, Thorner Mexborough, in the Wetherby & District League.

Thanks are also due to Frank Keating for supplying the Foreword. Frank is a sportswriter I admired long before he joined *The Guardian*. He writes with rare humanity, and is the self-styled father of the sports quoted world. And to Mike Averis, sports editor of *The Guardian*, for looking benignly upon the days when this book threatened to take over my life.

David Hopps
Wetherby,
West Yorkshire.

April, 2000

1

England,
My England

A natural mistimer of the ball.

Michael Atherton, as described by **Angus Fraser**, his England team-mate (quoted by Atherton himself in the *Sunday Telegraph*, 1998.

One of the few men capable of looking more dishevelled at the start of a six-hour century than at the end of it.

Martin Johnson, *Daily Telegraph*, celebrating Michael Atherton's century at Edgbaston against South Africa, in his first Test innings after conceding the England captaincy, 1998.

An earnest young man who probably believes what he reads in *The Guardian*.

Michael Atherton as seen by **Richard Littlejohn**, *Daily Mail*, 1996. Littlejohn later withdrew the accusation as a 'monstrous slur' after meeting Atherton in a London restaurant.

He's a hard beggar and he has a strong mind.

Raymond Illingworth, 1994, upon Michael Atherton.

He's tough. Tougher than I thought at first. He's stubborn, but that's no crime – so am I. I think we have more in common than perhaps either of us realized in the beginning.

Raymond Illingworth's farewell summary on Michael Atherton, in the postscript of *One-Man Committee*, 1997.

Concentration is sometimes mistaken for grumpiness.

Michael Atherton, concentrating hard, 1997.

My unicycle has broken down and I've left my red nose in the box.

Ally Brown, Surrey, after his century in a Texaco Trophy international against India. On his début four days earlier, he had been compared by Simon Wilde in *The Times* to Coco the Clown, 1996.

It's not hard to look at the way my life has developed and realize that there are things I should not have done.

Dominic Cork, Derbyshire and England, regretting, 1997.

A man more than worthy of filling my boots.

Ian Botham, on Dominic Cork, 1994.

He's a show pony. He's a prima donna. Cork may have talent but he does have an attitude problem. If you think I was bad, my God, he's three times worse.

Geoff Boycott, on Dominic Cork, 1997.

The man has not played cricket for a long time. He has no idea what sort of a person I am.

Cork's reaction, 1997.

Now that he's Derbyshire captain, he'll have to behave more like an adult than an over-tired kid.

Devon Malcolm, Dominic Cork's former Derbyshire and England team-mate, in *You Guys Are History*, 1998.

What Dominic really needed was a good housemaster.

Guy Willatt, one of Cork's predecessors as Derbyshire captain, and a former head teacher at Pocklington School. (Quoted by Michael Henderson in *The Times*, 1998.)

His most endearing quality is his patent and untrammelled joy in the game.

Frances Edmonds on Phillip DeFreitas, *Cricket XXXX Cricket*, 1987.

Maybe I should smile a bit more and do the old high fives and be Mr Bouncy; raise the profile and have a nice spin-off contract for wearing something or other. But that's not me. I look like I do on the field because what I do is knackering.

Angus Fraser, Middlesex and England, 1995.

Eeyore without the joie de vivre.

Mike Selvey on Angus Fraser, *Wisden*, 1996.

Fraser's approach to the wicket currently resembles someone who has his braces caught in the sightscreen.

Martin Johnson, *The Independent*, on one of Angus Fraser's fatigued days.

Though essentially good-natured, he had that vital weapon in the fast bowler's armoury, grumpiness.

Simon Hughes, on Angus Fraser, in *A Lot of Hard Yakka*, 1997.

I don't suppose I can call you a lucky bleeder when you've got 347.

Angus Fraser, after nearly finding the edge during Brian Lara's world-record innings of 375 in Antigua, 1994.

Fraser reminds me of my favourite things, aeroplanes. His bowling is like shooting down F-16s with sling shots. Even if they hit, no damage would be done. Like an old horse, he should be put out to pasture.

Colin Croft, former West Indies fast bowler, ridiculing Angus Fraser after England's defeat in the Guyana Test, 1994.

I'm just pleased to have bowled as well as Colin Croft did every day of his life.

Angus Fraser's response after leading England to victory in Barbados, the first at the Kensington Oval by a touring side for more than 60 years, 1994.

He's done very well has doo-da. But then if you look at any cricketer these days he just cracks up.

Brian Close, Yorkshire cricket chairman, upon Darren Gough's premature return from the Ashes tour because of injury, 1995.

He's a bigger star than Brian Lara.

Chris Hassell, Yorkshire's chief executive, after Darren Gough's successful 1994/5 Ashes tour. (It was quite a claim – Lara had broken both Test and first-class batting records with scores of 375 and 501 in the past year.)

The lad wi' nowt taken out.

If someone wore a chocolate bar on his head, Goughie would follow suit.

Steve Oldham, Yorkshire's director of cricket (as related by the former Yorkshire captain, Phil Carrick), capturing Darren Gough's appetite for gimmicks and crazes, 1993.

When I'm batting, I like to pretend I'm a West Indian.

Darren Gough, after an inspirational half-century in the Sydney Test, 1995.

Be natural, be yourself.

Fax message from Australia's **Shane Warne** which helped Darren Gough rediscover his form, 1997.

I've just spent a month working on training videos for the English Cricket Board. I'm pretty sure that they wouldn't have used me if they were worried about my action.

Darren Gough, responding to suggestions by his fellow Yorkshireman, Fred Trueman, that his action was suspect, 1997.

Before each World Cup match, we'd gather for a team meeting and I'd sit there, thinking, 'Please don't pick me, they're too quick for me.'

Graeme Hick, on fear of fast bowling, as Zimbabwe's junior pro in his first World Cup. (From *My Early Life*, 1991.)

I hope people aren't expecting too much from me. It's a big jump up to Test cricket.

Graeme Hick, with 57 first-class centuries behind him, after scoring four runs in his first Test, against the West Indies, 1991.

Hick is just a flat-track bully.

John Bracewell, former New Zealand spinner, dismissing the talent of Graeme Hick during England's 1991/2 tour.

At times he looks as though he has an artificial brain, slightly out of tune with his body.

Christopher Martin-Jenkins, *Daily Telegraph*, during a leaden-footed Hick innings on tour of West Indies, 1994.

They can't just let you walk by, a normal person with two arms and two legs. They have to pass comment.

Graeme Hick, on the price of fame, 1995.

What's money got to do with it? Why can't people just sit there and enjoy the spectacle in front of them? Why do they have to spoil it for everyone else?

Graeme Hick, still on the price of fame, 1995.

Mike said that he'd read Wilbur Smith when he was eight. That's why he went to Cambridge and I didn't.

Graeme Hick, comparing his reading habits with those of his captain, Michael Atherton, 1995.

At least we are safe from an intoxicated rendition of 'There's only one Graeme Hick'. There are, quite clearly, two of them. The first one turns out for teams like Worcestershire and New Zealand's Northern Districts and plays like a God. The second one pulls on an England cap and plays like the anagram of a god.

Martin Johnson, *The Independent*.

I'd like to think that I haven't got any weaknesses except chocolate and a bad back.

Graeme Hick, 1995.

I knew I could dismiss Graeme Hick virtually any time I wanted.

Waqar Younis, after causing the latest interruption in Hick's stop-start England career, 1996.

My natural instinct when I was young was to think with my fists.

Maoris and South Sea Islanders are very much like that. They're warriors, and that's my natural instinct too.

Adam Hollioake, hailed with his brother Ben as England's saviours. 1997.

If we went to the toilet together, I suppose we would see who could get it further up the wall.

Adam Hollioake describes the extent of his competitive relationship with Ben. The two brothers, called into England's Texaco Trophy squad, went on to become the first brothers to play together for England, 1997.

An inflatable Keanu Reeves.

Ben Hollioake, as depicted by **Allison Pearson** in the *Evening Standard*, 1997.

It was like seeing the future and realizing that it worked.

Steve Brenkley, *Independent on Sunday*, on Ben Hollioake's first runs at Test level, 1997.

'Very, very average, a sixth-grader.'
'A cricketing legend.'

Ben Hollioake, variously seen by **contributors to the Internet**, after his England début, 1997.

He has found success pretty easy so far and needs to fall on his face before he becomes a really good player.

Adam Hollioake, on younger brother Ben, 1997.

Ben Hollioake's self-regard is an open secret; even he doesn't mind who knows it.

Robert Winder, 1998.

I suppose I'm a bit of a slot-machine.

Ben Hollioake, on his sex appeal, *GQ* magazine, 1998.

He gives the impression that to talk in expansive sentences would spoil the image, and maybe he's right. Long sentences are ten-a-penny; polished images are harder to come by and need constant maintenance.

Robert Winder, 1998.

Until 2 a.m. we sat around a table strewn with bottles, pistachio shells and king-size Rizlas, talking rubbish through a thick fug.

That quote, in *GQ* magazine, plus a bit of laddish chat, was enough for the ECB to conduct an unofficial enquiry into the behaviour of Ben Hollioake on the England A tour to Sri Lanka. He was exonerated, but a general warning was issued about the standards expected on tour, 1998.

It's no pose, man. I'm f****** babooned. Look at my eyes.

Ben Hollioake's explanation for dark glasses, as alleged in *GQ* magazine, on the England A tour of Sri Lanka, 1998. (Hollioake, whatever the reason for the shades, was the star of the tour.)

The enigma with no variation.

Vic Marks on Chris Lewis, *The Observer*, 1994.

Chris Lewis baldly went where no other cricketer has gone before – and the prat without a hat spent two days in bed with sunstroke.

After the striptease came the shaven head ... England's tour of the West Indies, 1994.

Who is to say I can't achieve what Ian Botham has done? It's not too late.

Chris Lewis, at the beginning of the 1995 season for Nottinghamshire. Shortly afterwards he was injured again.

When you hear some people talk, you'd think he was a basket case.

Alan Ormrod, Nottinghamshire coach, on the enigmatic Chris Lewis, overlooked by England for the 1994/5 Ashes tour.

They really are a bunch of twits. According to them I was crap. We didn't gel at all. I was opposed because of my Calvin Klein underwear; I was opposed for wearing certain clothes and I was opposed because I didn't drink.

Chris Lewis, reflecting on life at Nottinghamshire, 1997.

You guys are history. You're going to pay for it.

Devon Malcolm, struck by a bouncer by Fanie de Villiers during the third Test at The Oval, 1994. Malcolm responded with 9 for 57, England Test figures surpassed this century only by Jim Laker's all-ten.

I know you. You are the destroyer.

Nelson Mandela, South African president, to Devon Malcolm in Soweto as England revisited the country for the first time after multi-racial elections, 1995. Mandela's memory of Malcolm's nine for 57 against South Africa at The Oval was apparently not shared by the England management.

I think he's developed a different walk.

Matthew Vandrau, Derbyshire off-spinner, searching for a change in Devon Malcolm's affable manner upon his return to Derbyshire after his nine for 57 against South Africa, The Oval, 1994.

Sometimes it takes him a fortnight to put on his socks.

Micky Stewart, England's team manager, frustrated with Devon Malcolm's laid-back ways at the start of the Ashes series, 1990.

He couldn't make up his mind which wedding to come to, so he fled the country.

Nasser Hussain, upon his friendship and rivalry with fellow England batting contenders, Graham Thorpe and Mark Ramprakash. The three became known as the 'brat pack'; Hussain and Ramprakash got married on the same day, and Thorpe was absent from both ceremonies, 1994.

To want something so badly that it hurts can be endured. To need something as much as breath itself can be dangerous. Ramprakash was troubled because he was obsessed.

Peter Roebuck, celebrating Mark Ramprakash's maturing as an England batsman, 1998.

Almost as good a bullshitter as Bob Woolmer.

Dermot Reeve, as seen by a Warwickshire insider, 1994. Reeve, as captain, and Woolmer, as coach, were widely praised for their part in Warwickshire's unprecedented treble.

I get quite deep and spiritual about my cricket career.

Dermot Reeve, 1995.

I don't like you Reeve. I never have liked you. You get right up my nose and if you come anywhere near me, I'll rearrange yours.

David Lloyd, then coach of Lancashire, in the Old Trafford committee room, 1995. (From Dermot Reeve's biography, *Winning Ways*.)

I regret that my mouth overtakes my brain.

Dermot Reeve, discovering new insights as coach of Somerset, 1997.

The type of self-flagellating bloke who could have scored every week, but he was so self-obsessed that he didn't notice anyone else. Even on the local nudist beach he only admired himself.

Simon Hughes, *A Lot of Hard Yakka*, 1997, on Dermot Reeve.

I listen to my children opening their presents and later listen to the Queen's speech, with the phone at home pressed against the television. I'm a great monarchist.

Jack Russell, describing Christmas in Harare, 1996.

You get called a fruitcake because others don't understand what you're doing.

Jack Russell, arguing that he is 'eccentric', not 'mad', in *Jack Russell Unleashed*, 1997.

I'm an instinctive player but at the moment I'm thinking too much and have become a gibbering wreck.

Robin Smith, 1994.

He is too interested in making money.

Robin Smith, as depicted by England's team manager, **Keith Fletcher** in the Caribbean, 1994. Smith was galvanized into making a Test century in Antigua.

After 130 games for England I still lack confidence.

Robin Smith, 1996.

You can't smoke 20 a day and bowl fast.

Phil Tufnell, about to embark upon his first England tour, on why he opted for slow left-arm, 1990.

Why go to the nets for two hours when all your mates are down the kebab house making career-best scores on the Galactic Defender?

Phil Tufnell, in his early days at Middlesex, 1990.

The other advantage England have got when Phil Tufnell is bowling is that he isn't fielding.

Ian Chappell, during the fifth Test in Perth, Ashes series, 1990/1.

He mistook notoriety for celebrity status.

Tufnell's attitude to crowd barracking on the 1991 Ashes tour – according to his captain, **Graham Gooch**, in *Captaincy*, 1992.

Whenever I look down the wicket at the batsman I see a geezer trying to ruin my career. I'm not going to let that happen am I?

Phil Tufnell, England tour of India, 1992/3.

Well, I'm not dead yet, know what I mean? Remembered? Blimey! Twenty-eight years old!

Phil Tufnell, asked on *Cover Point* video magazine how he would like to be remembered, 1994.

I was sitting there in a hospital with some bloke shining a light in my eyes and saying, 'Tell me about your childhood,' and I just thought to myself, 'What the hell am I doing here? This is ridiculous!'

Phil Tufnell, sent for psychiatric examination in Perth after flying into a rage in his hotel room because of personal problems. England tour of Australia, 1994/5.

I couldn't believe it when John used to get cut for four and just turn round, walk back to his mark and bowl the next one right on the spot. I used to get cut for four and I was fuming.

Phil Tufnell, 1996.

'Cor Jack, you ain't arf made me look miserable.'

'You are miserable, Tuffers.'

Exchange between **Phil Tufnell** and **Jack Russell**, while Russell sketched him during a rain break on the tour of Zimbabwe, 1996.

He walked into the dressing room and there's a lot of young guys in there and came over to me and said, 'All right, Cat, how are you son?' And I thought, 'Hold on a minute, this is good, I'm playing for England with f****** Ian Botham.'

Phil Tufnell, reminiscing, 1994.

My life is back to normal. In fact it's never been abnormal.

Phil Tufnell, back in the England side against South Africa at Headingley. Less than three months earlier, he had been found guilty on two charges of assault against his former live-in girlfriend, 1994.

I'm not OBVIOUSLY backing away am I?

Life as a no. 11 batsman, as expressed by **Phil Tufnell**.

2
The Old Guard

The saddest person who ever walked onto a cricket field.

Mollie Staines, the first woman to be elected to the Yorkshire Committee, on Geoffrey Boycott, 1984.

He is of the type who are likely to have enjoyed quite a fill of wine, women and song.

Fraser White, graphologist, analysing Geoffrey Boycott's handwriting in *The Cricketer*, 1975.

The only thing I'm bloody frightened of is getting out.

Geoffrey Boycott, Yorkshire and England, 1973.

What have you done? What have you done?

Geoffrey Boycott's lament to Ian Botham who had followed instructions to run him out, because he was batting too slowly, New Zealand, 1978. Botham's reply was unprintable.

His ability to be where the fast bowlers aren't has long been a talking point among cricketers.

Tony Greig, in churlish mood after Geoffrey Boycott had turned down an offer to join the Kerry Packer circus, 1978.

As I stood at the non-striker's end, I felt a wave of admiration for my partner; wiry, slight, dedicated, a lonely man doing a lonely job all these years.

Mike Brearley, on Geoffrey Boycott, 1979.

Nobody's perfect. You know what happened to the last man who was – they crucified him.

Geoffrey Boycott, under pressure for slow scoring, 1979.

I play best when I'm surrounded by people who appreciate me.

Geoffrey Boycott, 1980.

The Establishment seem to want my ability but not me.

Geoffrey Boycott, *In the Fast Lane*, 1981.

Given the choice between Racquel Welch and a hundred at Lord's, I'd take the hundred every time.

Geoffrey Boycott, 1981. (Boycott later added £50,000 – and still chose the hundred.)

The best slow batsman in the world.

Keith Fletcher, England captain, when Boycott left the India tour early, pleading illness, 1982.

The greatest tragedy of his troubled life is that, above all else, in the desire to be admired and loved by everyone, he has this enormous capacity for upsetting people.

Tony Greig, on Geoffrey Boycott, 1983.

You cannot motivate a team with the word 'I'. Geoff cannot fool anyone; they know he's totally, almost insanely, selfish.

Geoffrey Boycott in the view of **Ian Botham**, in *It Sort of Clicks*, Botham and Peter Roebuck, 1986.

Even the Yorkshire Ripper got a fair trial.

Geoffrey Boycott, on being overlooked for the England captaincy.

Brighter Cricket With Geoff Boycott – No. 1: The Backward Defensive Stroke.

Geoffrey Boycott's illustrated coaching series, 1985.

The greatness of Boycott the batsman and the gaffes of Boycott the man had common roots in an unceasing quest after perfection.

Frank Tyson, *The Test Within*, 1987.

His attention to the practical detail of equipment, and the minutiae of every stroke has probably never been rivalled.

Frank Tyson, *The Test Within*, 1987, on Geoffrey Boycott.

People have a herding instinct. If a guy does not drink and goes off to practice or have dinner they think you are weird. You are not. You are different.

Geoffrey Boycott on the problem of being an individual, 1987.

We sometimes argue about the cricketer we would choose to bat for one's life (consensus answer: Don Bradman for your life, Geoff Boycott for his own).

Matthew Engel, the *Guardian*, 1989.

If Geoffrey had played cricket the way he talked he would have had people queuing up to get into the ground instead of queuing up to leave.

Fred Trueman on Geoffrey Boycott's TV analysis of England's failings in India, 1993.

The only fellow I've met who fell in love with himself at a young age and has remained faithful ever since.

Dennis Lillee, on Geoffrey Boycott, 1997.

I know why he's bought a house by the sea ... so he'll be able to go for a walk on the water.

Fred Trueman, heading for 30 years of anti-Boycott jokes, as Geoffrey left his beloved Yorkshire for a new home overlooking Poole Harbour, 1997.

You should have stuck to soccer, lad.

Len Muncer, coach on the Lord's groundstaff, assessing the career prospects of Ian Botham.

He's like a big soft puppy really.

Tom Cartwright, one of Ian Botham's early influences.

I'm probably the worst practiser in the world. You look at me in the nets and you wouldn't think I was a player. I just slog.

Ian Botham, Somerset and England, on himself, 1982.

If something is not done to excess, it's hardly worth doing.

Peter Roebuck, 1982, on the Ian Botham approach to cricket – and life.

If you made him Prime Minister tomorrow, he'd pick this country up in ten minutes.

Bill Alley, umpire, in praise of Ian Botham, 1980.

He couldn't bat to save himself. I bowled to him with a dicky arm during the 1977 tour and he was either dropped four times or made nought.

Jeff Thomson, Australian fast bowler, unimpressed with Ian Botham in 1980.

He captains the side like a great big baby.

Henry Blofeld, on Ian Botham's leadership of England in the West Indies, 1981.

He always gets the benefit of my help. I haven't known him bothering asking much, have you?

Geoffrey Boycott, grumbling about Ian Botham before the tour of the West Indies, 1981.

I'd rather face Dennis Lillee with a stick of rhubarb than go through all that again.

Ian Botham, cleared of assault at Grimsby Crown Court, 1981.

It's not the fault of my cooking. He gets no potatoes, stodgy pudding or anything that's fattening. He simply hasn't played enough cricket. It's the weather.

Kathy Botham, responding to criticism that her husband, Ian, was overweight, 1981.

A waste of ten good pokes, but it was worth it.

Ian Botham's verdict on a practical joke which involved inserting condoms into the fingers of Derek Randall's batting gloves. Tour of Australia 1982/3.

The most overrated player I've seen.

Harold Larwood, scourge of Australian batsmen in the Bodyline series 50 years earlier, assessing Ian Botham in 1983.

He must have put more backsides on seats than any other cricketer since Denis Compton.

Bob Taylor, *Standing Up, Standing Back*, on Ian Botham, 1985.

He couldn't bowl a hoop downhill.

Fred Trueman, on Ian Botham, 1985.

The greatest matchwinner the game has ever known.

Ian Botham, as seen by **Mike Brearley**, former England captain, 1985.

The longest pub crawl in history.

Jimmy Greaves, on Ian Botham's first leukaemia charity walk, John O'Groats to Land's End, 1985.

The first rock-and-roll cricketer.

Sir Len Hutton, on Ian Botham, 1986.

If I'd been in the war I'd have won the VC, but it would have been posthumous.

Ian Botham, attempting self-recognition.

I don't ask Kathy to face Michael Holding, so there's no reason why I should be changing nappies.

Ian Botham on fatherhood.

If Botham is an English folk hero, then this must be an alarming time for the nation.

David Miller, sportswriter.

Who writes your bloody scripts?

Graham Gooch to Botham after he had taken a wicket with his first delivery on returning to Test cricket after suspension, England vs New Zealand, 1986.

Ian Botham would make a great Aussie.

Jeff Thomson, *Thommo Declares*, 1986.

You bastards have been out to get me since I arrived. All you Aussies are a bunch of hicks who don't know the first thing about cricket.

Ian Botham's farewell to a scrum of journalists as he left Australia after his sacking by Queensland, 1988.

I like the bugger. He's a grand lad. It's just a pity he spoils himself.

Brian Close after Ian Botham was sacked by Queensland, 1988.

Eyes to the front, shut up, or you'll be next.

Ian Botham's response to protests about his assault on a passenger, Adrian Winter, who had objected to Botham's language on an internal Australian flight. The upshot was a £320 fine.

He just happened to be on the wrong flight at the wrong time.

Botham's explanation re Winter, 1988.

He invariably has a high opinion of the cricketing merits of his mates.

Peter Roebuck, *Ashes to Ashes*, 1987, on the cricketing loyalties of Ian Botham.

Ian is a man who is very warm in friendship but very ugly in enmity.

Peter Roebuck, 1988.

Whereas Hannibal, 2000 years ago, came to this country to bring war, you have come to bring with you messages of hope.

Piazza Castello, mayoress of Turin, during Ian Botham's 'Hannibal' trek across the Alps with elephants, 1988.

Form is temporary. Class is permanent.

Inscription on Ian Botham's T-shirt, 1990.

A fat has-been.

The alleged remark by **Dermot Reeve**, Warwickshire all-rounder, after being dismissed by Ian Botham at Edgbaston, 1990. (In his autobiography, *Winning Ways*, Reeve would only admit to informing Botham: 'You've had your day, mate!')

Ian Botham represents everything that's the best in Britain. He's Biggles, the VC, El Alamein, the tank commander, he's everything. I mean, how could a schoolboy not want to be like Ian Botham?

Tim Hudson, Ian Botham's agent, 1985.

I think we have created a Frankenstein, bigger than life.

Maxi Hudson, as Ian Botham severed links with his agent and his agent's wife, 1986.

He doesn't give a damn; he wants to ride a horse, down a pint, roar around the land, waking up the sleepers, show them things can be done. As it is, he has to play cricket all the time, and worry about newspapermen, a Gulliver tied down by the little people.

Peter Roebuck, in *It Sort of Clicks*, Roebuck and Ian Botham, 1986.

He becomes like a Roman gladiator at the feast of something or other. Women find it more than difficult not to cross and uncross their legs under his gaze. They seem to breathe quicker and their chests begin to heave as the nipples push against the soft T-shirt fabric or the silk blouses. He's definitely every woman's piece of rough ... in the long, long grass ... by the lake ... under a full moon.

Tim Hudson's unpublished diaries, concerning the sex appeal of Ian Botham. (Recorded in *My Autobiography*, 1995.)

So far as I know there has never been a St Ian.

Kathy Botham, after her husband confessed to smoking marijuana, 1986.

I'm very pleased to be still considered one of the best 43 cricketers in England.

Ian Botham. He didn't reply to the TCCB letter enquiring about his availability for the Ashes tour, 1990.

I would rather like to spend an hour or two with Stormin' Norman – he seems to be my kind of bloke.

Ian Botham, asked whom he would most like to meet, 1993. (General Norman Schwarzkopf led the US assault in the Gulf War.)

I have never thought life was a dress rehearsal. I once saw an advert on Australian television which said 'Life: be in it.'

Ian Botham, announcing his retirement, Durham, 1993.

Sometimes it takes me five minutes to get out of bed in the morning.

Ian Botham, justifying retirement, 1993.

What I will miss most of all is the comradeship of the dressing room. I won't miss bowling 20 overs uphill into the wind when I could be out on the river catching salmon.

Ian Botham, announcing his retirement, Durham, 1993.

That's part of my childhood gone.

Durham's wicketkeeper, **Chris Scott**, as Ian Botham left the field for the last time, Durham vs Australia at Durham University, 1993.

Some might say that Ian is a talented thug, but I believe there is far more to him than that.

Dennis Silk, TCCB chairman, advocating Ian Botham's involvement in England's coaching set-up, 1995. It didn't happen.

Botham's idea of team spirit and motivation was to squirt a water pistol at someone and then go and get pissed.

Raymond Illingworth, resisting pressure for Ian Botham to return to the England set-up as a motivator, 1995.

A drug-crazed opium pusher.

Sarfraz Nawaz's wild allegation, as jokily recorded by Botham himself in *My Autobiography*, 1995. Sarfraz was responding to Botham's mother-in-law jibe.

Botham's biggest trick has been to convince people of his standing as an anti-establishment hero. Rarely has a cricketer been so protected by those in power.

Peter Roebuck, on Ian Botham's conservatism, 1995.

I want to be more successful than my father. I want to play Test cricket, take more wickets, score more runs and take more catches than he did in his career.

Liam Botham, during his debut for Hampshire 2nd XI, in the week that his dad, Ian, retired, 1993.

There was an element of good fortune about some of those wickets, so I suppose people will say it's typical Botham luck.

Liam Botham, after taking 5-67 for Hampshire on his first-class début, 1996.

I chose rugby because it will be going further than cricket.

Liam Botham, rejecting Hampshire for West Hartlepool, 1996.

Even the Pakistanis are nice to me.

David Gower, Leicestershire, Hampshire and England batsman, reflecting on his easy-going nature.

Perhaps Gower will eventually realize that cricket's not always about champagne. It's a bread-and-butter game.

Brian Brain, revealing an impatience with David Gower, not uncommon among bread-and-butter county cricketers, in *Another Day, Another Match*, 1981.

Gower might have been more at home in the 1920s or 1930s, cracking a dashing hundred for MCC, the darling of the crowds, before speeding away in a Bugatti and cravat for a night on the town.

Scyld Berry, *The Observer*, 1984.

Gower never moves, he drifts.

Peter Roebuck, *Ashes to Ashes*, 1987, on David Gower.

Real officer class. Languid self-possession. Confront him with a firing squad and he'd decline the blindfold.

Pat Pocock, after David Gower was appointed England captain, 1989.

The West Indies will be quaking in their boots now.

David Gower's sardonic assessment after England's defeat of the 1985 Australians. His dry wit was not appreciated by everyone.

Difficult to be more laid back without being actually comatose.

David Gower, in the eyes of **Frances Edmonds**, *Daily Express*, 1985.

From being a person who disregarded discipline – he wasn't a rebel, he just ignored it – he has been put in a situation where he has to determine the framework. And that is why we have called him TC (Turn Coat) because he has talked of compulsory nets.

Graeme Fowler, on David Gower's leadership in India, in *Fox on the Run*, 1988.

People say I'm too casual, but there are ambitions, fears, trials and tribulations all whirling around in there.

David Gower, *Declarations*, 1989.

A master in the art of non-communication.

Geoffrey Boycott's view of David Gower's captaincy, 1990.

It's like watching a swan. What you see on the surface bears no relation to the activity going on underneath.

David Gower, dismissing charges of being too laid back after a century in the third Test in Sydney during England's disastrous Ashes tour, 1991.

Of all the people I have worked with, whether in the police, in the armed services, in education, in local government, among the unemployed, even among the criminal fraternity, I have rarely had a more difficult task than David.

Brian Mason, personal counsellor and motivator, trying to solve David Gower's poor form for Hampshire in 1991.

He would have to take his journalistic gear ... corkscrew, spare corkscrew and Press box biro.

Martin Johnson, in *The Independent*, musing upon David Gower's impending addition to the cricket writing ranks, 1993.

A curly-haired kitten.

Frank Keating on David Gower.

'Do you want Gatt a foot wider?'

'No. He'd burst.'

Mike Gatting, Middlesex and England, as sent up by **David Gower**, the captain, and **Chris Cowdrey**, the bowler, during India vs England Test in Calcutta, 1985.

It couldn't have been Gatt. Anything he takes up to his room after nine o'clock, he eats.

Ian Botham's judgment on the barmaid affair which cost Mike Gatting the England captaincy.

How anyone can spin a ball the width of Gatting boggles the mind.

Martin Johnson, in *The Independent*, on the 'Ball of the Century', delivered by Australian leggie Shane Warne, which bowled Gatting in the 1993 Old Trafford Test.

If it had been a cheese roll, it would never have got past him.

Graham Gooch, Gatting's England team-mate, joins the fun on the same topic.

Hell, Gatt, move out of the way, I can't see the stumps.

Dennis Lillee, stopping in mid-run at Lilac Hill, opening match of England's 1994/5 Ashes tour.

Gatting at fine leg – that's a contradiction in terms.

Richie Benaud, Channel 9 commentary, 1995.

If Gatt plays he's got to be captain. Can you imagine being captain and having Gatt on your back?!

Michael Roseberry, after leaving Mike Gatting's county, Middlesex, to skipper his home county of Durham, 1995.

Journalist: 'Would you be interested in the post of chairman of selectors?'

Gatting: 'Not really, not while I'm playing. I'd have too much on my plate.'

A typically food-orientated exchange between **Mike Gatting** and an English cricket journalist, this time in 1997.

If Graham tried harder he could make a successful office boy.

Teacher's report on a young Graham Gooch.

The new Briton – forceful, plebeian, undeferential, a winner. He is cricket's Thatcher.

The *Sunday Telegraph*, on Graham Gooch, Essex and England, 1990.

I went and phoned Mum and Dad and then went into the bar. There was not a soul around. They had either gone early to bed at 8.30 or, more likely, out to a pub somewhere. Either way, they had not bothered to include me.

Graham Gooch, lonely at Edgbaston on the eve of his England Test debut at 21 against the Australians, 1975.

He is built like a guardsman and that expressionless face with its black moustache surely saw service in England's old imperial wars, defending Rorke's Drift and marching up the Khyber Pass.

Geoffrey Moorhouse, on Graham Gooch, 1978.

I know I look a totally miserable sod on television. I wish I didn't. But there you are.

Graham Gooch, during the series in which he established his influence as both batsman and captain, England vs India, 1990.

Hang on a minute pal, I haven't been down there for 20 years.

Graham Gooch, asked to field at fine leg by his replacement as England captain, Michael Atherton, Edgbaston, 1993.

I never saw a fitter, stronger and healthier cricketer ever become a worse cricketer.

Graham Gooch, defending his work ethic in *Gooch: My Autobiography*, 1995.

Masterful against spin, courageous against pace, he could shuffle so agonizingly against swing that the enduring image is of a large and drooping figure dragging himself from the crease – an image of frailty and majesty which is also inaccurate. After all he is England's heaviest ever scorer in Tests. It has been a marvellous career. Gooch was honest and humble. He could be mournful. But he was never half-hearted.

Peter Roebuck's tribute in the *Sunday Times* upon Graham Gooch's retirement from Test cricket, England's tour of Australia, 1995.

The old petrol tank has been flashing empty for about five years and now I know the tank is empty.

Graham Gooch, announcing his first-class retirement by falling back on his traditional imagery, 1997.

Until getting out he has actually looked the same old Gooch. I think it needed only one innings. A hundred and he would have been back.

Alan Lilley, Essex's development officer, and Graham Gooch's unofficial aider and abetter, taking a different view on his fuel levels, 1997.

Wheat beer, s'il vous plaît.

Graham Gooch, in France on a benefit jaunt for Michael Atherton, gives his schoolboy French a run out in a bar in Reims. He was rewarded with eight beers, 1997.

He did not sufficiently discourage the element of selfishness which is part of most professional cricketers.

Raymond Illingworth, Yorkshire, Leicestershire and England, this time as painted by **Mike Brearley** in 1973.

The trouble with Illy is that he always wants his own way.

Raymond Illingworth, as perceived by **Brian Close** (who also did).

On the field with him you sense that he knows every blade of grass by name. At Lord's, the Father Time weather vane turns by one degree behind his back and he will announce, 'wind's on the move.'

Tony Lewis, in the *Daily Telegraph*, 1994, in praise of Raymond Illingworth.

Say good morning to him as he leaves his hotel and he will twitch his nose, rub his hands and declare that 'wind is right direction for a few overs of outswing with second new ball from top end, though it might be too cold to swing and so England had better keep a fielder at deepish backward short-leg for so-and-so's pick-up shot.'

Tony Lewis, in the *Daily Telegraph*, 1994, on the same subject.

The face of a choirboy, the demeanour of a civil servant and the ruthlessness of a rat catcher.

Derek Underwood, England left-arm spinner, as seen by **Geoffrey Boycott** in *Opening Up*, 1980.

Small, pokey, as alert as a cat, as alive to the possibilities of misadventure as a boy playing French cricket on a bumpy lawn.

John Thicknesse on Alan Knott, Kent and England wicketkeeper.

The only bowler ever to require the services of a runner.

Anonymous verdict on Chris Old, Yorkshire and England seamer, talented but a trifle injury-prone, 1970s.

That frail appearance is deceptive, a cloak disguising a strong will. That pottering gait and shuffling feet, the tangled pads and the quizzical air create an impression of a quiet mystical leader, a

Napoleon of cricket. It is all nonsense! Fletcher is far from meek. He is a thoroughly professional, fighting captain. He asks nothing and gives less.

Peter Roebuck, *Slices of Cricket*, 1982, on Keith Fletcher, Essex and England.

I've never ever been any good at making gwavy.

Keith Fletcher's reply when asked by Graham Gooch if he had any regrets. (Related in *Gooch: My Autobiography*, 1995.)

Occupation: net bowler.

The immigration card as filled in by **Jack Birkenshaw**, Leicestershire off-spinner, during England's tour of India, 1972/3.

He's got a degree in people, hasn't he?

Rodney Hogg, Australian fast bowler, on Mike Brearley, Middlesex and England.

On Friday I watched JM Brearley directing his fieldsmen very carefully. He then looked up at the sun and made a little gesture which suggested that it should move a little squarer. Who is this man?

Letter to the *Guardian*, 1981.

The statistics suggest that he is one of the great England captains. The luckiest would be nearer the truth.

Ray Illingworth, not quite as impressed during Mike Brearley's first spell as England captain, 1980.

That man must be a bigger ass than I thought he was.

Clive Lloyd, dismissing Mike Brearley's criticisms of his own captaincy of the West Indies.

A bank clerk going to war.

Clive Taylor, in *The Sun*, as Northamptonshire's David Steele, silver-haired and bespectacled, defied the West Indian quicks in 1976.

If Greig fell off the Empire State building, he'd land on a furniture van full of mattresses.

England team-mate on Tony Greig, Sussex and England, 1976.

There's only one head bigger than Greig's – and that's Birkenhead.

Fred Trueman, with Tony Greig in his sights, 1970s.

The first England player I actively remember indulging in gamesmanship.

Bob Taylor on Tony Greig, Sussex and England, in *Standing Up, Standing Back*, 1985.

Hey, Greigy! This champagne's all right, but the blackcurrant jam tastes of fish.

Derek Randall, Nottinghamshire and England, sampling caviar on the MCC tour to India, 1976/7.

Twasack.

Mike Brearley's nickname for Derek Randall.

A fidgety player and a chirpy character who gave the impression of being very confident when, in fact, he was quite insecure and hopelessly nervous in the dressing room before going out to bat.

Richard Hadlee, New Zealand all-rounder, and a Nottinghamshire team-mate of Derek Randall, in Hadlee's autobiography, *Rhythm and Swing*.

The Sun Has Got His Hat On, Hip-Hip-Hip-Hooray …

Derek Randall's singing entry to the MCG before his innings of 174 in the Centenary Test, Australia vs England, 1977.

I hate bowling at you. I'm not as good at hitting a moving target.

Dennis Lillee, Australian fast bowler, after Derek Randall's 150 at Sydney in 1979.

That Randall! He bats like an octopus with piles.

South Australian to **Matthew Engel** during England's 1982/3 tour of Australia. (Recorded in 1994 *Wisden*.)

You'll be no good with that stuff – you'll best get some ale down you.

Brian Jackson, stalwart Derbyshire bowler, to Mike Hendrick, during Hendrick's early soft-drink days in the county side. He got the message.

In the Tests I sometimes break out into a sweat just putting on my boots.

Mike Hendrick, Derbyshire and England, 1970s.

When he strolls away to square leg, it is like an act of thanksgiving that the previous ball has been survived and a moment of prayer for the fibre to get through the next.

Bob Willis on Chris Tavare, Kent and England, *The Captain's Diary*, 1983.

I don't actually enjoy Test cricket that much.

Chris Tavare, after making 35 runs in five-and-a-half hours in Madras, England tour of India, 1981/2.

He personifies the best virtues of Yorkshireness – he doesn't give a toss for reputation, fights back when cornered and doesn't even contemplate defeat.

Michael Parkinson on David Bairstow, Yorkshire and England wicket-keeper.

You know three-quarters of seven-eighths of sod all.

David Bairstow's catch phrase, used mostly on unsuspecting journalists.

You don't want to be taking them pills, you want to get some good Tetleys down you.

David Bairstow's traditional recommendation – a few pints of ale – to an ailing Yorkshire fast bowler, 1997.

People say, do you think you would have played for England if you'd started at 18? And I say, I might. And I might have been sacked by Lancashire when I was 19 an' all.

Jack Simmons, a late starter at Lancashire, 1985.

At this stage I'm like the woman who is heavily pregnant – I've at last got used to the inevitable.

Jack Simmons, Lancashire spinner, contemplating retirement, in *Declarations*, 1989.

Bowler's name?

Cry from the Edgbaston crowd when Bob Willis came on to bowl for Warwickshire in 1985. Willis, an England hero, had taken only nine championship wickets the previous year.

A 1914 biplane tied up with elastic bands trying vainly to take off.

Frank Keating, the *Guardian*, describing Bob Willis.

Bob always led from the standpoint that if he put in 100 per cent effort, and if he bowled to his full potential and we fielded and batted to our full potential, we would beat any side in the world. Tactics ended at that. It was 'Follow me, men!'

Graeme Fowler, on Bob Willis, in *Fox on the Run*, 1988.

I don't go as far as that on my holidays.

Former Test bowler, on the length of Bob Willis's run-up.

I am a born pessimist.

Bob Willis, *The Captain's Diary*, 1983.

I can't play – I've been stung.

Chris Old, to his captain Ian Botham, 10 minutes before the start of the Bridgetown Test, 1981.

People no longer ask me if he advises me, because it's obvious that he doesn't ... or if he does, then I'm taking no notice.

Chris Cowdrey, Kent and England, on comparisons with his more illustrious father, Colin, 1980s.

A conversation with him would be 50 per cent shorter if he deleted the expletives.

Mike Selvey, describing his Middlesex and England colleague, John Emburey, in 1985.

Well, to be honest, the fackin' facker's fackin' facked.

John Emburey, on injuries. (From Simon Hughes's *A Lot of Hard Yakka*, 1997.)

I could never be a 100 per cent professional like John Emburey.

Phil Edmonds, his Middlesex and England spin partner, 1982.

Phil Edmonds needs two more field changes to get his 1000 for the season.

Jim Laker, BBC commentator, 1985.

Reputation for being awkward and arrogant, probably because he is awkward and arrogant. Works very hard at trying to be controversial and iconoclastic, but basically a pillar of the establishment.

Frances Edmonds, on husband Phil, in the *Daily Express*, 1985.

I just have to make a suggestion these days and it is interpreted as being antagonistic.

Phil Edmonds, 1984.

They wanted me to be a bloody doorman.

Norman Cowans, England and Middlesex fast bowler, walking out on a club side in Brisbane because they could not find him suitable employment, 1986.

I'm clumsy and I can't really be anything else. The only graceful sportsmen as big as me are basketball players.

Derek Pringle, Essex and England, 1991.

He takes an alternative view just for the hell of it.

Derek Pringle, in the view of **Graham Gooch**, in *Captaincy*, 1992.

Watching Roebuck was like being at a requiem mass.

Jim Laker, after Peter Roebuck's 34 in two-and-three-quarter hours against Surrey, 1985. Roebuck had previously criticized Laker's 'dirge-like' commentating.

I would love to sit in a deckchair and watch Malcolm Marshall knock his block off.

Ian Botham, asked if he would tour with Peter Roebuck in Australia, 1990/91. Neither of them were selected.

His biggest problem was an identity crisis. He wanted people to look up to him but he didn't know who he really was.

Peter Roebuck, summed up by his one-time colleague, now antagonist, **Ian Botham**, in Botham's autobiography, 1995.

If he could, he would mark man-for-man.

Peter Roebuck on Micky Stewart, England team manager, 1980s.

The Julie Andrews of cricket.

John Barclay, Sussex captain and later to become England tour manager, also as depicted by **Peter Roebuck**.

The only thing worrying me about Syd playing for England is that he may try to run in so fast he won't be able to let go of the ball.

David Graveney, David 'Syd' Lawrence's Gloucestershire captain, 1988.

Rather like facing up to a raging bull. The refined run-up still has a disconcerting chicane in it, there is a lot of puffing and blowing, a grimace or two, a huge leap and some serious pace to follow.

Simon Hughes, Middlesex bowler, on 'Syd' Lawrence.

Frank Bruno has a catch-phrase. Why can't I have one?

David Lawrence, asked about his repeated assertion that he was rockin' an' rumblin', Trent Bridge Test, 1991.

Allan Lamb kept me on the straight and narrow (to the nearest bar).

Ian Botham, on the Northamptonshire and England batsman, in his auto-biography, 1994.

One of the few men you would back to get past a Lord's gateman with nothing more than an icy stare.

Peter Willey, one of English cricket's hard men, as seen by **Martin Johnson** in *The Independent*.

3
Past Masters

He never played a Christian stroke in his life.

Ranjitsinhji, Sussex and England, as rated by Yorkshire's **Ted Wainwright**
... if we are to believe Neville Cardus, who told the tale.

After being warned for years of the danger of playing back on a fast
wicket, and especially to fast bowling, it came as rather a surprise
to see the great Indian batsman transgressing against a principle
so firmly fixed in one's mind.

Gilbert Jessop, on Ranjitsinhji.

I assure you that you will never see a batsman to beat the Jam
Saheb if you live for a hundred years.

WG Grace, addressing a public dinner in Cambridge, on the talents of
Ranji, 1908.

Jessop was a terror. We reckoned in this game we'd make him go
and fetch 'em. So we bowled wide on the offside. He fetched 'em all
right. He went off like a spring trap and, before you'd seen his feet
move, he was standing on the offside of his stumps, pulling 'em over
the square leg boundary.

Wilfred Rhodes, on Gilbert Jessop's century in each innings for
Gloucestershire against Yorkshire in 1900. (Recorded in AA Thomson's *Hirst
and Rhodes*.)

No man has ever driven the ball so hard, so high and so often in so
many different directions.

CB Fry on Gilbert Jessop, 'The Croucher'.

His speed of foot and eye and judgment, his strength of wrist, his timing and daring, all made him the most dangerous batsman the world will ever see.

Gilbert Jessop, as seen by **Sammy Woods**, in *The Cricketer*.

I never see a silly point positioned on a hard wicket without wishing that Mr Hutchings was at the wicket.

Frank Woolley, Kent and England batsman, on the fierce strokeplay of KL Hutchings, regarded in Kent as 'England's Victor Trumper'. Early 1900s.

Never mind, I've got a little kid at home who will make it up for me.

'Poor' Fred Tate, after dropping the catch that lost England the Old Trafford Test against Australia, 1902.

Mr Mayor and Gentlemen, I can't make a speech beyond saying thank you but I'm ready to box any man in the room three rounds.

Johnny Douglas, England cricketer and Olympic gold medallist at boxing, tour of Australia, 1911/12.

If you wanted to score runs off Barnes you had to score off good bowling.

Learie Constantine, after facing Sydney Barnes, Staffordshire, Lancashire and England, in the Lancashire League. (Barnes was 59 at the time.)

There's only one captain of a side when I'm bowling – me.

Sydney Barnes, a combative and opinionated soul.

At least if we go down we'll take that bugger Barnes down with us.

AC MacLaren, during a rough trip home from Australia, 1902. McLaren, England's captain, had called up Barnes from league cricket to make the tour.

He occasionally takes time to see the obvious.

Portrait in *The Cricketer*, upon JWHT Douglas's appointment to the England captaincy, 1921.

There's only one man made more appeals than you George, and that was Dr Barnardo.

Bill Reeve, umpire, on George Macauley (Yorkshire), 1920s.

One fears he does not possess the equable temperament requisite for Test matches.

Donald Knight, after a wild Macauley spell against Australia, 1926.

He pervaded a cricket pitch. He occupied it and encamped upon it. He erected a tent with a system of infallible pegging, then posted inexorable sentries. He took guard with the air of a guest who, having been offered a weekend by his host, obstinately decides to reside for six months.

RC Robertson-Glasgow, on Philip Mead (Hampshire, England).

Mead, you've been in five hours and you've just stonewalled.

RWV Robins to Philip Mead during a match against Middlesex. Mead made 218 not out in that time.

Hello, Mead, I saw your father play in 1911.

Confused Australian spectator in 1928. Philip Mead toured Australia with MCC on both occasions.

Easy to watch, difficult to bowl to, and impossible to write about. When you bowled to him, there weren't enough fielders; when you wrote about him, there weren't enough words.

RC Robertson-Glasgow on Frank Woolley, Kent and England batsman, *Cricket Prints*, 1943.

The most graceful of the efficient, and the most efficient of the graceful.

Ian Peebles, *Woolley – The Pride of Kent*, 1969.

I wasn't disputing your decision, Frank. I just couldn't believe that such an awful bowler could get me out twice.

Frank Woolley to umpire Frank Chester when asked why he had dallied at the crease after Bob Wyatt (Warwickshire, Worcestershire, England) had dismissed him, Kent vs Warwickshire at Dover, 1923.

Jack Hobbs could have scored thousands more runs, but he often was content to throw his wicket away when he had reached his hundred and give someone else a chance.

Wilfred Rhodes, suggesting that Jack Hobbs's record run-aggregate could have been even greater.

He could have made 400 centuries – and if he'd played for Yorkshire he would have done.

Wilfred Rhodes again. (Hobbs made 197, the most in cricket history, which kept Surrey and England contented enough.)

A professional who bats exactly like an amateur.

Sir Pelham Warner on Jack Hobbs. (He intended it as praise.)

Others scored faster; hit the ball harder; more obviously murdered bowling. No one else, though, ever batted with more consummate skill.

John Arlott, *Jack Hobbs: Portrait of The Master*, 1981.

It's not comforting to feel I will no longer be a power in the land. I have found personal success very gratifying.

Jack Hobbs, retiring from Test cricket, BBC Radio, 1930.

You know Fender, there is no man in England whose bowling I would rather bat against than yours; and there is no batsman in England I would rather bowl against either.

Johnny Douglas, MCC captain, during outward voyage on tour of Australia, 1920/1 to Percy Fender. Fender had been much touted prior to the tour as captain.

He used to play very seriously, you know, but he hardly ever watched. Whether he was saving his eyesight or not I never knew. Myself, I wanted to see every ball.

Wilfred Rhodes, by then blind, on his great Yorkshire and England colleague, George Hirst, 1954.

How the devil can you play a ball that comes at you like a hard throw-in from cover point?

Sammy Woods, on George Hirst's swerve.

It has been suggested tonight that no one may again do what I've been lucky enough to do this season. I don't know about that, but I do know this – if he does he'll be tired.

George Hirst, after scoring more than 2000 runs and taking more than 200 wickets in a season, for Yorkshire, 1906.

I have tossed my slow tripe at you till I grew weary, and I longed for the shades of eve.

DLA Jephson, a lob bowler, paying tribute to Hirst on his 50th birthday, in his retirement season of 1921.

When George Hirst got you out, you were out. When Wilfred got you out, you were out twice, because he knew by then how to get you out in the second innings too.

Roy Kilner, Yorkshire team-mate, comparing the merits of Wilfred Rhodes and George Hirst.

I got bowled by a slow full toss and I knew something was wrong with my eyes.

Wilfred Rhodes, playing in Scotland a year after his retirement, 1931.

Wilfred studied the game more than a financier ever studied the stock market.

Bill Bowes, on his Yorkshire and England team-mate, Wilfred Rhodes, in *Express Deliveries*, 1949.

Wilfred couldn't see the stumps at my end. I couldn't have been more than a blurred and distant image, yet, bowling from memory, with his arm upright, he flighted the ball beautifully and dropped on a good length six times out of six. I played through a maiden over on merit and was glad enough to survive it.

Brian Sellers, describing Wilfred Rhodes's ceremonious opening over, with weakening eyesight, to open a new ground near Wakefield at the age of 72, 1949.

A cross-batted village-greener.

Gerry Weigall, Kent, on Yorkshire batsman Maurice Leyland, when
Leyland was chosen ahead of Weigall's Kent team-mate Frank Woolley for
the MCC 1928/9 tour.

I can bowl so slow that if I don't like a ball I can run after it and
bring it back.

JM Barrie, 1926. (From Neville Cardus's *Autobiography*, 1947.)

There comes a time when a man must realize that his cricket days
are over. The thing first began to dawn on me when I noticed that
the captain of the side, whenever he started to set his fielders,
invariably began by saying, 'General, will you go to point?'

Brigadier-General **Hugh Headlam** in *The Times*, 1930.

My word, Herbert, if it hadn't been for my lumbago, we'd have
brayed 'em.

Percy Holmes (224) to Herbert Sutcliffe (313) after a world-record partnership of 555 for the first wicket, Yorkshire vs Essex at Leyton, 1932.

Ah well, my feet aren't what they used to be.

Harold Larwood, former England fast bowler, awarded nought for plenty
in a computer Test played at Lord's between England and Australia, 1971.

I could a bowt t'taxi for less.

Arthur Wood, Yorkshire wicketkeeper, after rushing by taxi from
Scarborough for his Test début against Australia at Lord's, 1938.

Go on Hedley, you've got him in two minds. He doesn't know
whether to hit you for four or six.

Arthur Wood, Yorkshire wicketkeeper, to left-arm spinner Hedley Verity as
the South African batsman, HB Cameron, took 30 off an over at Bramall
Lane in 1935.

He bowled as if in a mental abstraction, the batsman being the
obstacle.

Walter Hammond on Hedley Verity (Yorkshire and England left-arm spinner).

46

A daft old clodpole.

This was **Joe Hardstaff**'s verdict on his captain, Gubby Allen, after the 1947/8 MCC tour of the West Indies. Allen, infuriated, bet Hardstaff £100 that he would never play for England again. He did – but only once.

Someone remarked that perhaps he is too daring for the grey-beards. My own view is that he is also too daring for the majority of the black-beards, the brown-beards and the all-beards who sit in judgment on batsmen; in short, too daring for those who have never known what it is to dare in cricket.

RC Robertson-Glasgow on Harold Gimblett (Somerset, England), *Cricket Prints*.

A wonderful batsman, a very intelligent bloke, and a first-class hypochondriac.

Harold Gimblett, as seen by a Somerset team-mate. (Told in **David Foot**'s *Harold Gimblett, Tormented Genius of Cricket*, 1982.)

I can't sleep, I can't sleep, my head's buzzing, I'm making too many runs.

Gimblett, sleepwalking in a Paddington hotel, during a Somerset match at The Oval. (**Foot** is also the source for this.)

Thank goodness that's over!

Harold Gimblett, dropped by England after two Tests against India in 1936.

Hark at them silly buggers, they don't know what it's all about, do they?

Fred Trueman, after bowling a prearranged bouncer to Harold Gimblett to liven up the Taunton crowd watching a Somerset vs Yorkshire championship match. (From David Foot's *Harold Gimblett: Tormented Genius of Cricket*, 1982.)

The most lovable and ugly man there ever was.

Harold Gimblett on Patsy Hendren.

I'm going while you still ask why. I'm not waiting until you ask why not.

Patsy Hendren, Middlesex and England batsman, explaining why he was retiring.

Machines are taken for granted when they work as they should, and impatiently criticized when things go wrong. Hutton has never given the public any cosy human view of himself which will allow them to recognize him as ... capable, however rarely, of the same errors of nerve and judgment as themselves.

Jim Kilburn, on Len Hutton, in the *Observer*, 1951.

Unlike Boycott, he could make the forward defensive stroke look attractive.

Len Hutton's advantage over Geoffrey Boycott, a Yorkshire batting idol of a future generation, as claimed by **Trevor Bailey** in *The Ashes: Highlights Since 1948*, 1989.

I'm only setting up these records for Hutton to break them.

Herbert Sutcliffe, Yorkshire batsman, recognizing the talent of a young Len Hutton.

If it was a matter of life and death I would choose to play under Len Hutton. The object of the game was to him far more important than the game itself.

Godfrey Evans, *The Gloves Are Off*, 1961.

If my mother hadn't thrown my football boots on the fire, I might have become as famous as Denis Compton.

Len Hutton.

The greatest player we shall ever see – but a funny bugger.

Wally Hammond, as seen by a Gloucestershire team-mate.

I wouldn't say I coached him, but I didn't mess him up.

George Fenner, head coach at Lord's, on the early Denis Compton, 1958.

The boy will be alright, but I was dying for a pee.

Umpire **Bill Reeves**, apologizing for adjudging Denis Compton lbw to Jim Parks on his debut for Middlesex against Sussex, 1936.

Go off the field, Compton, and get a cap.

Walter Robins, Middlesex captain, banishing Denis Compton from the Lord's outfield after he dropped a catch out of the sun.

I was as fit as a flea; I did what came naturally and I enjoyed myself.

Denis Compton's recollection of his vintage 1947 season, which brought 3816 first-class runs and 18 centuries.

Already they are kings; benevolent kings appointed and acclaimed by like-minded subjects; champions in the fight against dullness and the commercial standard.

RC Robertson-Glasgow, on the batting feats of Denis Compton and Bill Edrich in the golden summer of 1947.

I doubt if one in a hundred understood that what they were really watching was total batsman-domination of mediocre bowling.

Colin Cowdrey, offering a less romanticized judgment of the same summer, immediately after the end of WW2, of flat pitches and depleted attacks.

The only player to call his partner for a run and wish him good luck at the same time.

John Warr, Middlesex colleague, on Denis Compton.

I'd like to thank Denis Compton, a boyhood hero of mine.

Sir Tim Rice, collecting an Oscar, and confusing America in the process, 1995.

We don't know who Denis Compton is. He doesn't appear to be at Disney Studios or have anything to do with them.

Bemused employee at Academy of Motion Picture Arts, after Rice's acceptance speech, 1995.

To watch Denis Compton play cricket on a good day was to know what joy was. I could have been in Hong Kong, but I think I made the right choice.

John Major, attending Denis Compton's memorial service, rather than the Hong Kong handover to China, 1997.

Do you want a pot? I'll get some if you like – free!

Denis Compton, enjoying the benefits of one of cricket's earliest sponsorships ... Brylcreem. (As told by **Godfrey Evans**, in *The Gloves Are Off*, 1961.)

I've never felt so glad in my life as when I saw who was coming in.

Peter May on Cyril Washbrook's entrance in his comeback match after a five-year absence with England 17–3 against Australia at Headingley, 1956.

That chap'll never keep wicket – he stands on his toes.

Sir Pelham Warner on Godfrey Evans, who went on to win 91 caps between 1946 and 1959.

Sorry Godfrey, but I have to do it – the crowd are a bit bored at the moment.

Apology from **Keith Miller** after bowling two successive bouncers to Godfrey Evans on Evans's first tour of Australia, 1946/7.

I can see I'm going to have to do a lot of bowling if I play for this lot. I think I'd better cut my run down.

'Bomber' Wells, who only bowled off three paces anyway, after his debut for Gloucestershire at Bristol, 1951.

Seeing Trevor Bailey prepare for a session in the field was like a lesson in anatomy.

Ray East, *A Funny Turn*, 1983.

I haven't done it right often.

Jim Laker, Surrey and England, asked if his eight wickets for two runs for England against The Rest, Park Avenue, 1950, was his best bowling analysis.

No bugger ever got all ten when I was at the other end.

Sydney Barnes after watching Laker take all ten wickets for England vs Australia, Old Trafford, 1956.

The older I get, the better cricketer I seem to become.

Jim Laker, *Cricket Contrasts*, 1985.

I don't think you were trying to bowl them out.

This remark, by his Surrey captain **Peter May**, after a defeat against Kent at Blackheath, provoked Jim Laker into refusing to tour Australia under May's leadership, 1958.

May, though not exactly shy, has a kind of English frozen-upness about him: to join a hearty cricketers' group at the bar is for him the social equivalent of climbing the Matterhorn.

Peter May, Surrey and England, as seen by **Michael Davie**, 1959.

He started wrongly – and never looked back.

Jim Laker's opinion of Freddie Brown's managerial success on the 1958/9 MCC tour of Australia.

A fag, a cough, a cup of coffee.

Brian Statham, Lancashire and England seam bowler, on his pre-match breakfast. (Source: Frank Tyson, *The Test Within*, 1987.)

Without rival, the ripest, the richest, the rip-roaringest individual performer on cricket's stage.

AA Thomson, on Fred Trueman, Yorkshire and England fast bowler, in *The Cricketer*, 1961.

I'm alright when his arm comes over, but I'm out of form by the time the bloody ball gets here.

Fred Trueman, done in the flight, by Hampshire slow left-armer, Peter Sainsbury, 1963.

England's always expecting. No wonder they call her the Mother Country.

Fred Trueman, asked for a final effort in a Test match.

I had asked the publishers to call my biography 'T' Definitive Volume on t'Finest Fast Bowler That Ever Drew Breath'. But the silly buggers just intend to call it 'Fred.'

Fred Trueman, 1971.

Tell me, Fred, have you ever bowled a ball which merely went straight?

Richard Hutton's lugubrious enquiry to Fred Trueman during their Yorkshire playing days.

Fred Trueman the mature fast bowler was a sharply pointed and astutely directed weapon; Fred Trueman the man has often been tactless, haphazard, crude, a creature of impulse.

John Arlott, in *Fred*, 1971.

Fred not only bowled fast. He was a fast bowler to the very depths of his soul.

John Hampshire on Fred Trueman in *Family Argument*, 1983.

People only called me 'Fiery' because it rhymes with Fred, just like 'Typhoon' rhymes with Tyson.

Fred Trueman, BBC radio, as recorded in *Private Eye*, 1983.

Bad luck, Peter lad. The Reverend has more chance than most of us when he puts his hands together.

Rev David Sheppard's version of Fred Trueman's celebrated one-liner. This time it occurs in the dressing room after Peter Parfitt's dismissal in the Gentlemen vs Players match, 1962.

They say the fool of the family always goes into the church.

Ted Dexter, referring to a series of run-out disasters involving Rev David Sheppard, Australia vs England, 1963.

If I bowled to Barrington, I would bowl a bouncer or two, just to please my own ego.

Bill Bowes, former England medium pacer, who watched Ken Barrington (Surrey and England) batting against South Africa in 1960 and concluded that he was not happy against the quicks.

Whenever I see Ken coming to the wicket, I imagine the Union Jack fluttering behind him.

Wally Grout, Australian wicketkeeper, 1965, taking a more charitable view of Ken Barrington, a renowned scrapper.

I felt as if I had come third in an egg-and-spoon race at school and been awarded the prize because the first two had been disqualified.

Colin Cowdrey, assuming the England captaincy after a time-wasting controversy that caused the removal of his predecessor, Brian Close, 1967.

I was fascinated by an adorable girl.

Ted Dexter, explaining his delayed arrival for his first season at Sussex following Cambridge University's tour of Copenhagen, 1957.

The only question that remained in one's mind about his fielding was the continual doubt as to which end he was throwing at.

Jim Laker, *Over to Me*, on Ted Dexter's fielding on the MCC tour of Australia, 1958/9.

Does a dandy chew gum? Who knows – nowadays.

GD Martineau, in *The Cricketer*, on Ted Dexter, Sussex and England.

There is no doubt that Dexter can handle a bat, but who is going to handle Dexter?

Doubtful England selector after Ted Dexter's appointment as captain, 1962.

As I grew older, the elastic snapped. I lost the pace, the zip and the sting had gone. I remember taking two catches off my own bowling against Glamorgan, and being complimented on my cleverly disguised slower ball.

Ted Dexter, bemoaning advancing years in *Wisden Cricket Monthly*, 1980.

Too high? If the ball had hit his head it would have hit the bloody wickets!

Alan Brown, Kent seam bowler, denied an lbw appeal against Lancashire batsman Harry Pilling (5 ft 3 in), 1960s.

That's not a drink, lad. Fetch me a decent drink.

Brian Close, battered and bruised by the West Indies pace attack at Old Trafford in 1976. England's 12th man, Derek Randall, exchanged the tot of whisky he had originally offered for nearly half a pint.

Cor, he doesn't half swear a lot.

A young member of the Yorkshire Academy team, adjusting to the return of Brian Close, as captain, at the age of 63, for the side's entry into the Yorkshire League, 1994.

I can't see the ball, but I can still hear it whistle.

Brian Close, after a match-winning 39 not out that same season.

I would have died for Yorkshire. I suppose once or twice I nearly did.

Brian Close.

I always told him that it was a good job he was left-handed and had his heart on the other side.

Ray Illingworth on Brian Close, 1994.

Eh up, Raymond, t'rudder's gone again.

Jimmy Binks, Yorkshire wicketkeeper, to Ray Illingworth, reflecting Brian Close's tendency to let his mind wander.

There were times when Closey could make Walter Mitty appear a modest realist.

Ray East, *A Funny Turn*, 1983.

To bowl this lad Denness you don't have to bowl fast. You just have to run up fast.

Brian Close, 1974, dismissing the talents of Mike Denness, Kent and England.

When he asked me if I wanted to turn out, I thought he wanted me to play him at golf.

Fred Titmus, after a phone call from Don Bennett, Middlesex secretary, offering a recall at 46, 1979.

I've always been a slogger and my father was a slogger before me.

Colin Milburn (Northamptonshire, England), 1966.

Shall we put our heads down and make runs, or get out quickly and make history?

Don Shepherd, joining Peter Walker with Glamorgan 11–8 versus Leicestershire, 1971.

4

Deadly Rivals

If the countless columns written about him were placed end to end, they would stretch, on a still day, from the pavilion end at Puckapunyal, and would reach beyond the bounds of credibility.

The effect of Don Bradman, Australian batsman, and reputedly the finest the world has ever seen, as assessed by journalist **Ray Robinson**.

It is strange, but I think true, that all the time, day and night, somewhere in the world somebody is talking about Bradman.

Jack Ingham.

Tell me, Mr Ferguson, do you use an adding machine when The Don comes out to bat?

King George VI's enquiry of the Australian scorer during the 1948 tour of England.

I want to know everything.

King George VI, asking to be kept informed of Don Bradman's critical illness in 1934.

Mandela's first words to me were: 'Fraser, can you please tell me, is Donald Bradman still alive?'

Malcolm Fraser, Australian Prime Minister.

Oh! I've just been talking to Don Bradman. He is as shy as a gazelle and as modest as a buttercup. I felt like taking him in my arms and kissing him, he's so nice.

London society woman.

The grin was the cheekiest, the most challenging and the most confident thing I have seen in sport.

Jack Fingleton, on Don Bradman.

No one ever laughed about Bradman. He was no laughing matter.

RC Robertson-Glasgow.

In the 20 years of the Australian's reign it has become the habit to think of cricket as the World vs Bradman.

AA Thomson.

A number of Bradmans would quickly put an end to the glorious uncertainty of cricket.

Sir Neville Cardus.

To bat with him was an exercise in embarrassing futility.

Don Bradman, as seen by his Australian batting partner, **Jack Fingleton**.

Bradman is living witness to the very important truth that men are not equal.

Christian Renewal magazine.

He was the best in making the placement of a field look foolish.

Jack Fingleton, Australian team-mate and journalist, on Don Bradman.

BRADMAN BATS
AND BATS
AND BATS

London *Evening News* headline.

One does well to try and analyse Bradman's mind because, in all cricket, I met no other like it.

Jack Fingleton.

The animal spirits in Bradman are never likely to go mad. He is a purist in a hurry: he administers the orthodox in long and apolistic knocks.

Sir Neville Cardus.

How to get Bradman out is developing into a pastime for rainy days.

Arthur Mailey, Australian spin bowler and team-mate.

There's no ruddy best ball to bowl at the Don.

Bill Voce, 1933.

Bradman probably sits up in the middle of the night and roars with laughter at such feeble attempts to get him out.

Arthur Mailey, Australian bowler.

Pin him down! Of course not! I bowled every ball to get the little devil out.

Maurice Tate, England bowler, on the futility of bowling to contain Don Bradman.

The bowler who is confronted by Bradman and doesn't think doesn't bowl for long.

Harold Larwood, England fast bowler in the Bodyline series.

He had all the strokes – and the will and the nerve to crush a bowler's heart.

Don Bradman, as seen by England bowler **Alec Bedser**.

My feet feel tired when I think of him.

Joe Hardstaff, England batsman, on fielding with Don Bradman at the wicket.

Bradman didn't break my heart in 1930, he just made me very, very tired.

Harold Larwood.

They said I was a killer with the ball without taking into account that Bradman with the bat was the greatest killer of all.

Harold Larwood, reflecting upon Bodyline.

Luckiest duck I ever made.

Don Bradman, after aborigine Eddie Gilbert summoned up the fastest ball he had ever faced, 1931.

Hollies pitches the ball up slowly and ... he's bowled ... Bradman bowled Hollies nought ... bowled Hollies nought ... and what do you say under these circumstances? How ... I wonder if you see the ball very clearly in your last Test in England, on a ground where you've played some of the biggest cricket in your life and where the opposing side has just stood around you and given you three cheers, and the crowd has clapped you all the way to the wicket. I wonder if you see the ball at all.

John Arlott's BBC radio commentary at The Oval, 1948. Don Bradman, in his last Test, was bowled for nought, second ball, by a googly from Eric Hollies.

It's not easy to bat with tears in your eyes.

Don Bradman, on his emotional state when Hollies bowled him, The Oval, 1948.

I didn't see any tears, and I was standing behind the stumps, right up close.

Godfrey Evans on the same incident.

Never, never have I heard more tragic words fall from the lips of any man.

Sir William Norman Birkett, upon Don Bradman's retirement.

All England feels that now, at last, we may be able to fight for the Ashes on more equal terms again.

Bill Edrich, England batsman, upon Bradman's retirement.

I spoke to Don Bradman and he said, 'You've got to end with a duck.' I said, 'If it's good enough for you, it's good enough for me.'

Desmond Haynes, whose last first-class match finished with a duck for Western Province in Cape Town, 1997.

I've seen someone who reminds me of you.

Alec Bedser, in a phone call to Sir Donald Bradman, after witnessing Michael Slater's century for New South Wales against Western Australia, 1992/3.

Bradman was a team in himself. I think the Don was too good: he spoilt the game ... I do not think we want to see another one quite like him. I do not think we ever shall.

Jack Hobbs, who counted himself 'human' by comparison, 1952.

The one player who came close to mastering the game.

Keith Stackpole, Australian batsman, on Don Bradman.

Because Bradman will always be remembered is no reason why Ponsford should be neglected; when the sun rises it is a mistake to forget the moon.

RC Robertson-Glasgow, remembering another fine Australian batsman, Bill Ponsford.

Come and see this. Don't miss a minute of it. You'll never see the likes of this again.

Don Bradman to the Australian side during Stan McCabe's 232 vs England at Trent Bridge, 1938.

Victor Trumper had the greatest charm and two strokes for every ball.

CB Fry, *Life Worth Living*, 1930.

There was no triumph in me as I watched the receding figure. I felt like a boy who had killed a dove.

Arthur Mailey, in *10 for 66 and All That*, on the bowling of his idol Victor Trumper in a Sydney Grade match.

If Arthur Mailey was not cricket's greatest bowler, he was its greatest philosopher.

Ben Travers, on the Australian slow bowler, 1967.

If I ever bowl a maiden over, it's not my fault.

Arthur Mailey, Australian spin bowler.

I used to bowl tripe, then I wrote it, now I sell it.

Notice above Arthur Mailey's butcher's shop near Sydney.

It was rather a pity Ellis got run out at 1107, because I was just striking a length.

Arthur Mailey, who took four for 362 while Victoria scored 1107 vs New South Wales, 1926.

One of the gentlest bowlers ever to lift a ball, he walked gently, picked up a cup of tea gently, arranged his tie with whispering fingers.

Arthur Mailey on Clarrie Grimmett (Australia) in *10 for 66 and All That*, 1961.

Clarrie Grimmett thought that a full toss was the worst form of cricket vandalism and the long-hop a legacy from prehistoric days when barbarians rolled boulders towards the enemy.

Arthur Mailey, Australian slow bowler, on a more serious-minded teammate.

To hit him for four would usually arouse a belligerent ferocity which made you sorry. It was almost like disturbing a hive of bees.

Don Bradman on Bill O'Reilly (Australia), *Farewell to Cricket*, 1950.

He is the only athlete I have ever known who, as he walked, sagged at ankles, knees and hips.

John Arlott on Ken Mackay (Australia) in *The Cricketer*, 1963.

He planned every move from the time he got up in the morning to the time he went to bed.

Bobby Simpson, Australia coach on Richie Benaud (quoted in Gideon Haigh's *One Summer Every Summer*, 1995).

He can be quite delightful because he is so charming. He can be quite impossible because he can be so selfish. And he is quite unpredictable because he has a touch of genius.

Keith Miller, as depicted by **Ian Johnson**, former Australian captain.

He was a great man at a party and played a part in ensuring no English brewery went out of business through lack of patronage.

Ray Lindwall, Australian fast bowler, as viewed by **Jim Laker** in *Over to Me*, 1960.

I could never read the scores on the board. The specialist said to me: 'Who leads you out to bat?'

Neil Harvey, Australian batsman, admitting defective eyesight.

It's in the eyes.

Harry Soloman, Sri Lankan cricketer, explaining why Steve Waugh's determination won him an Australian place before his brother Mark.

People don't pay to watch me anymore. They come to see me drop dead from exhaustion or old age.

Bill Alley, Somerset's Australian all-rounder, 1967.

He's not one of us. We can't understand him.

The view on Bobby Simpson, Australian batsman, as expressed by his team-mate **Neil Hawke** after a heavy defeat in South Africa, 1966.

If you threw a ball to Wally Grout a bit off target, you'd get the full treatment. One hell of a glare and something like: 'These hands are my life, protect them!'

Neil Hawke, Grout's Australian team-mate, on wicketkeeper's priorities, 1972.

The only bowler I've ever come across who never appealed.

Dickie Bird, on Garth McKenzie, Leicestershire and Australia seam bowler, in *Not Out*, 1978.

A corpse with pads on.

Bill Lawry, described by an **English journalist** on Australia's 1968 tour of England.

I don't try to be Joe Blow, the super-stud – it just happens.

Jeff Thomson, Australian fast bowler, in *Thommo*, 1981.

Chappell was a coward. He needed a crowd around him before he would say anything. He was sour like milk that had been sitting in the sun for a week.

Judgment on Ian Chappell, Australia, from **Ian Botham**, in *It Sort of Clicks*, Botham and Peter Roebuck, 1986.

Border is a walnut, hard to crack and without much to please the eye.

Peter Roebuck on Allan Border, Australian batsman.

Border has not so much a style as a *modus operandi*. He is utterly practical.

John Woodcock on Allan Border, *The Times*, 1985.

A terrier who barks and growls and will not give in. In trouble, Border spits and scraps, but hides his passion. Border inspires best those as regular and capable as himself.

Peter Roebuck, on Allan Border, 1989.

Boon appears a most contented cricketer. I can visualize him on a sheep farm in Tasmania, sipping lager on the verandah, the ideal temperament for dealing with fast bowlers.

Sir Len Hutton, on David Boon, Australian batsman, 1985.

All right, if that's the way you feel, let's get a Queenslander out here.

The jibe by **Allan Border**, Australia's captain, which dissuaded Dean Jones, a Victorian, from retiring through exhaustion during his epic double century against India in Madras in 1986. Greg Ritchie, a Queenslander, was due in next. Jones ultimately collapsed from dehydration and was rushed to hospital.

He might bully at times, but he would never hurt the game he loves.

One of the more positive assessments of Dean Jones, who resigned as Derbyshire captain after a players' revolt. It came from **Les Stillman**, the county's coach and a fellow Victorian, 1997.

Deano, you might be the greatest player Victoria has produced, but you'll retire without a friend in the game.

Darren Berry, Victorian wicketkeeper, to Dean Jones in the Perth dressing room, during a stormy Sheffield Shield season, 1996/7.

The mincing run-up resembles someone in high heels and a panty girdle chasing after a bus.

Merv Hughes, Australian fast bowler, profiled by **Martin Johnson**, in *The Independent*, 1993. (Johnson also remarked upon 'a heart the size of Ayers Rock'.)

A big sleep-in, a half decent round of golf, followed by a barbecue at home with my wife and a few mates sinking a few cans and then send out for dial-a pizza.

Merv Hughes's response in *The Cricketer*, 1993, to the question: 'How in your wildest dreams would you most like to spend a day/night?'

Merv spends more than that on a round of drinks.

Australian team-mate after Merv Hughes had been docked 10 per cent of his match fee by ICC referee Donald Carr for misbehaviour during the Test against South Africa, 1994.

The very model of the modern Australian fast bowler, a caricature that was big, bad and ugly.

Peter Roebuck, on Merv Hughes in the *Sunday Times*, 1988.

An ordinary bloke trying to make good without ever losing the air of a fellow with a hangover.

Peter Roebuck, again on Merv Hughes, in the *Sunday Times*, 1988.

I've completed my player profile now; I've finally got a biggest disappointment in cricket.

Ian Healy, Australia wicketkeeper, whose missed stumping off Shane Warne allowed Pakistan the winning runs and a one-wicket victory in the Karachi Test, 1994.

Use it as an experience – life's realities form the canvas. Must now get on with it.

Entry in **Ian Healy**'s diary after the Australian keeper missed a stumping to give Pakistan a one-wicket victory in the Karachi Test, 1994.

As great a spinner as ever was born. He does things no one else even thinks about and he does them standing on his head. In his hand a cricket ball curses and spits and sings and whispers and screams and shouts.

Shane Warne, praised by **Peter Roebuck**, *Sunday Times*, after bowling Australia to Brisbane Test win against England, 1994.

You haven't got it son.

Mike Tamblyn, captain of Brighton CC, a Melbourne sub-district side, to a young Shane Warne. (From Warne: *Sultan of Spin*, Ken Piesse, 1995.)

He used to hit the side of the net, the roof, everything. At one stage he said to me, 'I'll never be able to bowl this.'

Jack Potter, head coach at the Australian Cricket Academy, describing Shane Warne's earliest attempts at a flipper.

There are tons of easy pickings out there.

Bill O'Reilly, former Australian leg-spinner, assessing the challenge facing budding leggie, Shane Warne, during his Test debut, 1992.

I knew how I felt when I played my first Test. I couldn't feel my feet walking down the stairs at Adelaide. He probably couldn't feel his fingers. If a spinner can't feel his fingers, how is he going to bowl?

Geoff Marsh, Australian batsman, after Shane Warne's disastrous start to Test cricket – a double ton for India's Ravi Shastri at Sydney.

That must be the greatest heist since the Great Train Robbery.

Allan Border after Australia's amazing recovery, from 291 runs behind on the first innings, to beat Sri Lanka at the SSC in Colombo. Shane Warne made his first mark on Test cricket, finishing things off with 3–0 in 11 balls. 1992/3 season.

In the space of one delivery so much had changed. My confidence was sky-high. I was pumped up and rock'n'rolling.

Shane Warne, on the emotional fallout from the 'Ball of the Century' – Mike Gatting, bowled by a huge leg-break, Old Trafford, 1993 – Warne's first ball in an Ashes Test.

My theory is that he spins the ball too much. When Grimmett or O'Reilly beat your bat, they usually hit the wicket. Warne beats the bat, the wicket and everything. What's the good of that, eh?

RES Wyatt, former England captain, unimpressed by talk of Shane Warne as the best leg-spinner in history, 1995.

This secret new delivery starts off going down the legside, stops in mid-air, whistles the tune of Advance Australia Fair, reverses back to the bowler, then shakes the hand of every member of the fielding side before homing in on and uprooting all three stumps.

Peter Hayter, *Mail on Sunday*, on Shane Warne's supposed mystery ball, Ashes series, 1994/5.

Shooter and zooter, my foot.

Geoffrey Boycott, in *The Sun*, scoffing at Shane Warne's supposed new mystery ball, 1994.

I still have the butterflies, but I now have them flying in formation.

Mark Taylor, Australian batsman, escaping a bad run of form, 1997.

I enjoy the nightlife. I enjoy going out. I enjoy wearing an earring. I shave my head. But that's just me. I'm just there to please myself.

Colin Miller, Tasmania, shortly before his outstanding 1998 Sheffield Shield season brought an Australian call-up at 34.

My face is my own and I'll do what I like with it.

George John, the great West Indian fast bowler, accused of sulking during
the 1923 tour of England. (He was 38 at the time, and well past his best.)
Related in **CLR James**'s *Beyond a Boundary*.

Like trying to play a bunch of confetti.

The difficulties posed by Sonny Ramadhin, West Indies wrist-spinner.
(Ascribed to a Derbyshire batsman by **Ian Peebles** in *Batter's Castle*, 1958.)

All you see is a blur of black hand, a white shirt with sleeves
buttoned down to the wrist and a red blur.

Denis Compton's advice on reading Sonny Ramadhin to his great
Australian rival, Keith Miller, 1951.

I consider Worrell the sounder in defence, Weekes the greater
attacking force; Worrell the more graceful, Weekes the more devastating; Worrell the more effective on soft wickets, Weekes the more
so on hard wickets. Worrell gives the bowler less to work on, Weekes
has the wider range of strokes. Both are good starters, but Weekes
is the more businesslike; Worrell appeared to be enjoying an afternoon's sport; whereas Weekes was on the job six times a day.

Everton Weekes and Frank Worrell, West Indies batsmen, as seen by their
former captain, **Jeffrey Stollmeyer** in *Everything Under the Sun*, 1985.

I've come out here to develop a few photographs.

Frank Worrell to Godfrey Evans, England's wicketkeeper, in murky light at
Trent Bridge in 1957. Worrell, who made 191 in the first innings, had been on
the field for more than 20 hours, but still opened when his side followed on.

I suppose I can gain some consolation from the fact that my name
will be permanently in the record books.

Malcolm Nash, Glamorgan bowler, struck for an unprecedented six sixes in
an over by Gary Sobers, West Indies all-rounder, Glamorgan vs Notts,
Swansea, 1968.

It was not sheer slogging through strength, but scientific hitting
with every movement working in harmony.

Tony Lewis, Glamorgan captain, on Gary Sobers's six sixes.

Inspired by a mixture of pride and prejudice.

Viv Richards, Somerset and West Indies, assessed by **Frank Tyson** in *The Test Within*, 1987.

To see him take the field was to hear the beat of drums and to picture an African potentate, all chains and infernal eye, swaggering to the throne. His was a grand entrance, delayed and poised, one that said: 'See how far the little boy from a tiny island has risen, see he cannot be blown away.'

Peter Roebuck, former Somerset colleague, on Viv Richards, 1993.

His game embraced a contempt for his fate, a foaming fury, because to him, cricket was a game of kill or be killed, a street fight in which it was left to the umpires to keep peace.

Roebuck on Richards, 1993.

When he was a boy, a soak de bat and he drink de oil.

Shivnarine Chanderpaul's Uncle Martin, celebrating a Test debut at 19 years old, against England in his native Guyana, 1994.

A wise man doesn't sit with his back to the door.

Curtly Ambrose, West Indian fast bowler in a rare observation intercepted by a journalist, 1995.

For one hour, on an untrustworthy pitch, he performed like the very devil himself.

Mark Nicholas, in the *Daily Telegraph*, on Curtly Ambrose's destruction of England, dismissed for 46 in the Trinidad Test, 1994.

West Indies minus Ambrose = Poms.

Banner at Perth Test, 1997. West Indies, including Ambrose, won by a street.

Whispering Death.

The nickname of Michael Holding, West Indian pace bowler.

A perfect running specimen, but I don't go to a Test to see running; if I wished to see that I would go to Crystal Palace to see Coe and Ovett.

Jack Fingleton on West Indian Michael Holding, in *Batting From Memory*, 1981.

Blimey, the bugger can't bend as well can he?

Brian Close, witnessing Joel Garner, the West Indian fast bowler, for the first time at Somerset, 1977.

I will not be pushed by other people's agenda or ambition.

The remark by **Richie Richardson**, West Indies captain, that caused Brian Lara to walk out of their tour of England, 1995.

Pressure is what turns a rock into a diamond, but it can turn it into dust.

Wes Hall, West Indies team manager, after Brian Lara's withdrawal from the Benson & Hedges one-day series in Australia, 1995. Lara was protesting over his punishment for incidents on the tour of England earlier that summer.

Dermot Reeve: The more Tim bowls, the better he gets. He's a captain's dream.

Brian Lara: He's a bad captain's dream.

Testy exchange over Tim Munton between captain, **Reeve**, and star player, **Lara**, at Northampton, indicating the growing rift between them during Warwickshire's 1995 season.

Brian, you're turning into a prima donna.

Dermot Reeve's admonishment of Lara during the same Northamptonshire match. Soon afterwards, Lara announced that he had a knee injury and left the field, 1995.

Who the hell does Brian Lara think he is? Cricket has made him a superstar and he should never forget it.

Ian Botham, railing about Brian Lara's complaints of burn-out, 1995.

I'd just like to say that it's a privilege to be sharing the same sporting arena with someone who is bigger than the game.

England seam bowler, **Angus Fraser**, irritated by Brian Lara's behaviour, during the final Test against the West Indies, at The Oval, 1995.

I'm off to another world, via the bat room.

Aubrey Faulkner, of South Africa, in a suicide note left before he gassed himself, 1930.

In cricketing terms Graeme Pollock is a sadist.

Eddie Barlow, on his South African team-mate.

When I walk off a cricket field for the last time – whenever that will be – it will be with an enormous sense of relief.

Barry Richards, South African batsman, 1978.

I would have preferred fewer runs and more friends.

Barry Richards, recalling his time with Hampshire during a benefit match for Mark Nicholas, 1991.

I go to a party on Friday night, sometimes until 4 a.m., then score 50 and take five wickets.

Omar Henry, the first coloured player to represent South Africa, 1987.

Cronje is like a chilli – cool on the surface and hot once the skin has been removed.

Peter Roebuck, on South Africa's captain Hansie Cronje, 1998.

A great clockmaker would have been proud to have set Bedi in motion – a mechanism finely balanced, cogs rolling silently and hands sweeping in smooth arcs across the face.

Bishen Bedi, India and Northamptonshire slow left-armer, as seen by **Tony Lewis**.

In the country of the blind, the one-eyed man is king. But in the keen-eyed world of cricket, a fellow with just one good eye and a bit has to settle for something less than the perfection he once sought.

The **Nawab of Pataudi**, reflecting upon his eyesight limitations.

He didn't turn a single ball from leg to off. We shouldn't have much problem with him.

The verdict of **Keith Fletcher**, England coach, after a spying mission upon Anil Kumble in South Africa. The Indian spinner took 21 wickets in a three-Test series; England were whitewashed, 1993.

He was unstoppable. I'll be going to bed having nightmares of Sachin just running down the wicket and belting me for six. I don't think anyone, besides Don Bradman, is in the same class.

Shane Warne, mauled by Sachin Tendulkar, who averaged 113 against the Australian tourists in India, 1998.

He is sent from upstairs to play the game.

The talent of Sachin Tendulkar, witnessed at 15 years old, by his India team-mate **Ravi Shastri**, in *Declarations*, 1989.

Running with Miandad can be a dangerous business. He is lightning fast, and if he got rid of the extra ballast by removing the gold nuggets draped around his neck, he could look for two to short leg.

Martin Johnson on Javed Miandad, *The Independent*.

Some opponents get the wrong idea because I smile a lot.

Javed Miandad, on suggestions that he irritated his opponents, in *Declarations*, 1979.

I think he's a snob. He doesn't mix. And he gets very angry and picks on players for no reason.

Imran Khan, attacked by his Pakistani team-mate **Qasim Omar** in 1987. (Qasim had infuriated Imran by making drug allegations against international cricketers.)

A Pathan with the Khan genes has a vengeful fire in his belly. They also keep their eye on the ball.

Jonah Barrington, former world squash champion, on Imran Khan.

Gel is more macho than a hair band.

Wasim Akram, on his chosen method of keeping his hair out of his eyes, 1996.

You don't need a helmet facing Waqar so much as a steel toe cap.

Simon Hughes, extolling the swinging yorker perfected by Pakistan's Waqar Younis.

The only things that really keep me going are statistics.

Richard Hadlee, New Zealand fast bowler, *At the Double*, 1985.

It was like batting against the World XI at one end and Ilford Second XI at the other.

Mike Gatting on the comparative strengths of Richard Hadlee and his New Zealand colleagues, Lord's Test, 1986.

Imagine being enclosed in a small, illuminated space and being fed a barrage of searching questions by an indefatigable examiner. Your responses are nervous gibberish. It soon became clear that facing Hadlee was a bit like this.

Simon Hughes, reflecting upon the bowling of Richard Hadlee in *A Lot of Hard Yakka*, 1997.

His approach is calculating, commercial, bloodless, too much the chartered accountant to be heroic.

Scyld Berry, on Richard Hadlee in the *Observer*, 1988.

His secret is his action, which is faultless and almost robotically repetitive, regardless of the speed or length of delivery.

Simon Hughes, Middlesex seam bowler, on Hadlee, 1988.

He doesn't sledge you but he does intimidate you. He's actually one of the most aggressive bowlers I've ever faced. He uses eye contact – he has a presence.

Hadlee, as seen by **Greg Matthews**, Australian all-rounder.

He won't be great until he stops being a perfectionist.

Martin Crowe, New Zealand batsman, summed up by **Ian Botham** during their time together at Somerset, in *It Sort of Clicks*, Botham and Peter Roebuck, 1986.

All those rumours. He's supposed to have had marriage break-ups, Aids, homosexuality ... that's a lot to cope with. You'd have to be talking murder, rape or embezzlement to be much worse.

Sir Richard Hadlee on Martin Crowe's increasingly introverted personality.

The New Zealand public respects ruggedness, durability and humility. But mainstream New Zealand doesn't see Martin as having those qualities. He believes New Zealanders knock him for his cricket ability. In fact, they admire him for that, but only that. They knock him for his behaviour. The public believe he is a prima-donna, spoilt and pampered, neurotic.

John Morrison, former New Zealand cricketer, on Martin Crowe.

New Zealanders don't relate to excellence.

An alternative view, expressed by Martin's brother, and fellow international, **Jeff Crowe**.

He is New Zealand's ace tall poppy.

Dave Crowe, Martin's father, reflecting in *The Cricketer*, on why his son received so much criticism, 1994.

This tall poppy stuff is bullshit.

John Wright, Crowe's former New Zealand colleague.

Martin cultivates that class thing with his talk about wine and fine restaurants. That irritates the hell out of everybody outside Auckland.

John Bracewell, New Zealand team-mate, considering Crowe's patchy popularity.

His regard for New Zealand cricket is more selfish than mine.

Geoff Howarth, a predecessor to Martin Crowe as New Zealand captain.

One minute he's matey, the next it's like a bomb went off.

Mark Priest, New Zealand left-arm spinner, *Martin Crowe: Tortured Genius*, Joseph Romanos, 1995.

I guess he was a sensitive new-age guy.

Bruce Edgar, New Zealand team-mate, on Martin Crowe.

In their youth they feared they might never be able to test themselves in the highest company. Has not the poet written that 'full many a flower is born to blush unseen and waste its sweetness on the desert air'?

Grant and Andy Flower, Zimbabwe brothers, as depicted by **Peter Roebuck**, 1996.

Jayasuriya has bluffed the whole world. Everyone thinks he's a slogger, but he isn't.

Greg Chappell, on Sri Lanka's Sanath Jayasuriya, 1998.

5

Arts and Sciences

Batting
Bowling
Fielding and Wicketkeeping
Captaincy
Umpiring
Pitches

Batting

Tha knows one thing I learned about cricket: tha can't put in what God left out. Tha sees two kinds of cricketers, them that uses a bat as if they are shovelling muck and them that plays proper, and like as not God showed both of 'em how to play.

Wilfred Rhodes, from Michael Parkinson's *Cricket Mad*, 1969.

It were impossible to fault him. He got 'em on good 'uns, he got 'em on bad 'uns, he got 'em on sticky 'uns, he got 'em on t'mat, against South African googlers, and he got 'em all over t'world.

Wilfred Rhodes on Sir Jack Hobbs (Surrey, England).

A snick by Jack Hobbs is a sort of disturbance of cosmic orderliness.

Sir Neville Cardus.

If all living things in India are incarnations, Gavaskar is technical orthodoxy made flesh.

Scyld Berry, as Sunil Gavaskar equalled Bradman's world record of 29 Test centuries, India vs West Indies, Delhi, 1983/4.

Some challenged, like Trumper, some charmed, like Ranjitsinhji; Bradman devastated – deliberately, coldly, ruthlessly.

JM Kilburn, on Don Bradman's batting style.

Look at Border. He's scored 10,000 Test runs and he's only got three shots – the cut, the cover drive and the pull.

Jack Birkenshaw, Leicestershire manager, admiring the approach of Allan Border, 1994.

I never wanted to make a hundred. Who wants to make a hundred anyway? When I first went in, my immediate objective was to hit the ball to each of the four corners of the field. After that I tried not to be repetitive.

Sir Learie Constantine, speech to the Royal Commonwealth Society, 1963.

All I have to do is bowl loopy-doopies to them and they commit suicide.

Phil Tufnell on West Indies batsmen, 1994.

No man on this earth could ever get 300 runs in a day if the opposition set out to contain him.

Don Bradman, discussing his achievement of that feat, BBC radio, 1966.

The singles and the threes are the vital scoring shots in cricket, not the twos and the fours.

Bobby Simpson, Australian captain, on the advantages to batsmen of rotating the strike.

I saw Len Hutton in his prime.
Another time, another time.

'Poem' by **Harold Pinter**, 1986.

There's nothing we can teach this lad.

George Hirst, Yorkshire coach, on Len Hutton's first appearance at county nets, 1930.

There's not a batting coach in the world that would get a good technique out of me.

Ben Hollioake, accepting his limitations very early in life, 1998.

Ninety-nine per cent of cricket manuals belong in the dustbin.

Ian Botham, introducing his own.

Pisshole shot Botham, pisshole shot. But if you keep hittin' it son, you keep playing it.

MCC coach **Harry Sharp**, during Ian Botham's time on the ground-staff.

Enjoyment, given and felt, is the chief thing about Compton's batting. It is a clear-flowing stream, a breath of half-holiday among work days.

RC Robertson-Glasgow on Denis Compton (Middlesex, England).

He destroys bowlers nicely.

Bob Woolmer, Warwickshire coach, after witnessing Brian Lara's record-breaking innings of 375 and 501, 1994.

His innings had all the familiar traits: defiance, a terrible stillness at execution, chiselled defence ... Waugh's innings was clipped, capable, discriminating and withering. Every ball passed through the laboratory of his mind and no stroke was played without the most careful consideration.

Peter Roebuck, *Sunday Telegraph*, during Steve Waugh's match-winning century at Old Trafford, 1997.

Batting is a major trial before an 11-man jury.

Richie Benaud, Australian captain.

There is probably a greater premium on temperament for a batsman than for any player in any branch of sport.

Sir Donald Bradman, *The Art of Cricket*, 1958.

Nerves play as important a part in batsmanship as skill.

Gilbert Jessop.

Find out where the ball is, go there, hit it.

Ranji's three precepts of batsmanship.

The one and only way to foil a spin attack is by quick footwork, aggression and the spirit of adventure.

Charlie Macartney, Headingley Test, England vs Australia, 1938.

Footwork doesn't mean moving your feet all over the place. It's positioning.

Wilfred Rhodes, Yorkshire and England spinner, 1954.

If you're a good enough player, you don't need to leave your crease.

Coaching, Basil D'Oliveira-style. From **Graeme Hick**, *My Early Life*, 1991.

You were simply caught in two-man's land.

Ken Barrington, England manager on the 1980 West Indies tour, explaining a dismissal to Brian Rose.

You don't need footwork in batting, just hands and eye.

Majid Khan, to Glamorgan team-mates, 1969.

Any fool can play forward.

AC MacLaren, England captain, 1921.

They were nearly all made off the back foot.

Jack Hobbs, explaining why his 85 first-class centuries after the First World War did not match those made in his youth.

The best technique in the world is no good if you're backing away to square leg.

Geoffrey Boycott, coaching England's batsmen on attributes they would need in the West Indies, 1989.

There are many cries for the batsman to get behind the ball, but how can you hit it hard if you are behind it?

Ted Dexter, England batsman.

It is wonderful what a useful shield that narrow strip of willow can be if properly manipulated.

Ranjitsinhji, *Jubilee Book of Cricket*, on how to handle the dangers of fast bowling.

You're not Ranji, so aim at mid-on's nut and you'll find that the ball will go over the square-leg boundary.

Sammy Woods's advice to his Somerset colleagues.

It's hard work making batting look effortless.

David Gower, England batsman, 1989.

The cut was never a business stroke.

Wilfred Rhodes.

The cover drive is the most beautiful stroke in batsmanship. Does that throw any light on why I am a self-admitted lover of all things British and traditional?

Well, does it? **Colin Cowdrey**, in his autobiography, *MCC*, in 1976.

I tend to look for my runs using the wrong shot at the wrong time.

David Gower, England batsman.

For a long time the swinging ball filled me with the fear of God.

Colin Cowdrey, England batsman, on his early struggles at Kent.

Every batsman's dream should be a day with off-break bowlers.

Arthur Mailey, *10 for 66 and All That*, 1959.

There's more ways of getting out than is shown in t'rules.

Wilfred Rhodes, 1930.

Fender gave some amusement by hitting Armstrong back-handed on the offside for a couple.

Pelham Warner, perhaps recording the first reverse sweep, from Percy Fender in his report in *The Cricketer* on the Old Trafford Test of 1921 between England and Australia.

What do I think of the reverse sweep? It's like Manchester United getting a penalty and Bryan Robson taking it with his head.

David Lloyd, former England opening batsman. Lloyd had to grin and bear it when he became England coach.

I have thumbed through the MCC coaching manual and found that no such stroke exists.

Peter May, chairman of selectors, after observing Ian Botham play a reverse sweep, 1985.

I wonder whether Bradman will ever get tired of making runs?

Clem Hill, Australian team-mate, on Don Bradman's insatiable appetite for batting.

When you boiled Bradman down, when you analysed his eyesight, his footwork, his judgment, his range of strokes, there was still something left in which he was also superior to all others, and that was consistency.

Jack Fingleton.

As I ran up, Bradman seemed to know what I was going to bowl, where the ball was going to pitch, and how many runs he was going to score.

Jim Laker, England off-spinner.

You woke up in the night time and your arm was still going round.

L O'B Fleetwood-Smith, Australian left-arm wrist spinner, heavily punished during Len Hutton's 364 for England at The Oval, 1938. Hutton batted for 13hrs 20mins. (Fleetwood-Smith relived it on BBC Radio in 1970.)

I didn't even know the record existed.

Graeme Hick after scoring 405 not out for Worcestershire vs Somerset at Taunton, 19 short of what was then the record first-class score in England, set by AC MacLaren, 1988.

I woke up at 4 a.m. with my hands sweating and couldn't get back to sleep. I've been batting the innings since then, and now it's finished I'm very happy.

Brian Lara, upon beating Gary Sobers's record Test score, West Indies vs England in Antigua, 1994. Lara began the third day 320 not out, requiring another 46 (exactly the score for which the entire England team had been dismissed in Trinidad, two Tests earlier).

I don't think a better player could have broken the record. To me, Lara is the only batsman playing today who plays the game the way it should be played. He hits the ball with the bat, not the pad.

Sir Garfield Sobers, previous holder of the record score in Test cricket (365), celebrating Brian Lara's 375 vs England in Antigua, 1994.

I still don't think this 500 makes me a great cricketer. I've still much to learn.

Brian Lara, after his 501 not out (Warwickshire vs Durham, Edgbaston, June 1994) gave him the highest score in first-class cricket history.

I was thinking about declaring, but then at lunchtime Brian came and started talking about Hanif Mohammad's world record.

Dermot Reeve, Warwickshire captain, on the same innings, 1994.

He's had a fantastic season, but I wondered what was going on down there. Cricket's about trying to win a game.

Raymond Illingworth, England's chairman of selectors. (Scores in Lara's match: Durham 556-8dec, Warwickshire 810-4dec. Match drawn.)

We're still a good outfit.

John Morris, stand-in captain of the hapless Durham attack, and the bowler who conceded the record-breaking run, 1994.

Brian is short and so am I. It's all in the height of a batsman.

Hanif Mohammad, former Pakistan batsman, holder of the previous first-class record of 499.

I doubt whether the publishers will want to do a supplement straightaway, so it's probably down to me. I just don't know what to do. It's quite breathtaking really.

Robert Brooke, statistician, who had just updated a book of Warwickshire cricket records, and was aghast as Lara's 501 put more than twenty of them out of date in one go, 1994.

Frankly, I doubt whether I will ever call myself great.

Brian Lara, after his 152 against England (and with a Test average approaching 60), Trent Bridge Test, 1995.

We'll get 'em in singles.

George Hirst to Wilfred Rhodes before a last-wicket stand of 15 for England to beat Australia at The Oval, 1902. (Apocryphal.)

It's a tale. I don't think any cricketer would believe it. There'd have been just as much sense if he'd said: 'We'll get 'em in sixes.'

Wilfred Rhodes, on the 'We'll get 'em in singles' remark attributed to Hirst.

'Mr Jones, does it matter what I do?'

'No Alletson, I don't think it matters what you do.'

'Oh, then I'm not half going to give Tom Killick some stick.'

The result of this exchange – between **Edwin Alletson** and his Nottinghamshire captain, **Arthur Jones** – was that Alletson struck 189 in 90 minutes against Sussex at Hove in 1911. (Source: *A History of Cricket*, Benny Green.)

Well played Dickie lad, but get thee bloody 'ead down – tha's in't second team next week.

Brian Sellers, Yorkshire's chairman of selectors, after Dickie Bird's career-best 181 vs Glamorgan at Park Avenue. Ken Taylor, an England opener, was available again, so Bird lost his place, 1959.

Dear Hog!
Great stuff! But be there at tea. We can do this. The whole of the NZ boys need you to do it. Don't throw it away now. Brice is playing superbly for you (and us). God speed. 'Cones.'

Note sent out to Martin Crowe, by team-mate **Jeremy Coney** to help him keep his concentration during a West Indies Test. (Source: *Martin Crowe: Tortured Genius*, Joseph Romanos, 1995.)

I wasn't sure how successful I'd be – my batting is not that good anyway.

Fast bowler **Rowan Lyle**, after going out to bat at no. 11 for Eastern Province against Transvaal in Pretoria complete with crutches, a foot in plaster, a runner and a man carrying his bat. The umpires ordered the crutches back to the pavilion and Lyle hopped around for 0 not out in a last-wicket stand of 25, 1993.

It's very rewarding being a pain in the arse.

England 'keeper **Jack Russell**, after saving the Johannesburg Test against South Africa, alongside Michael Atherton, 1995.

It's always a good idea to aim the first ball right here at the bowler's head. They don't like it. It rattles 'em.

Charlie Macartney, in *Fingleton on Cricket*, 1972.

At the crease my attitude to three bouncers an over has been that, if I'm playing well enough, three bouncers an over should be worth 12 runs to me.

Ian Chappell, Australian batsman, opposing limitations on bouncers, 1970s.

No good hitting me there mate, nothing to damage.

Derek Randall, skulled by Dennis Lillee in the Centenary Test in Melbourne, 1977.

In future, I shall always be able to tell when the cricket season begins. All I have to do is listen to the sound of Brian Close being hit by a cricket ball.

Eric Morecambe, comedian, after Close withstood a barrage of West Indian bouncers on his emergency return to Test cricket, 1976.

Helmets are unfair to bowlers.

Viv Richards, 1985.

He looks like a cuddly little panda.

Tony Brown, England's tour manager, assessing the damage done to Mike Gatting's nose by the West Indian quicks, 1986.

I'll have quite a rugged countenance by the time I'm finished.

Mike Brearley, hit on the nose by the sedately paced Indian seamer KD Ghavri, MCC vs India at Lord's, 1980.

Johnnie, if you get hit again, make sure you drop inside the crease.

Brian Close's advice to John Hampshire after he was poleaxed by a bouncer from Charlie Griffith which gave him headaches for life, 1963.

Dear Mum, things are looking up. Today I got a half-volley in the nets.

David Lloyd, England batsman, in a letter home during the Australian tour of 1972/3.

As the ball whizzed past my head, I remember wondering whether my helmets were any good.

Robin Smith, putting his company's batting helmets to the test, in a courageous innings against the West Indies on a poor Edgbaston pitch, 1995.

Well, his mother was an actress, you know.

Mike Brearley, observing Mark Nicholas's pained response to being hit in the ribs by the Middlesex pace bowler, Wayne Daniel.

Don't give advice to a batsman going in: if he's inexperienced, it will only make him nervous; if he is an old hand, it is generally unnecessary. Give him credit and opportunity to use his own judgment; if he doesn't do so at first, he soon will.

Gilbert Jessop, in the foreword to James Thorpe's *Cricket Bag*, 1929.

When you are in all day the bat never feels heavy. It is only when you are in and out quickly that it weighs.

Colin Cowdrey, in *MCC*, 1976.

To stand ideally is either to inflict upon yourself a form of astigmatism or painful neck wrenching.

AE Knight, *The Complete Cricketer*, 1906.

When I'm coming, I say, 'Yes', and when I'm not, I say 'No'.

Wilfred Rhodes, explaining the mysteries of his excellent understanding over short singles with Jack Hobbs.

'Call, Bomber!'

'Heads!'

Traditional misunderstanding between Gloucestershire's lower-order batsmen, **Sam Cook** and **Bomber Wells**.

'Let's cut out some of the quick singles.'

'OK, Ken, we'll cut out yours.'

Exchange between **Ken Barrington** and **Fred Titmus** towards the end of a hot day in Australia.

I am working very hard on this relaxation business.

Graeme Wood, Australian opening batsman, 1985.

Pakistan's players are so lazy. You cannot give them home exercises. If you win the World Cup without hard work, why work hard? Inzy, he is so lazy! I told him, Inzy, you must lose weight!

Dan Kiesel, Pakistan's physio, risking the wrath of his portly batsman, Inzaman-ul-Haq, in 1988.

You lead in May, and I shall catch you in June.

Philip Mead, Hampshire batsman, to his team-mates having pre-season nets, 1920s.

I'll just have to get another one against the students.

Graham Gooch, informed in India in 1993 that his 100th first-class century was, in fact, only his 99th. The ICC had scrubbed a century scored on a rebel tour to South Africa. Gooch duly reached the landmark against Cambridge University the following May. Later that summer angry statisticians forced the ICC to backtrack.

When you're a batter and a bowler, you enjoy yourself twice as much.

George Hirst, Yorkshire all-rounder.

Bowling

Bowling is the most important thing in the game. It's the brainiest part of cricket.

HM Herman, writer, 1937.

They said to me at The Oval, come and see our new bowling machine. Bowling machine? I said. I used to be the bowling machine.

Alec Bedser, former England bowler, 1989.

Bill, get a notebook. Put down everything you learn about the batsmen, the way they play, their best shots, their weakest shots. For ten years, you'll learn something new every day. After that you'll remember something you've forgotten.

Emmott Robinson to his young Yorkshire colleague, Bill Bowes.

Desire is positive.

First law of **Richard Hadlee**'s cricketing philosophy, the whole of which could be found inside his cricket case – for motivational purposes.

I didn't need anyone to motivate me. Playing for England was all I needed.

Sir Alec Bedser, deriding motivational theories, 1990s.

I used to get bored with batting. All I ever wanted to do was bowl. I had one shot – the slog – and if I hit it, the ball went a long way and the crowd and I were happy. If I missed it, well I was that much closer to bowling.

'Bomber' Wells, Gloucestershire and Nottinghamshire spinner, in *The Spinner's Turn*, 1982.

There's more in bowling than just turning your arm over. There's such a thing as observation.

Wilfred Rhodes, Yorkshire and England spinner.

Bowling which does not get men out, like batting which brings no runs to the score, is an art abused.

AE Knight, *The Complete Cricketer*, 1906.

Ninety per cent of cricket is played in the mind.

Richard Hadlee, asked for advice on fast bowling by his Nottinghamshire team-mate, **Andy Pick**. (Related by Eddie Hemmings in *Coming of Age*, 1991.)

The thicker you are, the better your chances of becoming a quick bowler.

Stewart Storey, Surrey coach, in *From the Nursery End*, 1985.

Sorry, skipper, a leopard can't change his stripes.

Lennie Pascoe, the bellicose Australian fast bowler, apologizing to Ian Chappell for bowling bouncers in bad light and causing a suspension in play.

I used to give every new batsman four balls. One was a bouncer to check his courage, the second a fizzer to check his eyesight, the third was a slow 'un to try out his reflexes and the fourth a bender to see if he was a good cricketer. And if he took a single off each of the four balls, I knew I was in trouble.

Harold Larwood, England fast bowler, 1972.

I regard an over as having six bullets in a gun. I use those bullets strategically, to manipulate the batsman into a certain position or state of mind, so that I can eliminate him.

Richard Hadlee, New Zealand quick.

I never bowled at the wickets: I bowled at the stroke. I intended the batsman to make a stroke, then I tried to beat it. I tried to make the batsman move. The time a batsman makes mistakes is when he has to move his feet.

Sydney Barnes, former England fast bowler, 1953.

To bowl fast is to revel in the glad animal action, to thrill in physical power and to enjoy a certain sneaking feeling of superiority over the mortals who play the game.

Frank Tyson, England fast bowler, in *A Typhoon Called Tyson*.

As lovely a piece of movement as even cricket has ever produced.

John Arlott, on Maurice Tate's bowling action.

I hope you can hold a f****** blade, pal.

Dennis Lillee, struck on the hand by Jeff Thomson, his future fast-bowling partner, during their first meeting, NSW vs Western Australia, 1972/3 season.

There's no batsman on earth who goes out to meet Dennis Lillee and Jeff Thomson with a smile on his face.

Clive Lloyd, 1975.

I kept smiling at Thomson, hoping to keep him in a good mood.

Ranjit Fernando, 5ft 4in Sri Lankan batsman, as two of his team-mates were hospitalized by Jeff Thomson in a World Cup match, 1975.

Do you wish to prefer charges?

Police sergeant to Sunil Wettimuny when he arrived bruised in hospital, during Sri Lanka's clash against Australia in the 1975 World Cup, saying: 'Jeff Thomson did it.'

Ashes to ashes, dust to dust – if Thomson don't get ya, Lillee must.

Sydney Telegraph cartoon caption, 1975.

Wouldn't it be better if I got in the fridge?

Qasim Omar, Pakistan batsman, receiving ice-pack treatment for bruises caused by Australian fast bowlers, Perth Test, 1983.

'Is this a time for heroics or should we go off?'

'I'd eff off if I were you.'

Exchange between **John Barclay**, Sussex's Old Etonian, and the somewhat earthier Aussie fast bowler, **Jeff Thomson**, after Thomson had hit Barclay on the head with a bouncer, 1985.

The first time two batsmen have ever crossed in the toilet.

Tony Lewis, facing the pace of West Indian quick Wes Hall for the first time, Glamorgan vs West Indies, 1963.

I don't know why they bother to put the stumps out. None of those buggers are trying to hit them.

Graeme Fowler, suffering at the hands of the West Indian fast bowlers, Oval Test, 1985.

I don't think I would ever be comfortable against a bloke his size who has a Bible in one hand and a new ball in the other.

County opener, during Ian Bishop's time at Derbyshire, 1991.

I was interested to hear Michael Holding say that Curtly is still learning. I hope he doesn't learn too much more.

Australia's captain, **Allan Border**, after the Adelaide Test. Curtly Ambrose went on to settle the series in West Indies' favour with a devastating spell of seven wickets for one run in the final Test in Perth, 1993.

You never intimidate a good player.

Greg Chappell, Australian batsman, in *Howzat*, 1980.

None of us likes fast bowling, but some of us don't let on.

Maurice Leyland, Yorkshire and England batsman.

There's no sitting duck like a scared duck.

Ray Lindwall, Australian fast bowler.

Sir – 'Cricket' used to be a synonym for honourable conduct. It is now becoming a synonym for brute force. Is it not time that respected leaders in all countries spoke out?

Lord Brockway, letter to *The Guardian*, on short-pitched fast bowling, 1975.

Remember, with those speedsters bowling at 95mph, cricket can kill.

Australian TV advert for Packer Circus, 1975.

I want to hit you Bailey – I want to hit you over the heart.

Peter Heine, South African fast bowler, to Trevor Bailey.

When tha's laikin' wi Fred, tha's not laikin' wi' a soft ball, tha' knows.

Fred Trueman in *Fast Fury*, 1961.

I try to hit a batsman in the rib cage when I bowl a purposeful bouncer, and I want it to hurt so much that the batsman doesn't want to face me any more.

Dennis Lillee, *Back to the Mark*, 1974.

I enjoy hitting a batsman more than getting him out. I like to see blood on the pitch. And I've been training on whisky.

Jeff Thomson, Australian quick, 1974.

I know I'm a ruthless bastard and I always have a go. But I wouldn't deliberately put a ball like that on anybody. It slipped. It honestly slipped.

Dennis Lillee after a beamer to Bob Willis, England's no. 11, in Sydney, MCC in Australia, 1974/5.

I don't really like the new Dennis Lillee. There's no substitute for bowling fast and being able to make the good players jump.

Dennis Lillee, *My Life in Cricket*, 1982, after his back injury had forced him to substitute skill for speed.

The coming of guile to the fast bowler can be like the advance of creeping paralysis to the body. Outwardly, thought and cunning methods add to the armoury of the quick bowler and make him the complete, shrewd, mechanically perfect athlete. Inwardly, guile saps the physical foundations to the edifice of fast bowling until it takes away the real desire and very reasons for wanting to bowl quick.

Frank Tyson, *A Typhoon Called Tyson*.

It'll be all right if Dennis gets wickets, but if he doesn't the knockers will say 'silly old bastard.'

Jeff Thomson, on Lillee's 1988 comeback.

When I hear Colin bowl de bounces, I get vex. Two bounces an over okay, but when he bowl five I get vex bad. I tell him, what happen if he hit batsman and he fall dead on de spot.

Colin Croft's mother, during England's tour of the West Indies, 1981. (Recorded in Scyld Berry's *Cricket Wallah*, 1982.)

I don't want any bloody sympathy, do you understand that? It has happened. People who say 'I know how you feel' are just talking bullshit. They don't know, not at all. What I can't forget is that the ball was a deliberate short one. Not deliberately at his head, but still deliberate.

Peter Lever, England fast bowler, after felling New Zealand's last man, Ewen Chatfield, in the Auckland Test, 1975. Chatfield was hit on the temple and his heart stopped for several seconds.

You look a sight worse than I do.

Ewen Chatfield when Lever visited him in hospital, 1975.

Just remember one thing son, you've already been killed once on a cricket field.

Ian Botham's warning to Ewen Chatfield after the New Zealand seamer had run out Derek Randall, while backing up, Christchurch Test, 1977/8.

I have never felt it more likely that we should see someone killed.

John Woodcock, in *The Times*, after watching England's terrors at the hands of the West Indian quicks in Kingston, 1986.

Fast bowlers are bully boys. They dish it out but they can't take it.

Brian Close, Yorkshire batsman.

Denis, you were beginning to bore me, playing like that.

Keith Miller, Compton's drinking buddy, unleashing a beamer during the Adelaide Test, MCC tour of Australia, 1946/7.

I felt like phoning Devon Malcolm as he tried to flog life out of the pitch, to tell him that it was a law of diminishing returns; just try to kiss the surface with the ball. Be friends and the Headingley pitch responds.

John Snow, *Daily Telegraph*, Headingley Test, 1991.

The retaliation is simple and straightforward. Having successfully evaded the head-high bouncer, the batsman should feel entitled to straighten up, go into a hammer-thrower's crouch and hurl his bat at the bowler just completing his follow-through.

The solution to bouncers, as expressed by **Peter Walker**, Glamorgan all-rounder, 1962.

If anyone beats it, they'll be bloody tired.

Fred Trueman, becoming England's leading Test wicket-taker, 1964.

When Fred reached his 307 he said afterwards that anyone who passed him would be very tired. Well, you can tell him I'm not.

Bob Willis, surpassing Trueman's feat, in New Zealand, 1984.

Lillee will always be a better bowler than me.

Ian Botham, after breaking Dennis Lillee's Test wicket-taking record.

It's a bit like the four-minute mile or climbing Mount Everest. Someone is going to do it eventually, but no one forgets the person who did it first.

Sir Richard Hadlee, first to 400 Test wickets, 1990.

My effort should disprove that India cannot produce fast bowlers. For 15 years that has been my one great motivation.

Kapil Dev, passing Hadlee's record of 431 Test wickets when he dismissed Sri Lankan batsman Hashan Tillekeratne in Ahmedabad. Hadlee took 86 Tests, Kapil Dev 130, but half of Kapil Dev's wickets had been taken on unhelpful Indian pitches.

Kapil has not broken Hadlee's record – he has merely gone past it. That he is a great bowler is not in question, but it has been painful to watch him surpass it.

Raj Singh, former Indian chairman of selectors, 1994.

Kapil Dev now runs in with an almost baronial aspect, commanding respect more from his great record over 130 Tests than any of the youthful vigour he used to possess.

Don Cameron, *Sunday Telegraph*, on the respect afforded to a great fast bowler, 1994.

Alec rolled his fingers over the ball as he delivered it, and as it swung it pitched on the seam and became, as it were, a leg-spinner.

Godfrey Evans, crediting Alec Bedser (Surrey, England) with the invention of the leg-cutter.

It is just as important for a spin bowler to be aggressive as it is a fast bowler. We play at a very high level of arousal, on the edge of fury if you like.

Shane Warne, apologizing for his abuse of South Africa's Andrew Hudson in Johannesburg. Warne was fined and widely condemned. 1993/4 season.

When you're an off-spinner, there's not much point glaring at batsmen. If I glared at Viv Richards he'd just hit me even further.

David Acfield, Essex off-spinner, 1982.

A fast bowler either has the natural ability to hurl the ball down quickly or he hasn't. The reverse is true of spin bowling. I believe you can learn it from scratch.

Ray Illingworth, in *Spin Bowling*, 1980.

I shall bowl the first ball, but I don't know about a full over. I can't really spin 'em now. I can cut 'em, of course, but any fool can do that.

Sydney Barnes, bowling the first over of a match to mark his 80th birthday. Barnes XI vs England XI, 1953.

If a batsman thinks it's spinning, then it's spinning.

Wilfred Rhodes in Neville Cardus's *Autobiography*, 1947.

You can't light a ball, only an over.

Wilfred Rhodes.

Best ball on a sticky pitch is a spinnin' half-volley.

Wilfred Rhodes, who bowled a few.

As I'm walking back I think maybe I'll bowl a googly. Then, as I run in, I think, no, I'll bowl a leg-spinner. Then, do you know, just as I prepare to bowl, I decide it'll be a googly after all. And then, as I let go of the ball, I say, sod it, I'll bowl a top-spinner.

The thought processes of **BS Chandrasekhar**, Indian leg-spinner, as reported by Peter Roebuck, in *It Sort of Clicks*, 1986.

I am not unhappy to be hit for six sixes. I want batsmen to play shots. Only then can I get them out.

Bishen Bedi, Indian left-arm spinner.

Slow bowling is an art, Mr Kelly, and art is international.

Arthur Mailey, replying to a reprimand by the Australian manager for giving advice to England's leg-spin bowler, Ian Peebles, during the 1930 Old Trafford Test.

The great spin bowlers were personalities and men of character – not always pleasant but invariably interesting. They may have lacked the charm and friendliness of their faster confederates; they may have been more temperamental and less self-disciplined; but there seemed to be an absence of orthodoxy about them and they were able to meander through life as individuals not as civil servants.

Arthur Mailey.

It's always a blow when anyone who propels the ball at less than 50 mph calls it a day.

Jon Agnew, regretting the retirement of Vic Marks and Jack Simmons in 1989.

The bloody ball should never be changed until the string starts to fray from it and the four segments of it start to come adrift.

Bill O'Reilly, one-time Australian leg-spinner, 1986.

I remember playing in dozens of matches with Douglas Wright when he should never have been in the side. Not only did we find ourselves playing with ten men, but with every over of honest toil he was driving another nail into our own coffin.

Colin Cowdrey, Kent team-mate, on the perils of wayward leg-spin.

I can never forgive English cricket for trying to kill off leg-spin bowling.

Bill O'Reilly, former Australian leg-spinner. (Recorded in 1994 *Wisden*.)

If I was a young leg-spinner, I'd be playing tennis.

Ken Rutherford, New Zealand captain, rueing his country's green pitches, 1992/3 season.

It must be very humiliating for any skipper to see balls bouncing twice, with full pitches and long hops thrown in as a matter of course.

AC MacLaren on googly bowling.

Gone are the days when you bowled leg-spin at an Englishman and he just fell over.

Paul Strang, Zimbabwe leggie, during his first season in county cricket, at Kent, 1997.

Poor old googly! It has been subjected to ridicule, abuse, contempt, incredulity and survived them all.

BJT Bosanquet, inventor of the googly, *Wisden*, 1924.

Mentally, my stock ball pitches leg and hits off.

Phil Edmonds, England slow left-armer, in *A Singular Man*, 1985.

They say spinners mature with age. I just hope they are right.

John Childs, Essex slow left-armer, called up by England at 36, 1988.

When a spinner comes on, your eyes go round like dollar signs on a fruit machine. Everyone wants to hit him because they can't smash the fast bowler.

Allan Lamb, England batsman, 1982.

It's all a matter of inches – those between your ears.

Arthur Milton, former Gloucestershire opening batsman, on the secret of playing spin, 1982.

Look what the silly buggers have done now. Cost the club another 13s 6d.

Jim Smith, forced to take the new ball to end a prolonged last-wicket stand, Nottinghamshire vs Middlesex, 1938.

... at last
the bowler flails once more,
a final twitch for the dying day.

John Snow, England pace bowler, in *Moments and Thoughts*, 1973.

Neither of us were worried who got the wickets as long as we were in our favourite position – our feet up, watching England bat.

Brian Statham, recalling his fast-bowling partnership with Fred Trueman, 1989.

They can have my bloody slips!

George Macauley, testy Yorkshire seamer, upon hearing that Madame Tussauds had been struck by fire. Macauley had suffered three dropped catches in the first over against Middlesex at Lord's. (From *Cricket and All That*, Denis Compton and Bill Edrich, 1978.)

Fielding and Wicketkeeping

A wicketkeeper who is on his toes is likely to over-balance.

CB Ponsonby, Worcestershire, 1920s.

Jack, you're not going home just because of a hat are you?

Worried England off-spinner, **Robert Croft**, visiting Jack Russell's hotel bedroom during West Indies tour, 1998. Russell's preparations had been disrupted by the ECB's insistence that he abandoned his old floppy sunhat in favour of 'Team England's' new corporate issue.

I shall have to catch a later train tonight – that one knocked off the 7.30.

Fred Stedman, predecessor of Herbert Strudwick as Surrey wicketkeeper, after he was hit in the chest ... on the copy of the South Western Railway Timetable he used as protection.

Have there been any byes yet?

Herbert Strudwick, Surrey wicketkeeper, arriving late at Leyton in 1925. Surrey had taken the field with only two players after the professionals had been delayed in traffic.

You must rinse your hands in the chamberpot every day. The urine hardens them wonderfully.

Herbert Strudwick, former England wicketkeeper, offering advice to Tony Pawson of Oxford University.

No wicketkeeper should spare himself in taking throws, however wide they are.

Godfrey Evans, *The Gloves Are Off*, 1961.

I made it very plain to my fielders that I set the standard, and if anyone of them didn't reach it, I let them know I wasn't happy about it.

Rod Marsh, Australian wicketkeeper.

Men stand in the field today like so many 'little mounds of earth' ... the energy, the life, the ever-watchfulness of 10 years ago are gone, and in their place are lethargy, laziness and a wonderful yearning for rest.

DLA Jephson, Surrey captain and lob bowler, in *Wisden*, 1901.

Short boundaries, by decreasing the opportunities for good fielding, rob cricket of half its charm.

Wisden editorial, 1906.

Once I've got the fielders with their tongues hanging out I aim to run them into the ground.

Rohan Kanhai, West Indies batsman, 1966.

What is the good of an innings of 50 if that man drops a couple of catches and lets by 40 or 50 runs. He has not only wiped his own runs off the slate, but he has probably upset the bowlers into the bargain.

AER Gilligan, Cambridge University, Surrey and Sussex, getting wise to the advantages of good fielding, 1920s.

When I was quite young I made a boy, when out for a walk, throw stones into the hedge, and as the sparrows flew out, I caught 'em.

FR Spofforth, Australian fast bowler, explaining his skill at slip. (This version told by 'Buns' Thornton, *Wisden*, 1927.)

After working all day, I just go down to the river and catch the swallows as they flit by.

GJ Bonnor (Australia), explaining his prowess as a slip to Sammy Woods.

When we first married, Derek used to throw tea cups behind his back and catch them. That's one way he got out of doing the washing up.

Liz Randall, 1970s, on Derek Randall, the finest England fielder of his generation.

Thee get on with thi laikin', and I'll get on wi' mine.

Emmott Robinson, of Yorkshire, warned that he was standing dangerously close to the bat.

I only just have to perch myself at short leg and just stare at some of 'em to get 'em out. They fiddle about and look away and then they look back to see if I'm staring at 'em. I am. They don't stay long.

Brian Close.

Be ready for rebounds!

Brian Close (short square) to a bemused Ray East (forward short leg).

I just put my hand down as a pretence, which pleases the crowd, taking good care never to touch the ball, which pleases me, and everyone is satisfied.

George Giffen, South Australia, giving advice to Charles McLeod, Victoria, after the latter had injured himself stopping Giffen's straight drive.

The only thing I'm very keen to do before I leave Somerset is to throw myself at the ball and dive, as I see the other team-mates in the Somerset team do. And I'm sure when I do, when I really do dive, I'm going to get a big applause.

Sunil Gavaskar, BBC Eastern Service, 1980.

I persuaded them that to take a towel out to Viv Richards or to dry Clive Lloyd's socks is as good as scoring 20 or 30.

Wes Hall, West Indies tour manager in Australia in 1984/5, on how to keep inactive players happy.

Captaincy

Why do so many players want to be captain?

Derek Underwood, Kent left-armer, quoted by Mike Brearley in *The Art of Captaincy*, 1985.

Captaincy seems to involve half-hearing conversations which you'd rather not hear at all.

Peter Roebuck, Somerset batsman, in *It Never Rains*, 1984.

It is a strange fact connected with cricket that a good captain is but seldom met with.

AG Steel, *The Badminton Library – Cricket*, 1904.

Captaincy means more than vigorous arm-waving.

David Gower, 1986.

Captaincy is ninety per cent luck and ten per cent skill. But don't try it without that ten per cent.

Richie Benaud, Australian captain.

A captain can do nothing for his side other than win the toss.

Surrey captain, **KJ Key**, told by Streeton in *Fender*, 1980.

There is very little wrong that a captain cannot attend to.

Stuart Surridge, Surrey captain, in a letter to *The Times*, 1957.

From Douglas's captaincy, no idea ever emerged.

CB Fry on Johnny Douglas.

A pessimistic commander, I have heard old timers say he was liable to enter the dressing room clutching his head and saying, 'Look what they've given me this time,' or 'Gracious me! Don't tell me you're playing!'

Ian Peebles on Johnny Douglas.

My God, look what they've sent me.

AC MacLaren, on England's team to face Australia in the fourth Test at Old Trafford in 1902. The selectors had left out Fry, Jessop and Barnes; Australia won by three runs, and took the series.

England may have had worse captains, but I'd be hard pushed to name two or three.

Alan Gibson, in *The Times*, on the centenary of AC MacLaren's birth, 1971.

I've been saddled with a B-grade team.

Sachin Tendulkar, Indian captain, blaming it on the selectors during the Independence Cup, 1997.

Tendulkar knows the futility of crying over spilt milk in public.

Ramakant Desai, chairman of the Indian selectors, hits back, 1997.

He had that type of mind – cool logic was his great secret.

Sir Leonard Hutton, upon Don Bradman's captaincy.

A public relations officer, agricultural consultant, psychiatrist, accountant, nursemaid and diplomat.

DJ Insole's definition of a captain's duties.

Of how many cricketers may it be said, at the end of a long and distinguished career, that they made no enemies. No matter who he was with, or where it was, or when, he was always the same man – absolutely fair and as unselfish a captain as England ever had.

John Woodcock, in *Wisden*, upon the retirement of MJK Smith, former Warwickshire and England captain.

I find I am playing every ball, bowling every ball and fielding every ball. The captaincy has cost me over six hundred runs a season. I am snapping at my wife and children and sleeping no more than four hours a night.

Micky Stewart, the year Surrey won the championship, 1971.

It is easier for a football manager to 'play God', to read the riot act to the players, because he doesn't have to perform himself. Sales managers don't sell, foremen don't hump bricks. All cricket captains bat and field, and some bowl. We receive repeated intimations of our own fallibility.

Mike Brearley, *The Art of Captaincy*, 1985.

Captaincy is the ability to think ahead of play, not to be left responding to it.

Richie Benaud.

He was a cunning bugger, Fletch. He had a mental image of every opponent and a special field for each batsman pre-programmed. He knew exactly which bowler to put on when and what his strategy should be. He stood in the gully cackling at Gooch's jokes while he plotted each batsman's downfall. It's very disconcerting if you're that batsman.

Simon Hughes, *A Lot of Hard Yakka*, 1997, on Keith Fletcher.

Right, I'm batting no. 4 and the rest of you can sort yourselves out.

Keith Fletcher, on a bad Essex day.

One of you bugger off and the rest scatter.

Keith Miller, captaining New South Wales, and told that he had 12 players on the field.

We think you'll like the side Richie.

Communication from the Australian selectors to captain, Richie Benaud, after choosing the side to tour England, 1961. Benaud, as captain, had no say.

As a county captain, one seems to spend an inordinate amount of time filling in forms of which no one takes the slightest notice.

Ray Illingworth, *Yorkshire and Back*, 1980.

A kinder or more considerate captain never walked on to a cricket field.

Sir Len Hutton, on Norman Yardley (Yorkshire, England), *50 Years in Cricket*, 1984.

You'll have the most miserable time of your life.

Brian Close's warning to Ian Botham about the potential effect of the England captaincy, 1980.

England have at least nine captains out there. Unfortunately Bob Willis is not one of them.

Henry Blofeld, during the latter stages of England's three-run win over Australia in Melbourne Test, 1982/3 Ashes tour.

Hey, hey, hey, hey! I'm f****** talking to you. Come here, come here, come here, come here ... Do that again and you're on the next plane home, son ... What was that? You f****** test me and you'll see.

Australia's captain, **Allan Border**, in on-pitch exchange with his fast bowler, Craig McDermott, at Taunton, 1993 tour. McDermott wanted to bowl at the other end.

Can't you have a word with your captain without it being broadcast? This is 1993 not 1893.

McDermott's reaction when told that the exchange had been transmitted on Channel 7.

'A dynamic bowling change' you write about is probably sheer luck nine times out of ten. OK, you bring on someone and he gets a wicket – great, but I haven't solved the mystery of the universe, have I?

Graham Gooch, leading England in 1988.

If you've been hit in the face by a wet fish you will know how I've been feeling this week, ever since England's latest Test captain voiced his opinion on the business of captaincy.

Ted Dexter – on Graham Gooch. Dexter's opinion, expressed in the *Sunday Mirror*, did not prevent him chairing the England committee that appointed Gooch captain later that year, 1988.

Cricket teams have often suffered from captains who have arrived, done queer things, departed and been forgotten.

RC Robertson-Glasgow, *Cricket Prints*, 1943.

Reduced to subordinate rank, he looked forlorn and fettered, a great Prince in prison lying.

Ronald Mason on Percy Fender (Surrey), as Douglas Jardine assumed the county captaincy, 1932.

He could never make up his mind whether to call heads or tails.

Ray Illingworth on Colin Cowdrey (Kent, England).

I would guess that Dexter was more interested in ideas than people.

Mike Brearley, considering Ted Dexter's limitations in *The Art of Captaincy*, 1985.

Don't say too much.

Len Hutton's advice to Tony Greig, prior to him captaining England in India, 1976/7.

There are times when I've watched him at Cambridge when I've thought he could be more attacking. While he's a naturally conservative person, it could have been all those canings at Cambridge.

Alastair Scott, a Cambridge contemporary, 1995, on Michael Atherton.

It was Jung, I think, who said we learned from our failures, success merely confirming us in our mistakes. What can I learn from my failures at Test level?

Mike Brearley, 1981.

Umpiring

He is but a weak-kneed cricketer who in his heart approves of the umpires' decisions.

RC Robertson-Glasgow.

The only acceptable form of dissent is a dirty look. And we don't like that.

England Test umpire, 1982.

I don't understand why, in a democratic society, where government and all the accepted standards in every walk of life are being questioned, umpires should be immune.

Asif Iqbal, Kent captain, 1982.

Doubt? When I'm umpiring, there's never any doubt!

Frank Chester, Test umpire before video replays were even thought of, asked why he had given a batsman the benefit of the doubt.

Three kicks and you're out!

Umpire **Cec Pepper**, having no truck with excessive pad play.

I couldn't see why I should stand there and have players looking at me as if I were a leper.

Tom Brooks, retiring from Test umpiring during Australia vs England series, 1978/9.

It's not easy taking up umpiring after being an umpire baiter for over 30 years.

Bill Alley, on joining umpires' list, 1969.

Amateur players would rather sweep roads or sell newspapers in the streets than pretend to be first-class umpires.

'Cross-Arrow', *The Cricketer*, 1926.

I've always had to count the pennies.

Syd Buller, Test umpire, on an umpire's lot.

The 'Outer' – large of frame, rubicund of countenance, who drinks pints and eats vastly, is a gay, carefree fellow who, in his playing days, was a fast bowler and who now has only to hear somebody in the crowd clear his throat for his finger to shoot aloft.

Michael Stevenson, in *The Cricketer*, 1963.

The 'Not Outer' ... is small, wizened, misanthropic, drinks half-shandies and eats sparingly.

Michael Stevenson, as above.

Most umpires have good memories. If you stuff them once, they'll stuff you good and proper in the end.

Alan Oakman, Warwickshire coach, from the *Nursery End*, 1985.

You'll never die wondering, son.

Cec Pepper, umpire, reacting to numerous lbw appeals from Ashley Mallett, Australian spin bowler, 1968.

As God is my witness!

Alex Skelding, umpire, awarding a hat-trick of lbw decisions to Yorkshire's Horace Fisher vs Somerset at Scarborough, 1932.

Now all you want is a white stick.

Sidney Barnes, Australian batsman, handing a stray dog he had captured to umpire Alex Skelding on Australia's 1948 tour of England. Skelding had given Barnes out lbw.

Here's three ha'pence. Buy a paper and find out the score.

Alex Skelding, umpire, at odds with the scoreboard operators in a county match.

Derek Underwood could never bowl at my end – he could not get round me.

Swaroop Kishen, heavyweight Test umpire (related by Dickie Bird in *That's Out*, 1985).

That's out and we've won the championship!

Umpire and proud Welshman, **Dai Davies**, giving the decision as John Clay took the wicket which gave Glamorgan their first championship, 1948.

Pig's arse, two runs! We've been running up and down here all afternoon. Who are you kidding?

Jeff Thomson, Australian fast bowler, wanting a better return from umpire Tom Spencer during a last-wicket stand in the 1975 World Cup final, Australia vs West Indies. Confusion was due to a pitch invasion by fans mistakenly thinking that the game was over.

When I step across that boundary rope, it's the only time I feel in total control.

Dickie Bird, Test cricket's most famous umpire.

He has never exploited the game, he needed the game. He was a character who made the game grow and who grew himself because of the game.

Peter Roebuck on Dickie Bird, 1996.

He'd better not bite that – it's the finger I give 'em all out with.

Dickie Bird, attacked by Billy, an Amazon parrot from Aylesbury, while judging the annual talking bird contest at the NEC, Birmingham, 1989.

I've lost my marbles.

Umpire **Dickie Bird** during the Headingley Test, England vs West Indies, 1995. (The scoreboard had malfunctioned and Dickie couldn't find his counters.)

Umpiring at the top now is full of comedians and gimmicks. In the old days there used to be men you could respect.

Cec Pepper, resigning from the first-class umpiring list in 1980.

They sure like their tea, these English.

Scottish tannoy announcer, in Perth, as Dickie Bird's confusion over rule changes caused him to call two tea intervals in a Benson and Hedges tie between Scotland and Yorkshire, 1984.

Tell that fellow Lamb to play a few shots or get out.

Ian Botham's message, via mobile phone, to a shocked umpire Dickie Bird. England vs New Zealand, Trent Bridge, 1983. (The quote is Bird's version ... or one of them.)

Rain and bad light has followed me about all my life.

Dickie Bird, fearing the worst before officially launching the ICC's independent umpiring panel, New Zealand vs Pakistan, Auckland, 1994. It remained fine, Pakistan won, and Bird and his New Zealand colleague called several miscounted overs.

As soon as I walked off the plane a spot of rain hit me on the head. They had never seen rain like it. People were on their hands and knees, shouting 'Dickie Bird has arrived, it's raining, it's raining.' Everybody was celebrating, but we had terrible trouble with the run-ups.

Dickie Bird, Zimbabwe drought breaker, Zimbabwe vs New Zealand, Bulawayo, 1992.

It's not just wet, it's wet, wet, wet.

Dickie Bird, borrowing from contemporary pop music to explain a stoppage in the Headingley Test because of a blocked drain, 1988.

Oslear found something in the rules to get off the pitch because of the cold last year, but I can't find the bloody thing.

Dickie Bird, umpiring at Derby. (From *8 Days a Week*, Jon Agnew, 1988.)

Every morning I go down on my hands and knees and pray, 'Please, Lord, don't give us bad light today.'

Dickie Bird, Test umpire, in *Declarations*, 1989.

Maybe it's my false teeth, Dickie. I'll take them out if you like.

Old Trafford spectator as Dickie Bird searched frantically for the source of reflected sunlight which was holding up the Old Trafford Test, England vs West Indies, 1995.

I never watch TV replays. If I did, I'd go crazy.

Dickie Bird, in Hobart in 1995 to umpire in his 64th Test match, Australia vs Pakistan. The media did watch the replays – and were not impressed.

Cricket's my wife.

Dickie Bird, 1995.

I need to know. Counties want to know if it's my farewell so that they can give me something.

Dickie Bird, unnerved by the confusion over whether 1997 would be his last as a county umpire. He managed to delay his retirement for a further year, 1997.

I'm only happy stood in the middle of a cricket ground.

Dickie Bird, Test umpire, in *The Cricketer*, 1992.

He arrived on earth from the Planet Looney to become the best and fairest of all umpires. Great bloke, completely bonkers.

Ian Botham, in his autobiography, on Dickie Bird, 1994.

He was the first umpire to combine the distinct roles of top-flight umpire and music-hall comedian. He was the first umpire superstar.

Matthew Engel, on Test umpire Dickie Bird, 1996.

Ee lad, tha's a bit of a character. Tha could ave been a great comedian thissen.

Albert Modley, music-hall comedian, to another famous son of Barnsley, Dickie Bird.

The physique of a hat-pin and the only geriatric stoop I have ever seen on a 15-year-old.

Michael Parkinson, recollecting his first sight of HD Bird.

The players know I used to box, and that's probably why they don't stuff with me.

Cyril Mitchley, South African umpire, 1998.

'Ere Rupert, you've got to hit the ball to be lbw in this game. If you miss it, you can only be caught.

Keith Fletcher, Essex captain, to Somerset's Peter Roebuck, on a day of unusual umpiring, 1981.

Pitches

Too much crap cricket on crap wickets.

Tom Moody, Australian batsman, assessing English cricket's shortcomings, 1997.

The scientists fail us. They cannot do anything to supply men who are born to be groundsmen.

Colin Cowdrey, *MCC*, 1976.

We always picked balanced teams so we didn't worry about the pitch. These days they're always worrying about the pitch.

Sir Colin Cowdrey, 1994.

Men are too often picked for England on the strength of a hundred on a 'doped' pitch.

Patsy Hendren, Middlesex and England batsman, in *Wisden*, 1938.

A lotus land for batsmen, a place where it was always afternoon and 360 for 2 wickets.

Neville Cardus on the traditions of Trent Bridge.

I grew up here in the fifties and spent half my time watching people nod off and go home early. Just lately they bloody well haven't.

Ron Allsopp, Nottinghamshire groundsman, refuting criticism of Trent Bridge pitches, 1988.

If they want pitches that do bugger all, that's easy. If they want pitches that are dangerous, that's easy, too. Good cricket pitches, the sort we think we produce more often than not, are difficult. The dividing line between a flat pitch and a dodgy one is very thin, and occasionally you miscalculate. If the TCCB aren't careful, they will frighten groundsmen into being responsible for producing exactly the sort of cricket they used to moan about before.

Ron Allsopp, Trent Bridge groundsman, 1988.

Look at that: Parkin, 32 overs, 8 maidens, 92 runs, 1 wicket. And they send missionaries to China!

Cecil Parkin, Lancashire spin bowler, suffering a flat Worcester pitch in the late 1920s.

If those boat people want a job, they can come and bowl on this bloody wicket.

Norman Gifford, Worcestershire spinner, with similar troubles at Worcester in 1978.

Already the press are lamenting on the paucity of new faces among the bowling fraternity. Any wonder – what youngster in his right mind gladly looks forward to a life of little glamour, few rewards and days of being just 'cannon fodder' for opposing batsmen?

Peter Walker, on the 1958–62 experiment with covered wickets.

It was the loveliest of sounds.

Overnight rain – as recalled by **Ellis Robinson**, Yorkshire off-spinner in days of uncovered wickets, by then in his 80s, in 1995.

After I've retired, they should open the pitches to the elements.

Peter Roebuck, Somerset batsman, 1985.

What's the matter? Have you gone bloody religious?

Nottinghamshire's captain, **Clive Rice**, when groundsman Ron Allsopp resisted his pressure for yet another grassy pitch. c. 1982.

My immediate reaction was: 'How on earth can major cricket be played on this?'

Jim Fairbrother, Lord's groundsman, on his first sight of the slope, in *Testing the Wicket*, 1985.

It is a remarkable fact that every time a side has a bad innings it is the wicket that is blamed – never the player.

The Groundsman magazine, 1958.

Thank God Nasser has taken over the Suez Canal. Otherwise, I'd be plastered over every front page like Marilyn Monroe.

Bert Flack, Old Trafford groundsman, after Jim Laker's 19 wickets for England against Australia, 1956.

They've got it easy. They operate in the growing season.

Stan Gibson, Manchester City groundsman, on his cricketing opposite numbers, 1989.

There's a bastard in my family and it's sitting out there.

Keith Boyce, Headingley groundsman, at his wits' end about the Test wicket, 1985.

I'd throw them off the top of the pavilion. Mind, I'm a fair man, I'd give them a 50:50 chance. I'd have Keith Fletcher underneath trying to catch them.

Fred Trueman, on the saboteurs of the Test wicket. Fletcher's catching ability was not held in high regard in Yorkshire. 1975.

6

Cricket Culture

Philosophers All
Gents and Players
The Pastoral Game
Views From Elsewhere
The Gentler Sex
The Great Unwashed

Philosophers All

What do they know of cricket who only cricket know?

CLR James, *Beyond a Boundary*, 1963.

To some people cricket is a circus show upon which they may or may not find it worthwhile to spend sixpence; to others it is a pleasant means of livelihood; to others a physical fine art full of plot, interest and enlivened by difficulties; to others, in some sort, it is a cult and a philosophy.

CB Fry, foreword to DLA Jephson's *A Few Overs*, 1913.

Cricket is first and foremost a dramatic spectacle. It belongs with theatre, ballet, opera and the dance.

CLR James, *Beyond a Boundary*, 1963.

The very word 'cricket' has become a synonym for all that is true and honest. To say 'that is not cricket' implies something underhand, something not in keeping with the best ideals.

Sir Pelham Warner, laying down the moral law.

A chance to play the man and act the gentleman.

Sir Frederick Toone, *Wisden*, 1930.

To play cricket is synonymous with running straight.

Earl of Derby, Lancashire's championship dinner, 1926.

Use every weapon within the rules and stretch the rules to breaking point, I say.

Fred Trueman, *Fast Fury*, 1961.

The first consideration is the mental outlook of the individual who can, if he chooses, soil any game by his interpretation of its character.

Don Bradman, *Wisden*, 1939.

Cricket will never be left to be just cricket. It is always asked to 'stand for' something more than itself.

Mike Marqusee, *Anyone but England*, 1994.

You will do well to love it, for it is more free from anything sordid, anything dishonourable, than any game in the world. To play it keenly, honourably, generously, self-sacrificingly is a moral lesson in itself, and the class-room is full of God's own air and children. Foster it, my brothers, so that it may attract all who can find the time to play it; protect it from anything that would sully it, so that it may grow in favour with all men.

Lord Harris's speech to half-holiday cricketers, quoted in a letter to *The Times* on his 80th birthday, 1931.

A particular generation of cricketers thinks in a certain way and only a change in society, not legislation, will change the prevailing style.

CLR James, *Beyond a Boundary*.

The barriers to the regeneration of cricket techniques are mental, as are the barriers to the regeneration of its moral values.

CLR James, *Beyond a Boundary*.

Innovations invariably are suspect and in no quarter more so than the cricket world.

Gilbert Jessop.

Old cricketers become bores.

David Frith, after writing a history of cricket suicides, 1991.

Of course it's frightfully dull! That's the whole point! Any game can be exciting – football, dirt track racing, roulette ... To go to cricket to be thrilled is as stupid as to go to a Chekhov play in search of melodrama.

Robert Morley's character in *The Final Test*, film.

You can't treat cricket as a living, as a means of earning a living. It's got to be your life. You've got to love it.

Indian spinner **Dilip Doshi**, in *For the Love of the Game*, David Lemmon, 1993.

Equality of obsession. That's what's important in making a cricket marriage work.

John Minnion, captain of the *New Statesman* cricket side, 1991.

I'm not interested in sport. I'm interested in cricket. I'm always surprised to find cricket books in the library in the sports section, next to football.

John Minnion, ibid.

If I knew I was going to die today I'd still want to hear the cricket scores.

JH Hardy.

Bury me 22 yards away from Arthur, so I can send him down a ball now and then.

Last request of Nottinghamshire batsman, **Alfred Shaw**, to be buried next to his old team-mate, Arthur Shrewsbury. They buried him 27 yards away, to allow for Shrewsbury's five-yard run-up, 1907.

What can you have better than a nice green field, with the wickets set up, and to go out and do the best for your side?

George Hirst in his retirement speech at Scarborough, 1921.

Cricket is indescribable. How do you describe an orgasm?

Greg Matthews, Australian all-rounder, 1980s.

I'd rather have a game of cricket than watch England in the World Cup.

Chris Sutton, Blackburn Rovers striker, overlooked by England's manager, Glenn Hoddle, and planning instead to pad up for Drayton, a Norfolk club side, 1998.

I only ever think about cricket. I just worry that when I pack up I'll be dead within 12 months.

Dickie Bird, contemplating the end of his Test umpiring career, 1995.

Dear Mr Edrich, I would like you to know that, if I did want to have all my teeth extracted in one go, that is the way I wanted it done. Well played, sir.

Letter from *Times* reader, struck by a Bill Edrich hook shot against Harold Larwood, while reading his newspaper at Lord's, 1938. (From *Cricket and All That*, Denis Compton and Bill Edrich, 1978.)

A Test match is a good setting for something like murder.

Ted Dexter, on his new novel, *Testkill*, 1976.

The gesture demonstrates the sublimated socially acceptable face of the homo-erotic impulse that makes sport possible.

Oliver James, clinical psychiatrist, analysing a photograph of Chris Lewis and Alec Stewart celebrating the fall of a West Indian wicket, 1990.

To go to a cricket match for nothing but cricket is as though a man were to go into an inn for nothing but drink.

Neville Cardus, *Autobiography*, 1947.

If there is any game in the world that attracts the half-baked theorist more than cricket I have yet to hear of it.

Fred Trueman, *Fred Trueman's Book of Cricket*, 1964.

There is no other game at which the confirmed duffer is so persistent and so undepressed.

EV Lucas, *English Leaves*.

Who ever hoped like a cricketer?

RC Robertson-Glasgow, *Cricket Prints*, 1943.

If ifs and buts were pots and pans, we wouldn't need tinkers.

Christopher Martin-Jenkins, in the *Daily Telegraph*, upon cricketing excuses, 1995.

Cricket more than any other game is inclined towards sentimentalism and cant.

Sir Neville Cardus, *A Fourth Innings with Cardus*, 1981.

It's no use complaining that cricket is fuddy duddy because I'm afraid it's part of the game.

Doug Insole, former chairman of the TCCB, 1995.

Cricket is a game played on the edges of the nerves. It requires men of stoical and stout temperament yet attracts players with artistic yearnings who hover around it like a moth hovers around a flame.

Peter Roebuck, in *Ashes to Ashes*, 1987.

The scoreboard is an ass.

Sir Neville Cardus, *A Fourth Innings with Cardus*, 1981.

Hard-wicket cricket is like chess – there is no element of chance in it, and only those who perfect themselves survive.

Bill Edrich, 1948.

Cricket is a situation game. When the situation is dead, the game is dead.

Trevor Bailey.

I've heard it said that this game at Test level is 50 per cent in the mind, 50 per cent in the heart, and bugger technique, and that's not far off the mark.

Raymond Illingworth, chairman of selectors, 1995.

Golf is a game to be played between cricket and death.

Colin Ingleby-Mackenzie, ex-Hampshire captain.

Cricket dimensions will always defy the metric system.

Robin Marlar, *Sunday Times*, confident about cricket's traditions, 1979.

It is a good thing to carry a scarf to put round your neck between innings. It looks smart – and there is no harm in doing your side credit – and cools one off gradually.

'Cross-Arrow', *The Cricketer*, 1927.

If you like a white sunhat, always carry one with you. CB Fry played some of his greatest innings in a sunhat.

'Cross-Arrow', *The Cricketer*, 1927.

When I see a young man who has an expensive and pretty hair-do, I have doubts as to his ability to reach Test standard.

Ted Dexter, *A Walk to the Wicket*, 1985.

I can't understand Smith. Babies have been born for centuries, and he wants to come home in the middle of an Ashes series.

Geoffrey Boycott, aghast at Robin Smith's fatherly desires, England tour of Australia, 1990.

Being a Christian does not mean that you have to stand down from a conflict. God does not want me to be second best.

Jonty Rhodes, South Africa, 1998.

Gents and Players

We don't play this game for fun.

Wilfred Rhodes, Yorkshire and England spinner.

Cricket was never made for any championship. Cricket's a game, not a competition.

George Hirst, taking an untraditional Yorkshire view.

Amateurs have always made, and always will make, the best captains, and this is only natural.

AG Steel.

Pray God no professional may ever captain England.

Lord Hawke, Yorkshire autocrat.

A gratuitous insult to the main body of professional cricketers.

Percy Fender's response to Hawke's 'Pray God' speech. As Surrey captain, Fender insisted that amateurs and professionals passed onto the field of play through the same gate.

May I congratulate you on having buggered the career of another young cricketer.

Lord Deerhurst, president of Worcestershire, to Lord Harris in the Long Room at Lord's, 1922. Harris had succeeded in banning Walter Hammond from county cricket for the rest of the season after his defection from Kent to Gloucestershire.

'Sorry Sir!'
'Don't be sorry, Barnes, you're coming to Australia with me.'

Exchange between **AC MacLaren** and **Sydney Barnes** after MacLaren, England's captain, had been struck on the head by the Lancashire League fast bowler in the Old Trafford nets in 1901.

I have heard some English captains speak to their professionals like dogs.

Joe Darling, Australian captain, 1902.

There is hardly one first-class amateur bowler in England, and in my opinion, laziness is one of the main causes of this, and another is the employment of professionals at schools and universities. I have never heard an amateur say, 'I am going to have a bowl'; it is always a 'knock'.

FR Spofforth, former Australian fast bowler, 1906.

The only group of employees more right-wing than their employers.

Mike Edwards, former Surrey batsman, on The Cricketers' Association, 1990.

He's been at Cambridge. He's never really gone out to work and earned a living in his life. It's pretty hard going for him.

Raymond Illingworth, chairman of selectors, considering Michael Atherton's shortcomings as England captain, 1995.

His eyesight was so bad that he couldn't see from one end of the pitch to the other ... He eventually told me that he was having trouble seeing my slow-medium seamers and asked if I could yell 'bowled' once I had delivered the ball.

Former Australian wicketkeeper **Tim Zoehrer**, describing life on an MCC scholarship in 1981. The MCC member he was forced to bowl to in the Lord's indoor school was 91 years old. Zoehrer did shout 'bowled,' but sent down a bouncer which flew past the MCC member's nose. (From *The Gloves Are Off*, 1995.)

Bloody medieval most of them.

Ian Botham, on those running English cricket, 1995.

He always called everybody 'Sir'. There were a lot of 'Sirs' about from the moment he entered the room. I suppose it was a sign of respect, although after a while it could all become a bit overpowering.

Jack Bailey, former secretary of MCC, 1996

In all games where there is any pecuniary benefit to be derived, the professional invariably beats the amateur, and the reason is easily found in that the professional works much harder than the amateur.

FR Spofforth, in *Great Bowlers* (eds GW Beldham and CB Fry), 1906.

Well, if you're going to bowl with the new one, you can bloody well go on with the old one, too.

Sydney Barnes, sulking over Johnny Douglas's decision to take the new ball himself, MCC in Australia, 1911/12.

Johnny used to bowl them in, then chuck the ball to me to bowl them out.

Cecil Parkin, Lancashire and England bowler, with similar grievances in Australia nine years later.

One of the last of his kind – and certainly the finest specimen of it – the amateurs, the smiling gentlemen of games, intensely devoted to the skill and the struggle, but always with a certain gaiety, romantic at heart, but classical in style.

JB Priestley, on CB Fry (Surrey, Sussex, Hampshire), *The English*, 1973.

Mr Bloody Warner will go to bed when I've finished with him.

Charlie Parker, Gloucestershire left-arm spinner, after a public scuffle with Pelham Warner, whom he partly blamed for his lack of Test caps, 1929.

If these young men think they can field all day, on such a day as Thursday was, dance all night at the Hawks ball (which they were practically compelled to attend) and then do themselves justice with the bat the next morning, then they are very much mistaken.

'Cantab' on the weaknesses of Cambridge University cricket, in *The Cricketer*, 1925.

Whichever side it may be – and I fancy Eton were the principal offenders – the growing tendency to ebullitions of affection and exuberance in the field must be severely checked. They are not pretty at Wembley, but at Lord's quite intolerable.

'GMHC' shocked by the goings-on during the Eton vs Harrow match, 1955.

Ye gods, is the game to be ruled by young men, some of whom are prepared to take the unwritten law into their own hands?

Lord Hawke, following the first artificial declaration in first-class cricket, Gloucestershire vs Yorkshire, 1931.

Batsmen are the darlings of the committees; bowlers are cricket's labourers.

Don Bradman.

Of course, you appreciate, don't you Evans, that the last thing a cricketer wants is damaged eyesight.

Godfrey Evans's brief foray into boxing on the pier at Herne Bay brought this rebuke from Kent's secretary, **Gerald Hough**, in 1938.

We're still the lowest form of animal life!

Len Hutton, in a rare impassioned team talk, before a Gentlemen vs Players match at Lord's, shortly before the Second World War.

No human institution is perfect, but it would in my humble opinion be impossible to find nicer men than those who constitute the Government of Lord's.

Sir Pelham Warner, in *Lord's 1787–1945*, 1946.

Now look here Norman, when I tell you to do something, even if I tell you to run after the ball, you must do it.

Brian Valentine, Kent's captain, to one of his fast bowlers, Norman Harding. Harding, in the middle of a bowling spell, had been reluctant to chase a ball which had flown past his head at short leg, 1947.

But, beggin' your Lordships' pardon, it strikes me as bein' like this, beggin' your lordships' pardons – if Ah can go down to Lord's and get drunk and mek a century 'fore lunch, then Ah thinks it ud pay t'Notts committee to get mi drunk afore every match.

Billy Barnes, responding to a reprimand by Nottinghamshire after he had arrived late and drunk against Middlesex at Lord's. He still scored a century. (From Neville Cardus, *Autobiography*, 1947.)

Bradman was the summing up of the Efficient Age which followed the Golden Age. Here was brilliance safe and sure, streamlined and without impulse. Victor Trumper was the flying bird; Bradman the aeroplane.

Neville Cardus, *Autobiography*, 1947.

I would rather go to a pub with half a dozen Northern professionals than to all the studios, penthouses or Athenaeums and Saville Clubs in London.

Neville Cardus, who tended to go to the opera instead, 1947.

The outstanding characteristic of his captaincy was shrewdness. He made no romantic gestures; he lit no fires of inspiration. He invited admiration rather than affection and he would have exchanged both for effective obedience. A Test match rubber played under Hutton's captaincy became a business undertaking with its principal satisfactions represented by the dividends paid. Hutton did not expect his players to enjoy their Test matches until the scoreboard showed victory. He wanted his team-mates to be untiringly purposeful.

JM Kilburn, in *The Cricketer*, on Len Hutton's retirement, 1956.

A revision of our first-class programme, based on weekend matches only (except in the case of Test and representative fixtures) might well raise standards, both technical and financial.

Peter May, England captain, yearning for more amateurism in county cricket, 1957.

The love of cricket nowadays seems to be confined to those who watch it or read about it.

Arthur Mailey, *10 for 66 and All That*, 1959.

While the amateur status and professionalism still exist in cricket, I would prefer to be captained by an amateur.

Arthur Mailey, *10 for 66 and All That*, 1959.

A rebel is a person who disagrees with the committee.

Arthur Mailey, *10 for 66 and All That*, 1959.

Whilst recognizing that the Amateurs were fully entitled to the repayment of genuine out-of-pocket expenses incurred while playing, and that the counties themselves must be the final judge of such claims, the committee were disturbed by the apparent over-liberal interpretation of the word 'expenses' in certain cases that had come to their notice.

Report of MCC committee, chaired by the Duke of Norfolk, investigating amateur status, 1958.

By and large cricket is governed by a self-perpetuating oligarchy of willow-wielders! On almost every committee and at most conferences batters comfortably outnumber the game's honest toilers.

Robin Marlar, 1959.

Bad luck sir, you were just getting settled in.

Fred Trueman to an Oxbridge batsman. After a long, loosening-up exercise, he had been bowled first ball.

Don't get him out just yet, Johnny, he smells so bloody lovely.

Yorkshire wicketkeeper **Don Brennan** to left-arm spinner Johnny Wardle about a nervous Oxford undergraduate in The Parks.

Disraeli once stated that a country lives by its institutions. This is certainly true of Great Britain; it is full of institutions. Some, like the Royal National Lifeboat Association, are the envy of the world; others, like the House of Lords, are the target of venegary [sic] politicians and music-hall comedians. Midway between the two, more sedate than the former and less democratic than the latter, lies the MCC.

Lord Cobham, former MCC treasurer, 1964.

I had barely eaten my first meal on earth before my father wrote off to friends in England asking them to put my name down for MCC membership.

Colin Cowdrey, *MCC*, 1976.

Sir – Now I know this country is finished. On Saturday, with Australia playing, I asked a London cabby to take me to Lord's and had to show him the way.

Letter to *The Times*, 1970s.

Sir – I noticed one of the umpires today disgraced Lord's Ground by appearing with bicycle clips round his trousers.

Letter to the secretary of MCC, posted in the Lord's pavilion, 1923.

A welfare state cricketer.

EW Swanton, peeved by Warwickshire's dull championship cricket under the captaincy of MJK Smith in the 1960s.

His approach to a problem was to sit in a chair with the *Daily Telegraph* crossword, doze off, wake up, finish the crossword and then fire some broadsides.

Colin Cowdrey, on MJK Smith, (Warwickshire, England), in *MCC*, 1976.

I'm very glad we have an amateur again.

Middlesex committee man, mistakenly, to Mike Brearley on his appointment as county captain, 1971.

The single most important change has been the decline of the personality player and the rise of the professional attitude ... it is a product of the times, a tangent from Trade Unionism.

Colin Cowdrey, *MCC*, 1976.

His clarity of mind enabled him to pierce the woolly romanticism and anachronistic feudalism which for so long obscured the truth of cricket.

John Arlott, in praise of Mike Brearley.

England seem to have a fixation with so-called leadership qualities – and it usually means background.

Geoffrey Boycott, who felt he suffered as a result, 1981.

Good morning, Roy, good morning Peter.

Alec Bedser, chairman of selectors, greeting Ray East and John Lever in a lift during a Test trial, 1973.

Tell me, young man, have you ever played against the Australians before?

Sir Len Hutton, England Test selector, at breakfast, hours before Graham Gooch's Test debut against Australia at Edgbaston, 1975. Hutton was a selector; Gooch had hit 75 against Australia for MCC the previous week.

For God's sake, don't make a bloody fool of yourself!

Alec Bedser, chairman of selectors, to Alan Butcher before his only Test, against India, The Oval, 1979.

You've got to get on with the powers that be, to tug the forelock.

Phil Edmonds, Middlesex and England spinner, 1983.

I will just do a bit of telepathy with Frances and see what she thinks.

Phil Edmonds's jibe on the Wogan show against a TCCB contract which forbade him to comment on England's forthcoming tour of Australia. (Edmonds was summoned to Lord's for a ticking-off.)

This is a Test match. It's not Old Reptonians versus Lymeswold, one off the mark and jolly good show.

David Gower, England captain, refusing to condemn Malcolm Marshall's liberal use of bouncers, fifth Test versus West Indies, 1984.

The usual permutation of plebs: a few Gentlemen, some Professionals, a couple you'd rather not introduce to your mother – and at least one you'd cross Oxford Street to avoid.

Frances Edmonds, summing up the 1985 England team in the *Daily Express*.

Some people talk about 'Botham' and 'Allott' as though they were discussing the labourers on the farm. I used to get angry as soon as I walked into Lord's.

Ian Botham in *It Sort of Clicks*, Botham and Peter Roebuck, 1986.

They bring him out of the loft, take the dust sheet off him, give him a pink gin and sit him there. He can't go out of a 30-mile radius of London because he's normally too pissed to get back. He sits there at Lord's, saying 'That Botham, look at his hair, they tell me he's had some of that cannabis stuff.'

Ian Botham, speaking at a cricket dinner, describing the typical England selector, 1986.

Every time I champion Kim's cause at Lord's I am asked, 'Is he a gentleman?' and I reply, 'One of nature's!' Yet they keep asking the same question.

Guy Willatt, Derbyshire cricket committee chairman, on Barnett's failure to be tried as one of England's five captains in 1988.

There is no more amateurish professional game in the world than cricket.

John Emburey, Middlesex and England spinner, 1989.

I'm not anti-Establishment per se – I'm anti-stupidity.

Peter Roebuck, Somerset captain, 1989.

Everyone was a teenage tearaway unless they were a boring old fart.

Phil Tufnell, Middlesex and England, on his wild youth, 1992.

Allan Lamb is clearly more English than most, but wider issues may be involved, particularly if other South Africans join the trend. Black cricketing countries may well be unhappy if the England team begin to look like a side door round the apartheid boycott.

Matthew Engel, in the *Guardian*, recognizing the dangers of England's South African influx, 1981.

Getting like Glamorgan isn't it? When the weak link in the side is the only Welshman.

Anonymous county cricketer, observing the number of South Africans playing for England, 1980s.

From the humanitarian point of view, why should a cricketer born in Papua New Guinea, Zimbabwe, Israel or any of the other associate countries be denied the opportunity of a Test career by an accident of birth?

Alan Smith, TCCB chief executive, who was actually arguing for a reduction in the qualifying period for Graeme Hick, a Zimbabwean, in 1988.

The rat who joined the sinking ship.

Sydney Morning Herald's reaction to Martin McCague (born Northern Ireland, raised Western Australia) making his Test debut for England against Australia in 1991.

England could now have a New Zealander opening the bowling from one end and an Aussie coming in from the other. It takes the gloss off an Ashes Test.

Australia's captain, **Allan Border**, predicting England's new-ball attack at Trent Bridge, 1993; Caddick, nicknamed Kiwi by his Somerset team-mates, and McCague, known as Oz at Kent.

Why don't you say that to my face, you MCC twat?

Michael Atherton's alleged outburst to a MCC member who had described England's Sunday-morning session against Australia at Headingley as 'garbage'. (MCC member's version, 1997.)

I was just politely enquiring about the gentleman's health. Difference of opinion? Well, that's MCC members for you.

Atherton's version, 1997.

Image is crucial.

Lord MacLaurin, chairman of the ECB, considering a replacement after Michael Atherton's resignation as England captain, 1998.

Image is irrelevant.

Michael Atherton, former England captain, a few weeks later, 1998.

The Pastoral Game

It is more than a game this cricket, it somehow holds a mirror up to English society.

Neville Cardus.

Where the English language is unspoken there can be no real cricket.

Neville Cardus.

Cricket – a game which the English, not being a spiritual people, have invented in order to give themselves some conception of eternity.

Lord Mancroft, *Bees in Some Bonnets*, 1979.

Few things are more deeply rooted in the collective imagination of the English than the village cricket match. It stirs a romantic illusion about the rustic way of life, it suggests a tranquil and unchanging order in an age of bewildering flux.

Geoffrey Moorhouse, *The Best Loved Game*, 1979.

The Englishness is in the lie, in the cult of the honest yeoman and the village green, in the denial of cricket's origins in commerce, politics, patronage and an urban society.

Mike Marqusee, in *Anyone but England* (1994), charting the false vision and hypocrisy present in the English cricket idyll.

Cricket is a game stolen from the people who devised and popularized it; it is a game controlled for nearly 200 years by those who wanted it to become the pastime of an élite.

Alistair McLellan, *Nothing Sacred*, 1996.

There have always been many cricket cultures and those who try and narrow it down to one, who always claim to be the defenders of some inner purity, are the enemies of the game.

Mike Marqusee, opposing cricket's traditional Englishness, in Alistair McLellan's *Nothing Sacred*, 1996.

I object to having to scuttle backwards and forwards with our heads down to avoid being hit by a ball.

Design engineer, **David Lacey**, asking at Slough County Court for Jordans CC, Bucks, to be banned from playing cricket on the village green unless they erected 25ft safety netting in front of his house, 1994.

They should remove themselves during the afternoons when cricket is played.

Judge Nigel Haigh's advice to Mr Lacey, as he refused to ban cricket on the village green, 1994.

I'll watch a game or two. As a motorcyclist, I have a lot of crash helmets. Perhaps we'll wear those.

David Lacey, in amicable mood after losing his case, 1994.

Apart from a few donkeys behind the sightscreen, there were no problems.

Phil Bennett, spokesman for Churt Cricket Club, recalling the day when a home match clashed with the annual village fête – nearest stall 25 yards from the square, 1995.

The three stumps are the triplefold muse or three fates – which must be held in balance. The two bails, as a man and woman, are balanced on their fates to make up the fivefold wicket which must be defended against the fiery red sun.

Tim Sebastian, Arch Druid of Wiltshire, and off-spinner of local repute, before presenting a petition, in 1995, to the prime minister, John Major, pressing for Stonehenge Cricket Club to be given its ground back – a chance to play 'the sacred national game on the sacred site.' (Cricket was last played at Stonehenge in the 1860s.)

I think I probably had one or two drinks too many. During the meal I felt unwell and something snapped.

Local vicar, **Richard Allen**, the guest speaker at Minehead CC's annual dinner, who rose to his feet to swear, throw flowers and bowl roast potatoes at the diners, 1994.

Villagers do not think village cricket is funny.

John Arlott, foreword to Gerald Howat's *Village Cricket*, 1981.

We all started playing somewhere like this, and this is where we should all finish; back in village cricket that gave us the start.

Eddie Paynter, Lancashire and England, playing for Ingrow vs Denholme at the age of 58, 1960.

It is surely the loveliest scene in England and the most disarming sound. From the ranks of the unseen dead for ever passing along our country lanes, the Englishman falls out for a moment to look over the gate of the cricket field and smile.

Sir James Barrie.

Just a word of advice, Tommy, don't underestimate the women of Ambridge.

Advice to Tommy Archer during the annual single-wicket competition as *The Archers*, BBC radio's long-running soap, ensures that cricket remains a part of the social fabric as the end of the century approaches, 1998.

Views From Elsewhere

How can we interrupt such a noble activity as cricket?

French court president, **Marc Joando**, scoffing at Geoffrey Boycott's failure to attend a trial in France, where he faced charges of criminal assault on a former girlfriend, because of commentary duties, 1998.

The general atmosphere of Lord's is more like a prayer meeting than a ball game.

Alistair Cooke, journalist.

They looked on with some amusement, but don't really seem to understand the laws.

Ministry of Defence spokesman, describing the response of 200 Kurds to a game of cricket between British and Australian troops in Northern Iraq, 1991.

I taught my kidnappers cricket. They lent me a machete and I took great pains to carve a bat – a really heavy, Gooch-type bat. The first ball took ages to carve but I had to make a whole batch because every time a boundary was hit into the jungle it was as good as lost.

Phillip Halden, a British businessman keeping the upper lip stiff while kidnapped by Marxist guerrillas in the jungles of Colombia for eight months. (Halden admitted that neither his captors, nor the other hostages – a German, a Dane and a Colombian – appreciated the game), 1996.

What are the butchers for?

Pauline Chase, US actress, catching sight of the umpires at her first cricket match.

Nobody understands cricket. To understand cricket, you gotta know what a crumpet is.

Raphael, *Teenage Mutant Ninja Turtle*, 1990s.

Cricket-playing nations are capable of only limited amounts of sexual activity.

Letter to the *Bangkok Post*, 1991.

'Members and Friends.' That's the most ambiguous notice I've ever seen.

Groucho Marx, visiting Lord's in the 1960s.

I guess this homo business started earlier than I thought.

Groucho Marx again, looking at an ancient painting of cricket in the Long Room at Lord's.

Cricket? It's rubbish. I don't like it. It's not a very emotive game.

Juninho, Middlesbrough's Brazilian footballer, nominating a cricket match as the sporting event he would most pay to miss, 1996.

I want to play cricket. It doesn't seem to matter whether you win or lose.

Meatloaf, US rock singer, 1984.

Cricket is like sex films – they relieve frustration and tension.

Linda Lovelace, star of the pornographic film *Deep Throat*, visiting Lord's for the England vs India Test, 1974.

A cricketer – a creature very nearly as stupid as a dog.

Bernard Levin, *Times* columnist, 1965.

When I played in some friendly games, from the start the players shouted and yelled at one another, even at their own side. One day I explained cricket to friends at a camp and at their request organized a little game with bats hacked from pieces of wood, and a rubber ball. As soon as the fielders took position, they burst out with hue and cry, and when a ball was hit towards a fielder, his own side seemed to pursue him like the hounds of heaven until he had gathered the ball and thrown it in.

Selling cricket to the Americans, as seen by **CLR James** in *Beyond a Boundary*, 1963.

Cricket is the only game that you can actually put on weight while playing.

Tommy Docherty, former football manager, Piccadilly Radio, 1990.

The fact that cricket has to be left off during the winter months may be the reason for the fatality which seems to attend professional cricketers: they seldom live long.

James Cantle, *Physical Efficiency*, 1906.

Cricket is slow because that's what they want it to be.

Poem from *Punch*.

Baseball on valium.

Robin Williams.

I don't think I can be expected to take seriously a game which takes less than three days to reach its conclusion.

Tom Stoppard, English playwright and cricket buff, hitting back with a rejection of baseball in New York in 1984.

The Gentler Sex

You must treat a cricket ball like a new bride.

Micky Stewart's advice to bowlers, 1986.

The essence, the aristocracy of 0 is that it should be surrounded by large scores, that it should resemble the little silent bread-winner in a bus full of fat, noisy women.

RC Robertson-Glasgow, on the delights of making nought.

Pitches are like wives – you can never tell how they're going to turn out.

Len Hutton, explaining why he put Australia in to bat at Brisbane, MCC tour, 1954/5.

At Tunstall she came to the ground with me every morning and afternoon. I asked her to come there to bat at the nets so that I could practise my spin bowling. Day after day for two solid seasons she helped me in this way, and many the time she's gone home with her finger nails turned black and blue by blows from my bowling. Scores of times have I seen her crying with pain through these blows as she stood there patiently holding the bat and trying to defend herself against my spinners, but she never gave up.

Cecil Parkin, England spinner of the 1920s, in praise of his wife.

If possible tour with a bachelor team or a side of 'grass-widowers'. Ten out of eleven women care very little for cricket for cricket's sake, and though from the goodness of their hearts they insist on coming to the grounds and sitting through the weary hours till at length they grow tired, restless, fretful, it would be kinder to all concerned, and less like cruelty to animals, to leave them quietly at home.

DLA Jephson, on club tours.

There are men who fear women more than they love cricket.

Geoff Scargill, at Lancashire annual meeting of 1985, unsuccessfully proposing that women should be allowed in the Old Trafford pavilion.

Let them in and the next thing you know the place will be full of children.

Lancashire member, opposing the same resolution, 1985.

We are told that the speaker joined the club as Mr K Hull.

Bob Bennett, Lancashire chairman, explaining to the 1989 annual meeting how the county's first woman member, Stephanie Lloyd, had sneaked in by virtue of a sex-change operation.

The MCC should change their name to MCP.

Diana Edulji, Indian women's captain, branding the MCC as male chauvinist pigs after being refused entry to the Lord's pavilion during the men's Test, 1986.

If a lot of people thought it was a frightfully good idea, we would follow it through, but I feel that there is not a hope in hell of that.

Lt Col. **John Stephenson**, secretary of MCC, on the ballot asking members whether women should be admitted, 1989.

Popular opinion would be wrong if it ever thought that the M in MCC could stand for misogyny. Quite the reverse is the case. But it may well be that in this changing world there would be one small part of a small part of London which affords refuge for the hunted male animal.

Jack Bailey, former MCC secretary, arguing against the admission of women into the Lord's pavilion, 1989.

MCC have never yet subscribed to the freedom of thought which goes hand in hand with the unisex sauna.

Jack Bailey.

We want our good dykes on board so that we can get more lottery money.

Tim Lamb, ECB chief executive, *categorically denied* ever saying this. But **Theresa Harrild**, a former Lord's receptionist, made the claim anyway while winning a sexual discrimination case at an industrial tribunal. (Harrild claimed she had been pressed to have an abortion after becoming pregnant in an affair with a member of the ECB staff, 1998.)

I've urged cameramen to seek out a bronzed Aussie male, but there doesn't appear to be too many of them, especially among those who drink 15 tinnies a day.

Tony Greig, defending Channel 9's cutaway shots of scantily clad female spectators, 1987.

The ladies, curiously enough, must bear some of the blame at Lord's for the decline in popularity of the Varsity match. If top hats and tail coats were *de rigueur* as of yore, and these things depend on the ladies, the crowds would be infinitely more numerous.

Douglas Jardine, on the 100th Varsity match, 1938.

My friend Imran Khan, who is a famous cricketer and a very popular man with the ladies, has bodyguards outside his room, warding women off. I have guys warding them in.

Zia Mahmood, who chose bridge instead, 1990.

If it is embarrassing then it is wrong. But if it is private, and hopefully delightful, then what could be better – even in the middle of a Test match?

Ted Dexter, a month before his appointment as chairman of the England committee, on players' nocturnal activities, in the wake of the Mike Gatting barmaid affair, 1989.

If Margaret Thatcher had been running English cricket, England would be better off than they are.

Ted Dexter, on leadership qualities, 1989.

You can't come in here – you are a lady.

Brisbane gateman, refusing Frances Edmonds entry to a press conference, despite full accreditation, Ashes series, 1986/7.

I don't want to see knitting needles in the pavilion.

Martin Wood, MCC member, on the club's vote to continue banning women from membership.

One of my greatest pleasures is meeting many old friends at the Lord's Test matches. I cannot see this being enhanced by the presence of women.

Geoffrey Copinger, octogenarian, in a letter to *The Cricketer*, opposing women members of MCC, 1997.

You should treat women the same way as a good Yorkshire batsman used to treat a cricket ball. Don't stroke 'em, don't tickle 'em, just give 'em a ruddy good belt.

Fred Trueman (quoted by Frances Edmonds, 1994).

Have you tried a bunch of red roses?

Magistrate to a man who streaked at Lord's to try to save his marriage, 1991.

Oh God, if there be cricket in heaven, let there also be rain.

Lord Home, from *Prayer of a Cricketer's Wife*.

We've always set the trend. Remember, women cricketers were the first to bowl overarm.

Rachel Heyhoe-Flint, England captain, pressing for a game at Lord's to mark the women's association's 50th anniversary, 1975.

Ladies playing cricket – absurd. Just like a man trying to knit.

Len Hutton, former England captain.

I cried all the way to the wicket. We had arrived.

Rachel Heyhoe-Flint, recalling when Lord's hosted the 1976 women's international between England and Australia. *My Lord's*, ed. Tim Heald, 1990.

The days of women's cricket being seen as a knicker parade must be over.

Norma Izard, manager of England's World Cup-winning side, 1993.

Professional coaching is a man trying to get you to keep your legs close together when other men had spent a lifetime trying to get them wider apart.

Rachel Heyhoe-Flint, former England cricket captain.

I wasn't trying to put our opponents off. Every time I put 100 per cent into a ball it just slips out.

Shamin Umarji, of Oxford University, barred from the 1993 Varsity match for emitting a grunt which was construed as 'unladylike behaviour.'

Men just don't like women umpires. They really do prefer to be given out by a man. When a woman gives them out, they fume, they walk up and down, they get very cross indeed.

Teresa McLean, female umpire, 1987.

Statistics aren't everything.

Ann Mitchell, president of the Australian Women's Cricket Council, defending the omission of Denise Annets (average 81.9 in 13 Tests) from their tour of New Zealand. Annets claimed she was dropped because she was not a lesbian, 1994.

Lord Hawke, had he been asked about it, might have taken the same view as I do about having families on tour. It is no more the place for them than a trench on the Somme.

John Woodcock, *The Times*, MCC tour of Australia, 1975.

Our hotels were turned into kindergartens.

Bob Taylor, *Standing Up, Standing Back*, on the presence of wives and children on England's Australian tour, 1974/5.

Wives and families must never tour again with players ... there is little team spirit and even less fight. Women and children come first for those players who have families. To hell with the pride of England seems to be their motto.

Keith Miller, former Australian all-rounder, in 1975.

I have played my best cricket when I have been with my wife. If wives are accepted into the happy family, things will be very much better.

Alan Knott, England wicketkeeper, on the advantages of women on tour, 1977.

The authorities should consider that a cricketer is more likely to have a proper night's sleep with his wife in bed beside him, rather than a temporary stand-in and all the parallel gymnastics that would follow.

Lindsay Lamb, in Allan Lamb, *My Autobiography*, 1996.

Don't take for granted the English weather or the English women.

Sir Frank Worrell's advice to Bishen Bedi, India's left-arm spinner, before his first tour of England, 1969.

The Great Unwashed

The public need to be educated up to cricket.

Roy Kilner, Yorkshire cricketer.

It is to be feared that a good many people who find their pleasure in watching cricket are very ignorant of the game. In no other way can one account for the unseemly 'barracking' that sometimes goes on.

Sydney Pardon, editor of *Wisden*, 1919.

Edgbaston was awash with social inadequates, bawling, brawling, caterwauling; slating, baiting, hating. The Rea Bank was a cave of sullen youths, for whom insolence, ugliness and selfishness are basic facts of life.

Michael Henderson, in *The Times*, reflecting cricket's uncertainty about the nature of its Test crowds as the century nears its close, 1998.

At about two o'clock the sun came out and a great crowd assembled outside the ground. What I hadn't thought of was that two umpires and two captains would sit and wait for so long without making a decision. The crowd broke in, and to save our skins we started to play at 5.20 on a swamp.

Robert Ryder, Edgbaston administrator, on England vs Australia, 1902.

Owing to the pitch being deliberately torn up by the public, I, as captain of the Lancashire eleven, cannot see my way to continue the game, the groundsman bearing me out that the wicket could not again be put right.

AC MacLaren's statement to the press, 1907. MacLaren refused to continue the Middlesex vs Lancashire match at Lord's after a few spectators walked across the pitch.

The one thing that strikes me about the average crowd – and this is more true of the South than the North – is its ignorance, its startling and fathomless ignorance of the game in general and the match that is going on in particular.

Dudley Carew, *The Cricketer*, 1928.

Since cricket became brighter, a man of taste can only go to an empty ground and regret the past.

CP Snow, 1932.

I'm this side of the line, you're that, and never the twain shall meet. If they do I'll break your f****** teeth.

Rodney Marsh, Australian wicketkeeper, to a spectator who fielded the ball inside the boundary rope, 1981.

I could have cleaned the fellow up, but all I wanted to do was to frighten him a bit.

Merv Hughes, also in disciplinary trouble for threats to a spectator, Jo'burg Test, 1994.

Waugh! What is he good for? Absolutely nothing!

Adaptation of **Edwin Starr**'s soul song – one of the more humorous crowd chants during the 1993 Ashes series in England.

Please sir, can you make Kepler Wessels disappear.

Plea to a magician in the crowd in Pontypridd, Glamorgan vs South Africa, 1994. (Wessels batted three hours for 45 not out.)

Where's an original line?

Phil Tufnell, on the tired wit of Australian crowds, 1994.

The best time ever with the crowd was when me and Angus [Fraser] went out there in the World Series in Melbourne and Angus knocked about 40 and on the way out to the ground everyone was chanting 'Tufnell's a wanker'. I went to the middle and talked to Gus and I was laughing my head off. They don't like to see you laugh.

Phil Tufnell, 1994.

A limit to youthful enthusiasm is reached when these delightful young rascals career over the playing area after scalps.

The Cricketer's comment on the depredations of autograph hunters at Lord's, Middlesex vs Sussex, 1921.

We must be the only working-class family who have gone ex-directory.

Bill Donnison, whose son, Gary, was rugby-tackled by Australia's Terry Alderman when he invaded the pitch, causing Alderman to damage a shoulder, 1983.

We have got a freaker [sic] down the wicket now, not very shapely as it is masculine and I would think it has seen the last of its cricket for the day. The police are mustered, so are the cameramen and Greg Chappell. No! He has had his load, he is being embraced by a blond policeman and this may be his last public appearance. But what a splendid one. And so warm!

John Arlott, BBC radio commentary, Lord's Test vs Australia, 1975. For 'freaker', read Test cricket's first recorded streaker.

It is a sign of decreasing self-esteem and increasing moral turpitude.

Wes Hall, the West Indian tour manager in England, and born-again Christian, on the subject of streaking, Old Trafford Test, 1995.

After all, Lord's is Lord's.

Lord's steward, requesting that men replace their shirts after complaints from women members, Middlesex vs Yorkshire, 1959.

It's been a reasonable day for us boozers up here in the private boxes, but what about the geezers queueing and those blokes munching their sandwiches up there at the Nursery End?

Mick Jagger, after Saturday's play in the Centenary Test at Lord's between England and Australia was abandoned, 1980.

Official hospitality is an organized conspiracy to prevent the uninterrupted watching of cricket, based upon a constant invitation to 'have a drink' or 'meet our sales manager from Slough.'

Roy Hattersley, Labour MP, in *The Guardian*, 1983.

You have to clap yourself on at the WACA.

Gary Gilmour, Australian bowler, on the parochialism of Perth crowds, 1970s.

I enjoyed it, but if I go back again I'll wear a tin hat.

Laurie Lee, poet and author, knocked unconscious by a beer bottle on Sydney's Hill, watching Australia vs New Zealand, 1974.

Lord's was a little more civilized. Spectators used to carry most of their rubbish home.

Denis Compton, on the difference between Arsenal FC and Middlesex. (From *Cricket and All That*, Denis Compton and Bill Edrich, 1978.)

It will be nice to go to Lord's again and prove that there's somewhere in England where you can fall asleep and wake up without finding that your hat and stick have gone.

Elderly spectator, quoted in *The Observer*, at the end of the Second World War, 1946.

On Sundays in particular, we are subjected to the moronic chanting beloved of soccer crowds and decent folk are being driven away by the kind of mindless exhibitionism that has dogged football.

Bob Taylor, *Standing Up, Standing Back*, 1985.

A banal bunch of louts.

Ian Wooldridge's verdict in the *Daily Mail*, in 1995, on The Barmy Army, England's younger and more boisterous travelling fans.

It will be interesting to see how Captain Schultz of the Capetown police reacts to their jumping up and down.

Jon Agnew, BBC cricket correspondent, observing the Barmy Army's excesses in Australia, 1995.

We are changing the merchandising to 'England's Barmy Army' – just in case Michael Atherton gets sacked.

Paul Burnham, Barmy Army Productions, proving that even the Barmy Army were short of loyalty when it came to hard cash, 1995.

I would like to ask your support in preserving the traditional atmosphere of sportsmanship at this ground by acknowledging the good play on both sides.

MCC secretary, **Roger Knight**, at the start of the Lord's Test. England's win at Edgbaston had taken place to the backdrop of an exuberant and partisan crowd, 1997.

I didn't know he was the England captain, and he didn't tell me. I'm afraid I don't follow cricket; boxing's my game.

Headingley gateman, after refusing Chris Cowdrey admission to the ground the day before he was due to skipper England for the first, and only, time, England vs West Indies, 1988.

As our contribution to the UN's response to the Iraqi invasion of Kuwait, the government is sending a detachment of MCC gatemen with instructions not to return until they have ejected President Saddam Hussain by the scruff of his neck.

Ned Sherrin, Radio 4's *Loose Ends*, 1990.

We had never sent them on such a course before. It taught them that there are two ways of saying 'No' and that the other way – 'No, Sir, you can't do that' – is more polite.

Col. **John Stephenson**, MCC secretary: the Lord's stewards had been sent to a charm school, 1991.

7

Culture Clashes

Australians
The West Indies
The Pakistanis
The Indians
Miscellany

Australians

The aim of English Test cricket is, in fact, mainly to beat Australia.

Jim Laker, *Over to Me*, 1960.

You are carrying all the prejudices of England. You are representing deep and paranoid urges, jingoistic sentiments you may prefer to distance yourself from. But it is unavoidable.

Mike Brearley, 1987.

The Australian temper is at bottom grim. It is as though the sun has dried up his nature.

Sir Neville Cardus.

When in England, and particularly at English social functions, it is best for Australian ebullience to be toned down.

Arthur Mailey, *10 for 66 and All That*, 1959.

They are capital winners out here, but I'm afraid that I cannot apply the same adjective to them as losers.

Lord Harris on Australians.

You fellows should never have played cricket if you hate it so much! If I were Sid Smith, I'd bundle you moaning cows off home straight away.

Edgar Mayne, lambasting discontented team-mates at The Oval during the 1921 Australian tour. (Sid Smith was the manager; the story is related by Arthur Mailey in *10 for 66 and All That*.)

The formation of a players' committee to deal with the social engagements of the team will, I hope, prevent a repetition of some unfortunate 'incidents' last year, when invitations, accepted for the players, were either totally ignored or treated in a 'casual Australian' manner that must have been intensely irritating to their hosts.

Clem Hill, former Australian captain, in *The Cricketer*, 1927.

I have from the very outset regarded these tours primarily as imperial enterprises, tending to cement friendships between the Mother Country and her Dominions. Players should not be chosen for their cricket qualities alone. They must be men of good character, high principle, easy of address and in every personal sense worthy of representing their country in all circumstances, irrespective of their work on the field.

Sir Frederick Toone, three-time manager of Australia, in *Wisden*, 1930.

Don't give the bastard a drink – let him die of thirst.

Douglas Jardine's favourite piece of barracking from the Sydney crowd during the Bodyline series, 1932/3.

All Australians are an uneducated and unruly mob.

Douglas Jardine, to Australian wicketkeeper, Stork Hendry, during Bodyline series, 1932/3.

A cricket tour in Australia would be the most delightful period in your life – if you were deaf.

Harold Larwood, England fast bowler, 1933. (He later settled there.)

I know plenty of professionals whom I would delight to have as guests in my own home, but I am afraid I cannot say the same thing about most of the Australians I have met.

AW Carr, Nottinghamshire and England, in *Cricket with the Lid Off*, 1935.

In all this Australian team, there are barely one or two who would be accepted as public school men.

CB Fry, then a journalist, on the 1938 Australians.

Where's the groundsman's hut? If I had a rifle, I'd shoot him now.

Bill O'Reilly, Australian spin bowler, during England's 903–7 at The Oval in 1938.

Remember lad, one day we'll have a fast bowler – and I hope that day isn't too far off.

Len Hutton to Ray Lindwall after some torrid overs, MCC in Australia, 1950/1.

I shouldn't have done that.

Ray Lindwall, upon hitting Frank Tyson (the fast bowler Hutton had dreamed about) on England's next tour to Australia in 1954/5.

At 1.22 p.m. Lindwall bowled the first bouncer. Immediately a clatter of typewriters broke out from the press tent.

Jack Fingleton, in *The Ashes Crown the Year*, on the first bouncer bowled on the Australians' tour of England, 1953.

Bailey, I wish you were a statue and I was a pigeon.

Sydney Hillite, MCC's 1954/5 tour of Australia.

I don't think we'll ever see a better fielding side. Eight of your team ran like stags and threw like bombs.

Peter May, England captain, on the 1955 Australians.

It was built in Yorkshire by a firm called Dorman Long – and it isn't paid for yet.

Fred Trueman, asked for the umpteenth time what he thought of Sydney Harbour Bridge, MCC tour of Australia, 1958. (Source: *Over to Me*, Jim Laker.)

FR Brown was of that type of Englishman not always finding favour in the dominions.

Bill Bowes on Freddie Brown's management of the 1958/9 MCC team to Australia.

I would rather the Australians won 2-1 or 3-1 than go through the dismal business of four more draws.

David Clark, MCC manager in Australia, after the first two Tests were drawn on the 1970/1 tour. Raymond Illingworth, the captain, did not agree.

'They're not bouncers!'
'Well, somebody's bowling them from this end, and it's not me!'

Exchange between England captain, **Ray Illingworth**, and the Australian umpire, **Lou Rowan**, Perth Test, Ashes tour 1970/1. Rowan had warned John Snow about excessive bouncers.

He couldn't speak – he was stoned.

John Snow, asked what had been said when a spectator grabbed him during Sydney Test, 1970/1. Snow had bounced Australian tail-ender Terry Jenner and caused him to retire. Raymond Illingworth led England in the first walk-off in Test history.

I've seen people hit by bottles and it makes a bloody mess of them.

Ray Illingworth, England captain, defending his decision to take players off the field during crowd trouble at Sydney, 1971.

There you are, skip. I reckon you deserve this.

Keith Fletcher, handing a stump to Ray Illingworth in Sydney upon successful defence of Ashes, 1971.

I will not join the group at any wailing wall.

Umpire **Lou Rowan**, refusing to join the post-Test recriminations, Sydney, 1970/1.

He is everything most Australians are not ... a good model of batting technique.

Ray Illingworth on Ian Redpath, 1972.

G'day, howya going?

Dennis Lillee's address to the Queen at Lord's, 1972.

I have on occasions taken a quite reasonable dislike to the Australians.

Ted Dexter, former England captain, 1972.

Good Lord, he's knocked old George off his horse now.

Geoff Arnold, watching from the dressing room as Dennis Lillee hit Keith Fletcher on his touring cap, MCC in Australia, 1974/5.

I don't think we have met – my name's Cowdrey.

Colin Cowdrey, introducing himself at the crease to Australia's tearaway fast bowler, Jeff Thomson, after being pressed into service at a dangerously advanced age on England's 1974/5 tour of Australia.

Yeah, I'd drink with 'em. Trouble is, ya can never find any Poms to drink with, eh Dennis?

Jeff Thomson, scourge of England's batsmen during 1974/5 Ashes series.

Who's this then? Father Bloody Christmas?

Jeff Thomson, Australian fast bowler, as David Steele, silver-haired and bespectacled, emerged for his England début at Lord's, 1975.

If I live to be 95 I'll never forget this day.

Tony Greig, England's captain, after Australia were bowled out for 138 in Centenary Test, Melbourne, 1977. England were then bowled out for ... 95.

Come on Brearley, for God's sake! You make Denness look like Don Bradman.

Melbourne barracker, Australia vs England, 1978/9.

Gold Medallion Award for Greatest Whinger Would Have To Be Won By JM Brearley, Classical Music Lover.

Banner at Melbourne Cricket Ground, England's 1979/80 tour.

They gaily revive every prejudice they ever knew, whether to do with accent, class consciousness or even the convict complex, and sally forth into battle with a dedication which would not disgrace the most committed of the world's political agitators.

Ted Dexter, upon Australians.

The Hill at Sydney used to be amusing, sharp and cutting, but not unfriendly; now it's simply foul-mouthed and crude.

Geoffrey Boycott, 1979.

The latest news is that the Hill at Sydney is to be replaced by a stand. So much the better.

EW Swanton, *Follow On*, 1977.

First the convicts, then the rabbits and now Botham.

Australian banner, 1978.

Playing against a team with Ian Chappell as captain turns a cricket match into gang warfare.

Mike Brearley, lecture at St John's College, Cambridge, 1980.

I think you're struggling, Skip. Best thing to do is put the spinners on and get us home early.

Dickie Bird's assessment of England's chances in the Headingley Test against Australia in 1981. Mike Brearley put Ian Botham on instead, the last five wickets fell for seven runs and Australia, needing 130 for victory, lost by 18 runs.

Goochie hadn't used it much and I thought there were a few runs left in it.

Ian Botham, explaining why he had borrowed Graham Gooch's bat for his miraculous Headingley innings, 1981. (Gooch had made 2 and 0.)

If I played and missed he was standing at the other end, grinning. If I tried a really big heave and made no contact he would just lean on his bat and laugh out loud.

Graham Dilley's memory of their Headingley partnership.

That's better – all the other stuff has made me puke.

Peter Willey, sampling champagne in a victorious England dressing room for the first time, Ashes Test, Headingley, 1981.

It will be remembered in 100 years – unfortunately.

Kim Hughes, Australia's captain, on the 1981 Ashes series.

Well, Bob, this must be the worst English team ever to reach these shores?

Bob Willis's first question on arriving with the England team for the tour of Australia, 1982.

When appealing, the Australians make a statement; we ask a question.

Vic Marks, Somerset and England all-rounder, comparing different approaches in Australia, 1982/3.

You know a few Afrikaans swear words. Have a go at him.

Ian Botham to Allan Lamb during Kepler Wessels's 162 for Australia vs England in Brisbane, 1982/3.

I'm making sure you go this time and don't change your mind.

Rodney Marsh, Australian wicketkeeper, grabbing England batsman, Allan Lamb, by the arm and ushering him towards the pavilion as he 'walked' for a catch in the Perth Test, 1982/3. Lamb had been given 'not out' for an earlier nick, and stayed put.

I acted as pacemaker on the first leg – from Melbourne to Honolulu – then others helped out on the last two stretches as I enjoyed a good sleep. When we got to London, Graeme Wood and I were fresh enough to help him off the plane. The man needed some help after 45 cans!

Dennis Lillee, recalling in *Declarations* (1989) Rodney Marsh's successful assault at the start of the 1985 Ashes tour on Doug Walters's beer-drinking record during an Australia–England flight.

In my day 58 beers between London and Sydney would have virtually classified you as a teetotaller.

Ian Chappell, former Australian captain, informed that David Boon had consumed 58 beers on the team flight to England, 1989. Boon said that he was afraid of flying.

It's going to be very hard to convince people back home that we really do have a lot of promising players.

Allan Border, after his 1985 Australian side lost the Ashes.

The air is thick with gestures, the cheating is on a massive scale and the threatening gestures are rife.

Bob Taylor, in *Standing Up, Standing Back*, on Sydney schools cricket, 1985.

Passengers are reminded that they should be as quiet as possible on this trip because Mike Gatting is trying to catch up on his sleep.

Air hostess on the Melbourne–Adelaide flight. Gatting, the new England captain, had arrived late for play in Melbourne after oversleeping, 1986.

Not bad for the worst team ever to leave England.

Mike Gatting, winning the Ashes in Australia in 1986, after facing the usual suggestions about the weakness of the squad.

At least I have an identity. You're only Frances Edmonds's husband.

Tim Zoehrer, Australia's wicketkeeper, in slanging match with England's slow left-armer, Phil Edmonds, 1986/7 Ashes tour. (From Zoehrer's autobiography *The Gloves Are Off*, 1995.)

There was a young glove-man named Zoehrer,
Whose keeping got poorer and poorer.
Said AB from first slip,
'Please, stop giving lip,
And with extras stop troubling the scorer.'

Limerick read by **Phil Edmonds** to Australian dressing room during Melbourne Test, Ashes series, 1986/7. Edmonds and Tim Zoehrer had been involved in a long-running feud.

There was a balding old man called Philippe,
Who stands in the gully too deep.
When his turn came to bat
He opened his trap.
And his innings just fell in a heap.

Zoehrer's response.

162

There was a strange, white laundry bag sitting in the bedroom on my arrival at the Menzies at Rialto, Melbourne. On further inspection it revealed its contents: a life-sized doll's head, with a very large open mouth attached to an ingenious pumping device. Phil, it transpired, had won the Wanker of the Series award.

Frances Edmonds (wife of the England spinner Phil), *Cricket XXXX Cricket*, 1987.

There are few remaining English prophets in Australia forecasting anything but doom, but for heaven's sake let's not panic. England have only three major problems. They can't bat, they can't bowl and they can't field.

Martin Johnson, *The Independent*, shortly before the first Test in Brisbane, on the Ashes tour of 1986/7. The comment provided constant motivation as England won the series.

I dunno. Maybe it's that tally-ho lads attitude. You know, there'll always be an England, all that Empire crap they dish out. But I never could cop Poms.

Jeff Thomson, Australian fast bowler, 1987.

What do you think this is, a f****** tea party? No you can't have a f****** glass of water. You can f****** wait like the rest of us.

Allan Border, getting tough with England batsman Robin Smith, Trent Bridge Test, Australia tour of England, 1989.

David, the last time I came here, I was a nice guy who came last.

Allan Border's explanation of his hard-line approach to England's captain, David Gower, 1989.

I'm very proud, very proud of my heritage – and, unlike Mr Keating, I do have one.

Ian Botham, 1992, on the eve of the World Cup final in Melbourne. Botham had flounced out of a pre-final banquet after an entertainer took the mickey out of the Queen. Keating, Australia's prime minister, had accused him of being 'precious'.

163

If they call me a 'Pommie bastard' or something I'll say: 'You're right, mate, now buy me a beer.'

Phil Tufnell, 1992, on Australians.

The only reason our fieldsmen were sledging your batsmen at Lord's was to try and stop you being so meek and defeatist. We were just furious at you not making a game of it. We wouldn't sledge if you started standing up for yourselves and didn't just lie down and die all the time.

John Newcombe, Australia's three-times Wimbledon champion, after Lord's Test, 1993.

When England come out here next time they should be treated like Sri Lanka and Zimbabwe and given only three Tests each.

Rodney Marsh, former Aussie wicketkeeper, and head coach of their Institute of Sports' Cricket Academy, after England had been beaten by an innings at Lord's, 1993.

Under the Southern Cross I stand,
A sprig of wattle in my hand,
A native in my native land.
Australia, you bloody beauty!

Australia's **traditional dressing-room song**, following a Test victory. The tradition, begun by David Boon, was handed down upon his retirement to Ian Healy. 'When my moment came to take over, I was more nervous than I ever have been playing Test cricket,' Healy said.

We certainly have got the pace of Dennis Lillee and we are getting near the pace of Jeff Thomson as well.

England's team manager, **Keith Fletcher**, proclaiming the strength of England's pace attack, start of 1994/5 Ashes series.

I think Keith Fletcher is right. England's fast bowlers are as quick as Lillee and Thomson ... now.

Greg Chappell, rubbishing his claims, with good reason, 1994.

Fletch has had a memory lapse ... all coaches have those.

Jeff Thomson, former Australian fast bowler, responding to Keith Fletcher's suggestion.

Man for man, on paper, the Australian side stand out like dog's balls.

Greg Chappell, 1994, predicting the outcome of the Ashes series.

No worries, Paul mate, we beat the bastards.

Spectator in Canberra, interrupting speech from Australian PM, Paul Keating, after his Prime Minister's XI beat the England tourists, 1994.

If the Poms win the toss and bat, keep the taxi running.

Banner at Melbourne Test during England's disastrous 1994/5 Ashes series.

You'll never have a better chance of getting a hat-trick.

Alec Stewart's comment to Shane Warne as Devon Malcolm strode out to face the hat-trick ball at the SCG, England's 1994/5 tour of Australia. Warne got the hat-trick, too.

Tufnell! Can I borrow your brain? I'm building an idiot.

Australian barracker addressing England's Phil Tufnell in Newcastle, Ashes series, 1994/5.

The Aussies try to present a tough-guy image, but this present generation are a bunch of cissies.

Tony Greig, former England captain, 1996.

If you're playing against the Australians, you don't walk.

Ian Botham, in court during Imran Khan libel action, 1996.

A fairly weak sort of player who relies on you to make a mistake. He's not going to get you out.

Phil Tufnell, as seen by **Mark Waugh** ... a few months before he bowled England to victory in The Oval Test, 1997.

Of course Shane Warne doesn't sleep with sheep. He could sleep with whoever he likes.

Paul Burnham, of the Barmy Army (English supporters group), defending taunting songs during England's Ashes tour, 1997.

Taylor is in no fit state to be captain of the Australian cricket team. If he was mentally fit, I know he would have stood down long ago.

Greg Chappell, pressing for Mark Taylor's sacking as Australian captain following England's Texaco Trophy whitewash, 1997.

We're too stunned to give you a reaction. Everyone is either in the pub getting smashed or lying down on couches, saying: 'What the hell happened?'

Australian journalist, in the aftermath of England's win at Edgbaston, 1997.

I'm pretty good at keeping my feet on the ground.

A deadpan **Michael Atherton** after England's Test win at Edgbaston, 1997.

Lightning won't strike twice. It was just one of those days when we seemed to nick everything. We'll retain the Ashes. Definitely.

Greg Blewett, Australian batsman, after England's astonishing start to the Ashes series at Edgbaston, 1997.

England's batsmen seem to get whipped more often than a saucepan full of spuds these days and when you look at the England attack, it looks like a makeshift outfit that couldn't win an argument with a drover's dog.

Jeff Thomson, former Aussie fast bowler, enjoying his annual dig at The Poms, 1997.

I'll have a few drinks in a very short space of time.

Jason Gillespie, Australia's fast bowler, explaining how he planned to celebrate his match-winning performance in the Headingley Test, 1997.

When you come back from Australia, you feel you've been in Vietnam.

Glenn Turner, New Zealand batsman, 1983.

I know the reason he likes the one-day game. He thinks it's great because nobody gets the ball above stump-high.

Kim Hughes on Glenn Turner (Worcestershire and New Zealand). (Turner retorted that Hughes's Australian side were 'simply block-bash merchants'.)

I just wonder what your Prime Minister thinks about the crowd abuse. I wonder whether he's very proud of the Australian spectators during this series. It's a gladiator sport out there. It's like being thrown into the lion's den, and we're on a hiding to nothing. The crowd have got the thumbs-down situation – kill, kill, destroy.

Richard Hadlee, New Zealand bowler, on TV news in Sydney, 1987/8.

We're prepared to try and protect our players from organized character assassination.

Alby Duckmanton, New Zealand team manager, lodging a complaint about Australian crowds' abuse of Richard Hadlee, 1987/8 tour.

Hadlee spits the dummy.
Hadlee's worse than whingeing Pom.
Even six-year-olds get on top of Hadlee.
Hadlee's ego – even bigger than Ken Rutherford's nose.
We're sorry Mr Hawke for calling Hadlee a wanker.

Selection of banners responding to Richard Hadlee's publicized complaints about Aussie crowds, 1987/8.

A deep underlying streak of cruelty and intolerance.

Dr Bill Wilkie, Australian psychiatrist, on why Aussie crowds were hostile to Hadlee, 1988.

This series could be to cricket's box office what *Attack of the Killer Tomatoes* was to the cinema industry.

Queensland official, dismayed by poor ticket sales for the Brisbane Test between Australia and New Zealand, 1997.

The only time an Australian walks is when his car runs out of petrol.

Barry Richards, South African batsman, 1980.

What people didn't realize about South Africa was that from the 'snake pit', where the dressing room was, there were 30 or 40 metres where you had to walk through the middle of Bay 13. You'd be walking down and the South Africans would be right up next to you, on either side, shouting abuse, grabbing your shirt, grabbing your hat and throwing it away, giving you a back-hander, throwing things at you. By the time you were on the field, you could tell everyone was thinking 'F*** this. Let's just get these guys.'

Shane Warne, Australian leg-spinner, defending his unruly behaviour in the South African series, 1994.

What was once to him an insipid form of recreation is now a new religion and such is his temperament and personality that in years to come he will become an even more faithful patron than his less volatile English counterpart.

Peter Pollock, South African quickie, on the increasing fondness for cricket among Afrikaners, 1967.

Go and deflate yourself, you balloon.

Darryl Cullinan's sledging of Shane Warne that began a long-running on-field feud between them. Sydney one-day international, Australia vs South Africa, 1997.

The West Indies

I recommend that future tours to the West Indies should take a good umpire to teach them the laws of the game, of which at the moment the majority are a bit doubtful.

Hon FSG Calthorpe, MCC captain, tour of West Indies, 1926.

No, we'll stay. We want another wicket or two this evening.

Len Hutton, refusing to leave the field in Guyana for fear of a crowd riot, MCC tour of the West Indies, 1953/4.

In England people do not speak to you unless they are firmly introduced with no hope of escape.

Learie Constantine, in *Cricket in the Sun*.

Gilchrist's idea of playing League cricket was to bowl bouncers and beamers at 16-year-old boys.

Jim Laker, *Over to Me*, 1960 on the introductory tactics of Eddie Gilchrist.

That's a fine bloody way to play cricket. If those bowlers don't watch out they'll bloody well kill someone.

Kenny Barrington, after surviving a short-pitched barrage from Wes Hall and Chester Watson, West Indies vs England, Trinidad, 1960 – arguably the birth of the West Indies' fast-bowling era.

If the West Indies are on top, they're magnificent. If they are down, they grovel. And with the help of Brian Close and a few others, I intend to make them grovel.

Tony Greig, England captain, before the 1976 series. The West Indies won the series 3-0.

After all that Closey's only made a single!

John Edrich, in fit of hysterical laughter, after he, at 39, and Close, at 46, had survived a fearsome 70-minute battering from the West Indies quicks, Old Trafford Test, 1976. Neither played for England again.

That was not great captaincy, it was barbarism.

Sunil Gavaskar, on Clive Lloyd's handling of the West Indies pace attack, 1976.

To call a crowd 'a crowd' in Jamaica is a misnomer. It should be called a mob ... these people still belong to the jungles and forests instead of a civilized society.

Sunil Gavaskar, in *Sunny Days*, on India's tour of the West Indies, 1976.

We have a saying in the West Indies – if you want to drive, buy a car.

Michael Holding, in his Derbyshire days, defending the proliferation of short-pitched bowling in the 1980s.

In their disregard of anybody being hurt and hit some West Indians appeared callous and reminded me of bully boys.

Jack Fingleton, appalled by the West Indians' short-pitched fast bowling at The Oval, 1980.

In the field the most boring team I had seen, with their super-abundance of fast bowlers who bowled so many bouncers (and therefore unplayable balls), their slow over rates with their incomprehensible long run-ups.

Jack Fingleton, expanding upon his dislike of the 1980 West Indians in *Batting from Memory*, 1981.

Even when they are just spectators, there is something intimidating about their presence.

Sir Len Hutton on West Indian cricketers, 1981.

Without being unkind, a donkey could lead West Indies at the moment. But put Clive Lloyd in charge of Australia and even he'd struggle.

Keith Fletcher, responding to Kim Hughes's resignation of Australian captaincy, 1981.

There's no rule against bowling fast.

Clive Lloyd, West Indies captain, 1985.

I've been a professional for 18 years and what happened out there had nothing to do with cricket.

Geoff Howarth, New Zealand batsman, reacting to the short-pitched methods of West Indian pace bowlers, Jamaica, 1985.

I may be black, but I know who my parents are.

Viv Richards, leaping into the crowd at Weston to confront racist hecklers, 1980s.

The drums. I miss the drums.

Viv Richards, after the TCCB decision to ban musical instruments, hooters etc at Test matches, 1988.

We don't breed brutal cricketers.

Clive Lloyd, West Indies manager, rejecting charges that his side played brutal cricket, Australia, 1988.

Twenty years ago, we were the frivolous calypso cricketers. Now the players just tend to go out and do a job.

Jackie Hendriks, West Indian manager and former wicketkeeper, 1988.

When I was captain I always told my bowlers that if they bowled bumpers they had to expect a few in return.

Clive Lloyd, West Indies manager, showing no sympathy towards the Australian quick, Geoff Lawson, after Curtly Ambrose had broken his jaw, second Test, Perth, 1988.

We bowl short at them, they bowl short at us, it's as simple as that.

Geoff Lawson, his jaw broken by Curtly Ambrose, capturing the mood of the 1988 series between Australia and the West Indies.

It's definitely worse than Bodyline, because there is no let-up and it is just as fierce.

Keith Rigg, former Australian player, on the West Indies' pace attack in Australia in 1988.

If every country had an attack like the West Indies, Test cricket would die pretty quickly. You can only think of survival, not playing shots.

Allan Border, Australian captain, after a fraught Melbourne Test, 1989.

Players will not be allowed on the field with coloured tams or hats, long plaited hair or dreadlocks.

Rules of Leeward Islands Cricket Associations, discriminating against Rastafarians. Introduced when Victor Eddy became the last Rasta to play for the Leewards in the 1970s.

As soon as I got into the West Indies team in the early Seventies it was clear to me that the Asian guys were not going to get fair treatment. It has always been there, but it has just grown and grown.

Alvin Kallicharran, *Declarations*, 1989.

Until we can breed seven-foot monsters willing to break bones and shatter faces, we cannot compete against these threatening West Indians.

David Frith, *Wisden Cricket Monthly*, 1990.

More fast-twitch muscle fibres and relatively shorter backbones.

Derek Pringle, on why West Indies' fast bowlers are quicker than their English counterparts, 1991.

They must have fallen asleep in a greenhouse with their feet in a growbag.

Fred Trueman, Test Match Special, Leeds Test 1991, explaining the size of the West Indian fast bowlers.

Kids in the West feel a bit peckish and buy a carton of junk-food. Plenty here can't afford to do that. So they have to eat lots of fruit and other good wholesome grub that happens to be the cheapest and the best for them. Add all the bits and pieces together and you get a long, long queue of fit, lean, loose-moving youngsters who are superbly fitted to the job.

Dennis Waight, West Indies' physio, explaining the side's surfeit of fast bowlers in the 1980s.

They are the most unpopular team in the world. Their game is built upon vengeance, violence and arrogance.

David Frith, editorial in *Wisden Cricket Monthly*, on the arrival in England of the West Indies, 1991.

When you are black you never really know what is inside another man's heart.

Viv Richards, *Hitting Across the Line*, 1991.

We have always been a peace-loving people, and I don't think that has changed.

Viv Richards again.

What we are looking for is a nice peaceful tour. We would like to start and finish on a wonderful note and hope that everybody will be happy. I just hope that we don't throw the first stone.

Viv Richards, start of West Indies' tour of England, 1991.

He is a moaner and bad loser. He is a very sour sort of guy. Bobby Simpson ain't our cup of tea at all.

Viv Richards, West Indies captain, following West Indies' victory against Australia in the Barbados Test, 1991. Simpson, Australia's team manager, said his previous contacts with Richards had been pleasant ones.

I just hope nobody shakes a coconut tree and a black Shane Warne falls out.

Robin Smith, unable to mask his South African upbringing, before England's tour of the West Indies, 1994.

You can't rent a room, you can't hire a car, and if you're dining out tonight, you'd better make a reservation ... last week.

Local newspaper on English fans' invasion of Barbados for the 1994 Test.

Some become arrogant. Some become difficult. Some forever will remain social misfits. It doesn't concern them. Their only concern is staying on board the team because the alternative is anonymity.

Ian Wooldridge, *Daily Mail*, linking magnificent West Indian fast bowling (in the 1994 series vs England) to poverty, drugs, violence and all manner of social evils.

Ambrose – he the West Indian Minister of Defence.

Trinidad taxi driver after Ambrose (six for 24) had bowled out England for 46, 1994.

English and Australian journalists have asked if Curt would quit. He don't even start doing anything. He has already given me what is mine. He has to work now on things for himself, for when he isn't playing.

Hillie Ambrose, mother of Curtly Ambrose, after England collapsed to 46 all out against him, Trinidad Test, 1994.

If we feel like praying together, we pray.

Richie Richardson, West Indies captain, on his side's sense of religion and unity, 1994.

We must stick together both politically and socially. We come from small communities and we have an insularity problem. The West Indies team can give our people a great example of unity.

Richie Richardson, West Indies captain, 1994.

I would be disappointed if we had not made 300.

Andy Roberts, West Indies cricket manager, after his side had bowled on the Lord's pitch, first day, second Cornhill Test, 1995.

It is one of the worst wickets I have ever seen in England. I am fearful for the game of cricket with wickets like that.

Roberts, adjusting his view ever such a little after the West Indies had batted on it, the next day, 1995.

We have to protect the majority from the mindless minority. A drum can be a missile or classified as a dangerous object.

Glyn Woodman, chief executive of Surrey, using the Safety of Sports Grounds Act to justify the banning of West Indian musical instruments, 1995 Cornhill Test series, England vs West Indies.

Twenty years ago parts of this ground were almost no-go areas. They could sit where they liked and all get together and they can't do that now because of the pre-selling of tickets. Now they've got to get organized. They can't just roll up on the day and sit together in a mass.

Glyn Woodman again, explaining why the West Indian spectators had vanished along with their drums, 1995.

Black people in Britain will always support the West Indies, whether it's the second, third or fourth generation. It's not disloyalty or lack of patriotism. West Indies cricket is part of our culture. It's one of the things that gives us our identity. It doesn't make us less British than anyone else.

Ron Shillingford, news and sports editor of *The Voice*, Britain's biggest Afro-Caribbean newspaper, 1995.

An Asian or negro raised in England will, according to the liberal, feel exactly the same pride and identification with the place as the white man. The reality is somewhat different. It is even possible that part of a coloured England-qualified player feels satisfaction (perhaps sub-consciously) at seeing England humiliated because of post-imperial myths of oppression and exploitation.

Robert Henderson, in *Wisden Cricket Monthly*, 1995. His racist analysis of 'foreigners' playing cricket for England understandably caused an outcry.

What they should do is get a younger individual. To be honest this present mob are a little bit shy in terms of fast bowling. I mean, very bashful. We have competed against Australia for a number of years and we have seen guys who have shown a little bit more of this [pointing to his heart]. For some reason we don't see that this time. Someone should set an example by getting in line. I think you would need your captain to have a little bit more heart.

Viv Richards, on the opening night of his 'King and I' talk show with Ian Botham, in Perth, 1993. Richards caused a storm by questioning Allan Border's reputation for unflinching courage. Border had dropped himself to no. 6 against the West Indies.

They set out to get the captain ... then they target the man they regard as the senior batsman. We saw it on the Caribbean tour last year when they got after Atherton. That was cricket's version of assault and battery.

Robin Smith, his cheekbone fractured by Ian Bishop, Old Trafford Test, 1995.

It's Test cricket; it's tough. If you want an easy game, take up netball.

Steve Waugh, resisting the West Indian fast bowlers, during Australia's historic series win in the Caribbean, 1995.

They are getting older and on good batting tracks they are getting slower. They have got to start listening to me.

Andy Roberts, former West Indies fast bowler, and team manager, on his current crop; Australia had just inflicted West Indies' first home series defeat for 22 years. 1995.

'Ah wonder which lottery game these numbers belong to?'
'Dem aint no lottery numbers. Dat is de West Indies scorecard against Kenya.'

Exchange in cartoon in the *Sunday Sun*, Barbados, after Kenya beat the West Indies in one of the greatest shocks in cricket history, World Cup, Pune, 1996.

When I started playing in 1970, we used to improvise with maize cobs, using sticks as bats. We graduated to tennis balls and carved our own bats.

Steve Tikolo, after Kenya's defeat of the West Indies in Pune, 1996 World Cup. Kenya had only 1500 registered players.

The kitchen and the bar are in roaring form. The orders are high for beers, for snacks such as burgers, the soft drinks are selling real hot. People are in celebration mood. I am so excited I cannot concentrate upon my work. It is joy and happiness.

Chander Thakar, manager of the Nairobi Club, base for many of the Kenyan players, after Kenya had beaten the West Indies in the 1996 World Cup.

You know, if you have a good team and a bad management, you can maybe get along, but a bad team and bad management and you're f*****. After this defeat they will be forced to sort out the shit.

The gospel according to **Brian Lara** (as alleged by *Outlook* magazine) following the West Indies' shock defeat against Kenya in Pune, World Cup, 1996.

It wasn't that bad losing to you guys. Now a team like South Africa is a different matter altogether. You know, this white thing comes into the picture. We can't stand losing to them.

Brian Lara's controversial remarks to Kenyan players after their defeat of the West Indies in the 1996 World Cup, as alleged by India's *Outlook* magazine.

Key elements of life in the West Indies include rum and coke, bananas, sugar and laid-back black men.

The England Cricket Board had recognized that its Test players needed educating about the countries they were about to tour. According to the *Mail on Sunday*, this banal and condescending summation of the West Indies was about as good as the lecture got, 1997.

They don't need a captain, they need a cross between Nelson Mandela and George Headley.

The *Barbados Daily Herald*, considering the West Indies' problems replacing Courtney Walsh, 1997.

If anyone starts throwing punches I'll be out there.

ICC referee, **Barry Jarman**, making light of a V-sign by England captain Michael Atherton to the departing West Indian batsman, Barbados Test, 1998.

I was going to give Philo a one-fingered send-off, which I knew was wrong. But all of a sudden the second finger appeared. It just slipped out.

Atherton's explanation, several months later, 1998.

The lions have been pussycats.

Michael Atherton, bemused that the English media corps had not pressed him to explain his V-sign to West Indian batsman, Philo Wallace, during the Barbados Test, 1998.

The Pakistanis

Pakistan is the sort of place every man should send his mother-in-law to, for a month, all expenses paid.

Ian Botham, returning from England's 1984 tour.

Why don't you send in your mother-in-law now? She couldn't do any worse.

Aamir Sohail, taunting Botham after his dismissal for a duck in the 1992 World Cup final in Melbourne.

The sooner we're out of this country the better.

Bill Athey, England batsman, before the Karachi Test on a disruptive England tour of Pakistan, 1987/8.

We'll not carry any flag – black or white. If anyone tries to prevent us getting there that will be it – we just won't be there.

Les Ames, England tour manager on the 1969 tour of Pakistan, during the Karachi Test. England had been told that, in the event of a general strike, they would have to march to the stadium behind a black flag.

They weren't very hard, but I think they were my only decent strokes up until then.

Tom Graveney, after swinging his bat at invading Pakistani spectators, Karachi Test, Pakistan vs England, 1969.

Come on Knotty, let's get out of here, quick!

David Brown to his England team-mate, Alan Knott, during a pitch invasion in the Karachi Test. Knott, on strike, was four runs away from his maiden Test hundred. Knott never made his hundred – the Test became the first to be abandoned because of riots, 1969.

Words spoken by William Pitt in 1805 may be precisely applied to cricket today: 'Roll up that map. It will not be wanted these 10 years.'

EM Wellings, in the London *Evening News*, patently reluctant to return to Pakistan after abandonment of the 1969 tour. (Pitt had been referring to Europe, overrun by Napoleon.)

They've always had a lot of talent, a lot of good players, but they're like eleven women. You know, they're all scratching each other's eyes out.

Ian Botham on Pakistani sides he had known.

I am surprised he left one stump standing.

Australia's captain, **Kim Hughes**, responding to questions about Rodney Hogg's behaviour in kicking down his stumps in the Melbourne Test against Pakistan, 1979. Hogg had been run out by Javed Miandad while he was inspecting the pitch.

If we had given them everything they asked for, England would have been out for single figures in each innings and Pakistan would have scored 500 runs in one.

Ken Palmer, English umpire, complaining about incessant Pakistani appealing, first Test at Edgbaston, 1982.

One problem was that gentlemen with white and brown faces confronted each other quite determined to have a punch-up. I have never seen it before on a Test ground.

Raman Subba Row, TCCB chairman, after crowd trouble during the England vs Pakistan one-day international at Edgbaston, 1987.

At one stage I was out on the boundary with Mike Gatting trying to count the number of Pakistani players on the field. But I gave up because I don't possess a calculator.

Micky Stewart, England manager, accusing Pakistan of time-wasting by constant substitutions, Old Trafford Test, 1987.

It's so depressing out here. Shout something encouraging you chaps!

Phil Edmonds to The Oval crowd as Pakistan scored 708 in the fifth Test, 1987. A spectator duly replied: 'This could be your last Test.'

I have never upset anyone in my life.

Javed Miandad, Pakistani captain, at the start of a stormy tour of England, 1992.

The whole thing was just a fly in the ointment.

Haseeb Ahsan's description of an altercation between Mike Gatting and Javed Miandad in the World Cup, 1992.

I knew that God was on our side.

Imran Khan, captain of the Pakistan team that beat England in the 1992 World Cup final.

An excitable kind of mob.

Phil Tufnell, on the Pakistanis, 1992.

See those bloody vultures up there. They're waiting for that bloody umpire. He's got to be dead.

Sam Loxton, Australian manager, to Pakistan army representatives when Hanif Mohammad was given 'not out' against Ray Lindwall in the Dacca Test, 1959/60.

If you don't play some cricket, they'll kill us.

Plea by the **deputy commissioner of Gujranwala** to the Australians, during their tour of Pakistan, 1994. Australia played in borderline conditions and the feared riot did not materialize, 1994.

'I've waited six years for your autograph, Mr Wog.'
'Well, another ten minutes won't hurt you, mate.'

Exchange between **Steve Waugh** and a Pakistani autograph hunter as Waugh left the field during the Pakistan vs Australia series, 1994.

At least when a side like Australia tries to rattle you, they do so in a language you can understand.

Bill Alley, Australian, upon the 1992 Pakistanis.

We enjoy touring different countries and appreciate experiencing different cultures.

One of a suggested list of media responses prepared for the Australian players before their tour of Pakistan, 1994.

While racist chanting went on unchecked, spectators were treated to the surreal sight of a pantomime cow being ejected from the ground for parading up and down while play was in progress.

Inside Edge magazine, 1996, on Headingley's appalling stewarding during the Test match against Pakistan.

I was calling him 'potato' in Punjabi because he is a little fat.

Spectator at the World Friendship Cup in Toronto after the Pakistani batsman, Inzaman-ul-Haq, waded into the crowd. The spectator was armed with a megaphone, Inzaman was armed with a cricket bat, and the ICC match referee, Jackie Hendricks, was armed with a two-match ban, 1997.

The Indians

England is not ruined because sinewy brown men from a distant colony sometimes hit a ball further and oftener than we do.

JB Priestley.

It is in the matter of patience that I think the Indian will never be equal to the Englishman.

Lord Harris, *A Few Short Runs*, 1921.

To wear down good bowling, and patiently wait for a run here and there, is easier for the phlegmatic Anglo-Saxon than for the excitable Asiatic.

Lord Harris, assessing the early performances of the Parsis at the turn of the century.

At Peshawar I stayed with a cousin of Jardine. On the first morning we parted on the doorstep, I to play cricket, he to settle a tribal war.

Lionel Lord Tennyson, describing the 1937/8 tour of India.

Stop the game. We can't see the game. Smoke is getting in our eyes.

GK Menon, Indian reporter, striding onto the Bombay outfield from the press box as the stands were set alight, India vs Australia, 1969.

They'll shoot you in the leg so they can get you lbw again.

Keith Fletcher to his England colleague, Tony Lewis, in Bombay after a PLO murder threat, MCC tour of India, 1972.

Hello, Colonel, glad to see you've got your colour back.

Fred Trueman to Lt-Col. Hemu Adhikari, the Indian manager, during the 1974 tour of India. Adhikari had suffered a traumatic experience against Trueman 22 years earlier when India had lost their first four wickets for no runs.

You can't muck around with eggs and you can't muck around with chips.

Ken Barrington, England batsman and later tour manager, explaining his eating habits in India. Quoted in Frank Keating's *Another Bloody Day in Paradise*, 1981.

In Bombay when England batting there are forty to fifty thousand people shouting every time ball hitting the pad, and in Calcutta, my God, there are ninety thousand people all shouting. But you must concentrate. It is a selfish thing but you must concentrate to save your skin.

Swaroop Kishen, Indian Test umpire, in Scyld Berry's *Cricket Wallah*, 1982.

It's 8.30 on a Friday night; what am I doing in Ahmedabad?

Graeme Fowler, as portrayed in **Vic Marks**'s *Marks out of Eleven*, enduring a quiet night on England's 1984/5 tour of India.

You're the instigator of all this. If you feel like that you can take your passport and f*** off.

England manager, **Tony Brown**, accusing Allan Lamb, in a players' meeting, of lobbying for the tour of India to be cancelled following the assassination of Prime Minister Indira Gandhi, 1984/5.

There was nothing else to do but drink. I saw so many balls I couldn't miss.

Frank Worrell, after his double hundred in Kanpur, West Indies' tour of India, 1952/3.

We were fascinated by the milling mass of humanity below and we took to dropping rupees to them and watching them scramble. Unkind I guess, but it was irresistible. We went a step further and started pouring water onto them as they fought each other for the rupees. We'd fill all available receptacles in the hotel room with water, drop the coins and whoosh.

Allan Border, Australia's captain, in autobiography of the same name, on dubious hotel entertainment in Kanpur, India, 1986.

We failed Tebbit's cricket test and we're proud of it.

Banner among English-born Indian supporters, Texaco Trophy international, England vs India, Headingley, 1990.

As the greatest run-getter of all time in Test cricket you have undone all your deeds at one stroke by ridiculing the greatest institution of cricket in the world. You have proven that only the mighty can be petty. I feel personally quite disgusted and ashamed I ever played cricket with you and like so many cricketers I have met in the last few days I wonder what kind of person you are. Not only have you let yourself down, but you've let down the Indian cricket team, world cricket and more importantly, the Indian people in Britain.

Bishen Bedi, Indian team manager, in an open letter to Sunil Gavaskar during the tour of England, 1990. Gavaskar's crime had been to refuse MCC life membership because of past brushes with Lord's officialdom.

Bad cricket – sweep shot not good. Play straight, good cricket.

Indian umpire to Dermot Reeve, after the England batsman had questioned an lbw decision during the 1993 tour of India. Reeve, who played very little else but the sweep (unless it was the reverse sweep) was not best pleased.

The players have quite reasonably talked about levels of pollution and how it has affected levels of performance ... I've decided to commission an immediate report into pollution levels in Indian cities.

Ted Dexter, chairman of the England committee, after the first of England's three successive, overwhelming defeats on the 1993 tour of India. This one was in fume-ridden Calcutta. The report never materialized.

In view of Mr Dexter's unease, I've decided to commission a report into the effect of pollution levels upon the trajectories of India's spinners.

Kamal Nath, India's forests and environment minister, suggesting that Dexter could not see the wood for the trees, 1993.

In India you are confined to your hotel. You've just got to accept it.

Graham Gooch, failing to adjust to the Indian lifestyle during England's 3-0 Test defeat, 1993.

While they were in this palace with gold tigers and everything there were crippled blokes on the streets of Calcutta who couldn't even get anything to eat. It made me sick.

Phil Tufnell, describing what he told his Indian hosts at a reception during England's 1992/3 tour.

Done the elephant. Done the poverty. Might as well go home.

Phil Tufnell, in joshing mood, after a fortnight in India, 1993.

People object to being beaten by volunteers rather than the police. We have told the volunteers that if they wanted to beat someone they should take them outside and do it.

GY Lele, joint secretary of the Indian Cricket Board of Control, responding to crowd disturbances during the India vs England one-day international, Jamshedpur, 1993.

I mean, look at our cricket team. One man's bowl of prawns is a nation's humiliation.

Arthur Daley, in *Minder*, using England's defeat in the 1993 Madras Test after a food-poisoning episode to illustrate how history's great disasters are caused by one small error, 1994.

I have signed a contract with the Reebok company, but I haven't autographed or signed on the shoes. If I have hurt the feelings of the Muslim fraternity, I apologize.

Mohammad Azharuddin, India's Muslim captain, denying that he wrote the Prophet's name on unholy footwear – even if they were Reebok's. (His name consists of the Prophet's name, and 'Azhar', one of nearly 100 appellations for Allah, 1995.)

Oh, that's India, stop worrying, I'm not.

John Barclay, England A's team manager, in determinedly admirable form in India in 1995.

I like the same routine. I once had steak and chips for 28 consecutive nights in India and I was the only one who wasn't ill.

Jack Russell, England wicketkeeper, 1995.

Miscellany

If cricket is regarded, even unconsciously, as an imported game, a freak amusement of an alien race, its roots are shallow.

Sir Hilary Blood, on the slow progress of cricket in Ceylon, 1955.

If you get one F, give two Fs back.

Advice given by **Mumtaz Yusuf**, manager of Sri Lanka A, to his players in a testy series against England's A tourists, 1991.

Dennis Silk told me the Sri Lankan boys are playing an excellent game. They are dedicated and they mean business, while the English are like a bunch of old women.

Tyronne Fernando, president of the Sri Lankan Board of Control, and Government minister, relating a conversation with MCC's president during Sri Lanka's first Test win against England, Colombo, 1993.

If we have appeared to have batted in a hurry, it is because the batsmen want to make the most of their short stay before the umpires do them in.

Bandula Warnapura, Sri Lankan team manager, excusing a heavy Test series defeat in India, 1994.

I'm not going to dance the way they want.

Sri Lanka's captain, **Arjuna Ranatunga**, refusing to guarantee the Australian Cricket Board 'an atmosphere of goodwill' in the final Test of the series, 1996. The ACB, astonishingly, had insisted that Australia's participation in the ensuing World Cup was conditional on that promise.

We don't look for revenge … it's not in our culture.

Arjuna Ranatunga, Sri Lanka's World Cup-winning captain, asked after the final in Lahore if he had sought revenge against Australia for their refusal to play in Colombo in the wake of a terrorist bomb blast, 1996.

Time stands still. Business is suspended. Chief executives and trainees slap each other on the back. Wives forgive husbands. Guys forget girls. At every watering hole euphoria overflows. History writes a new chapter in golden letters. Every Sri Lankan wherever in the world he lives, is roaring like a lion …

Union Assurance advert, in the *Colombo Daily News*, the day after Sri Lanka won the World Cup, 1996.

When I see English schoolboys thrusting their autograph books in my face and using bad language in front of adults, I think they could do with a few terms at Prince Edward's.

Graeme Hick, extolling the virtues of a Zimbabwe public school education. (From *My Early Life*, 1991.)

I had this strange negative feeling about England. I'd got this idea in my head that it was a country full of drug addicts and muggers and I had no intention of going out of my hotel unless I had to.

Graeme Hick, *My Early Life*, 1991.

We didn't tell them about the country or its culture. It's not fair on them. We have a responsibility to make them better people.

Lord MacLaurin, broadening England's horizons after the tour of Zimbabwe, 1997.

We're professional sportsmen, we can't get drunk every night. We've had up to 12 of us playing Balderdash, laughing and joking for hours. We've had a grand time.

David Lloyd, England's coach, defending his squad against accusations of unsociability, tour of Zimbabwe, 1996.

We murdered 'em. We got on top and steamrollered 'em. We have flippin' hammered 'em. One more ball and we'd have walked it. We murdered 'em and they know it. To work so hard and get so close, there is no praise too high. We have had some stick off your lads. We flippin' hammered 'em.'

David Lloyd, in a state of great agitation, after England failed by one run to beat Zimbabwe in the Bulawayo Test, 1996. The final hour was characterized by persistently wide bowling which remained unpunished by the umpires.

Wanted
David Lloyd
For Murder of Zim Cricket Team
last seen with his finger up his nose
talking complete bollocks
He knows it and we know it

Anti-Lloyd banner at the following Test, in Harare, 1996.

Up, breakfast, stretch, practise, play, bathe, bar, steak, bed. Same company, day in, day out.

Ian Botham, on the boredom of touring in *It Sort of Clicks*, Botham and Peter Roebuck, 1986.

Did I find Test tours too strenuous? The very question is sacrilegious.

Arthur Mailey.

Three to six months of constant packing and unpacking, living out of suitcases with home a succession of impersonal hotel rooms, some good, some bad, the majority indifferent. The tourist's life is in the open, with every move made under the spotlight of publicity. The television lens watches everything on the field, the curious eyes of strangers watch in hotels and streets, at receptions, cocktail parties and a succession of dinners. The moments of complete freedom are few and far between.

John Snow, *Cricket Rebel*, 1976.

Players cannot expect to sit on their backsides and be paid for just being Test cricketers.

Bobby Simpson, former Australian captain, later coach, insisting in *Howzat*, 1980, that long tours are inevitable.

8

Political Pitch

Political Cricket balls
The Apartheid Years

Political Cricket Balls

Cricket shouldn't be used as a political football.

David Graveney, Gloucestershire captain.

Say that cricket has nothing to do with politics and you say that cricket has nothing to do with life.

John Arlott, journalist.

High and low, rich and poor, greet one another practically on an equality, and sad will be the day for England if Socialism ever succeeds in putting class vs class and thus ending sports which have made England.

Lord Hawke, *Recollections and Reminiscences*, 1924.

Bolshevism is rampant, and seeks to abolish all laws and rules, and this year cricket has not escaped its attack.

Lord Harris, in *The Cricketer*, 1922. The outburst was caused by Wally Hammond's decision to play for Gloucestershire rather than his native Kent.

Cricket has become a part of the national life and, if the Bolsheviks get their way with her, it will be nationalized with the cinema and the theatre and Association Football.

Alec Waugh, 1922.

If the French noblesse had been capable of playing cricket with their peasants, their châteaux would never have been burnt.

GM Trevelyan, *English Social History*, 1944.

The second day was played under the cloud of the General Strike, and since then serious cricket at Oxford has been seen no more. Legge, after covering incredible distances at illegal speeds in his Vauxhall, transporting workers, ended up by driving a 'bus in London; Holmes, Stephenson and Abell joined the constabulary; Richardson, Greenstock, Surrurier and McCanlis have been acting as dockers at Bristol, Hull and Liverpool.

Oxford University cricket's contribution to crushing the General Strike of 1926, as recorded by **'Isis'** in *The Cricketer*.

Private enterprise in cricket might not be regarded as the last word, and ultimate State direction would not do it any harm.

Manny Shinwell, Labour MP, proposing nationalization to solve English cricket's problems, 1950.

No country which has cricket as one of its national games has yet gone Communist. On this I found my trust that the new regime in Grenada will turn out to be not so extreme Left-Wing as predicted.

Woodrow Wyatt, the *Sunday Mirror*, 1979.

At home and abroad, in politics and sport, Britain will do better without the Tories and their friends of the Marylebone Cricket Club. Twenty years ago Tribune first made the demand that the MCC should be nationalized. Now everyone can see the wisdom of our policy.

Michael Foot, Labour MP, in *Tribune* after a poor start to MCC's tour of Australia, 1958/9.

If there were a revolution in this country, I'd now be in the first 10,000 to the guillotine.

John Warr, elected MCC president in 1987.

It was his dream to build a kind of socialist cricket republic where all players would be equal. If he had had his way we would have stood up before the start of each match and belted out a couple of choruses of the Red Flag.

Ian Botham, on Geoff Cook's management of Durham, in *My Autobiography*, 1995.

There was a social prejudice against the scorer who was a direct descendant of the baggage man.

Vic Isaacs, Hampshire scorer and statistician. (Quoted by Ted Dexter and David Lemmon in *A Walk to the Wicket*, 1985.)

When we gave your association our blessing we didn't expect it to be militant.

Tim Lamb, TCCB cricket committee chairman, to Ted Lester, chairman of the Association of County Cricket Scorers, 1995. Militancy was a word no one would associate with county scorers, but their loud protests over the appointment of scorers on England tours surprised everyone.

Comprehensives don't produce cricketers.

Jim Laker, former England and Surrey spinner.

All the time I keep telling myself and telling the others, 'It could be worse, fellas. We could be putting a helmet on for a shift down the pit.'

Geoffrey Boycott, on bad days.

This miners' strike is ridiculous. There's tea ladies at the top of the mine who are earning more than county cricketers. Arthur Scargill ought to come down here and try bowling 20 overs.

Ray Illingworth, Leicestershire captain, 1975.

There's no pressure in Yorkshire cricket. My mate gets up at half-past four every morning to go down t'pit. That's what you call pressure.

Steve Oldham, upon his appointment as Yorkshire cricket manager, 1989.

I'm going to threaten them with going back down t'pit.

Les Taylor, to his Leicestershire bowling colleague, Jon Agnew, who had threatened to take up a career in broadcasting if he wasn't picked by England, 1988.

It is an institution, a passion, one might say a religion. It has got into the blood of the nation, and wherever British men and women are gathered together there will the stumps be pitched.

Lord Harris, with the First World War looming, 1914.

This modern scoffing at tradition is a product of super-democracy. Tradition is a good thing. It's what takes a regiment through hell.

Sir Pelham Warner, 1933.

No Lord's this year: no silken lawn on which
A dignified and dainty throng meanders.
The schools take guard upon a fiercer pitch
Somewhere in Flanders.

Bigger the cricket here: yet some who tried
In vain to earn a colour while at Eton
Have found a place upon an England side
Which can't be beaten.

The link between chivalry in cricket and war was ever-present in England until at least 1945. **EW Hornung**, the creator of Raffles, made his contribution with 'Lord's Leave: 1915'.

Did you see that, sir? That means war!

MCC member at Lord's when a green baize was placed over one of the Long Room busts, start of the Second World War, 1939.

A visit to Lord's on a dark December day was a sobering experience; there were sandbags everywhere, and the Long Room was stripped and bare, with its treasures safely stored beneath ground, but the turf was a wondrous green, old Time on the Grand Stand was gazing serenely at the nearest balloon, and one felt that somehow it would take more than totalitarian war to put an end to cricket.

Major HS Altham, *Wisden*, 1940.

I once saw a bowler in Australia thunder to the wicket and bowl a flat-out underarm to the batsman. No warning given. Quite right, too. In my profession you have to mystify the enemy.

Field-Marshal Viscount Montgomery.

Australians will always fight for those 22 yards. Lord's and its traditions belong to Australia just as much as to England.

John Curtin, Australian prime minister, towards the end of the Second World War, 1945.

There should have been a last line of defence during the war. It would have been made up entirely of the more officious breed of cricket stewards. If Hitler had tried to invade these shores he would have been met by a short, stout man in a white coat who would have said: 'I don't care who you are, you're not coming in here unless you're a member.'

Ray East, Essex spinner, in *A Funny Turn*, 1983.

Cricket is certainly one of the most powerful links that keep our Empire together. It is one of the greatest contributions which the British people have made to the cause of humanity.

Ranjitsinhji.

Cricket has done more to consolidate the Empire than any other influence.

Lord Harris, *A Few Short Runs*, 1921.

On the cricket grounds of the Empire is fostered the spirit of never knowing when you are beaten, of playing for your side and not yourself, and of never giving up a game as lost ... the future of cricket and the Empire is so inseparably connected.

Lord Hawke, in an introduction to Sir Pelham Warner's *Imperial Cricket*.

There was so much prejudice against a nigger showing us how to play cricket.

Sir Home Gordon, explaining (wincingly) why Prince Ranjitsinhji, one of the best batsmen in the land, had to wait until his third year for a Blue at Cambridge University.

The gradual exclusion of white folk is a bad thing for West Indies cricket.

Len Hutton, the first professional to lead England overseas, in the West Indies, 1953/4.

It is the constant, vigilant, bold and shameless manipulation of players to exclude black players that had so demoralized West Indian teams and exasperated the people.

CLR James, *Beyond a Boundary*, 1963.

He revolted against the revolting contrast between his first-class status as a cricketer and his third-class status as a man.

CLR James, on the great West Indian, Learie Constantine, in *Beyond a Boundary*, 1947.

Do not bump the ball at that man! He is the MCC captain, captain of an English county and an English aristocrat. The bowling is obviously too fast for him, and if you hit him and knock him down, there'll be a hell of a row!

CLR James's plea to Learie Constantine during an interval, MCC tour of West Indies, 1926. Constantine reluctantly complied. (Related in *Beyond a Boundary*, 1963.)

I haven't the slightest doubt that the clash of race, caste and class did not retard but stimulated West Indian cricket. I am equally certain that in those years social and political passions, denied normal outlets, expressed themselves so fiercely in cricket (and other games) precisely because they were games. Here began my personal calvary. The British tradition soaked into me was that when you entered the sporting arena you left behind the sordid compromises of everyday existence. Yet for us to do that we would have had to divest ourselves of our skins.

CLR James, *Beyond a Boundary*, 1963.

You can't depend on a man like that. Who knows, when you are looking for him for an important match, you will find him boozing.

The excuse for overlooking Piggott, a black West Indian, for his white wicketkeeping rival, Dewhurst, for the West Indies' 1923 tour of England. (As related by **CLR James** in *Beyond a Boundary*, 1963.)

I'm as full as a coon's Valiant.

Queensland batsman **Jimmy Maher**, celebrating the State's Sheffield Shield win. His remark caused rage among Aboriginal groups. 1995.

I'd say, don't give up hope. If it wasn't for the English, the Australians, the Sri Lankans and the Indians wouldn't be playing cricket. You are the masters. Maybe you are on a break right now, but you will be back. You're going to fall in love with the sport again because you're going to get jealous that everyone else is falling in love with your women.

Ted Haynes, skipper of the Homies and the Popz cricket team, drawn from inner-city Los Angeles, 1997.

It's rather like sending in your opening batsmen only for them to find that their bats have been broken by the team captain.

Sir Geoffrey Howe, resigning as Conservative deputy leader, in the conflict over Margaret Thatcher's attitude to Europe which precipitated Michael Heseltine's challenge for the Tory leadership, 1990.

It's new bats that are wanted.

Mrs Thatcher on the same issue, 1990.

THATCHER OUT
lbw Alderman 0

Graffiti in a London loo, Ashes tour, 1989.

There will be no stonewalling, no ducking the bouncers, no playing for time. The bowling's going to get hit all around the ground.

Mrs Thatcher at the Lord Mayor's banquet, warning off potential challengers for the Conservative leadership. Only 16 days later, Michael Heseltine had bowled the maiden over, but John Major was Prime Minister, 1990.

In my day, governments required the occasional use of the handbag. Now it will doubtless be the cricket bat and that will be a good thing because it will doubtless be harder.

Margaret Thatcher, in one of her last House of Commons speeches, encouraging her successor as Prime Minister, John Major, to play tough with Europe, 1991.

If I had a hand strong enough, I would break your fingers.

PM John Major, greeting Curtly Ambrose during the second Test at Lord's, 1991. Ambrose had taken the first six England wickets.

I wish he had used a runner.

Norma Major, after her husband, the Prime Minister, ricked his back in a charity cricket match during a Commonwealth summit in Harare. Discussions between Commonwealth heads led to South Africa's participation in the 1992 World Cup.

The long shadows falling across the county ground, the warm beer, the invincible green suburbs, dog lovers and pool fillers ... old maids cycling to Holy Communion through the morning mist.

Prime Minister **John Major**'s vision of Britain, in a speech to a group of Tory Euro MPs, St George's Day, 1993.

Major likes cricket. Watching it seems to be the only time he enjoys himself.

Hugo Young, on Prime Minister John Major in *The New Yorker*, 1996.

It does not require the skills of Nostradamus to predict the result of two forthcoming events: the general election and the Ashes between England and Australia. Like the Tories, the England Test side seems assured of defeat at the hands of a confident, well-organized opposition. With a structure dating back to the 19th century and an ageing group of supporters, the Tory party and English cricket appear in serious trouble.

Prospect magazine, 1997.

The Conservatives played like English cricketers – too many rash strokes and run-outs, dropped catches and bowling anywhere but the stumps.

Norman Tebbit, in the wake of the Tories' defeat in the European elections, 1989.

You think my run-up was long. Now you should hear my speeches.

Wes Hall, former West Indies quick, now a Barbados senator, 1987.

Sport is politicized the moment nation-states take the decision to enter the sporting arena under their national banners. England, Australia, India, Pakistan – these are nation-states, not sporting clubs.

Asif Iqbal, former Pakistan captain, opposing the plea that politics should be kept out of sport, 1989.

We play the game and, if we lose, we should go out because we are a civilized people.

Sri Lankan voter, aged 88, as the 1988 elections went ahead despite widespread political unrest.

It puts a lot of pressure on the chaps to train 365 days a year just to play one Test match.

Ranjan Madugalle, Sri Lankan batsman, describing the problems caused by terrorist warfare, 1988.

Cricket can be a bridge and a glue ... cricket for peace is my mission.

General Zia of Pakistan, on a goodwill tour to India during the Test series between the two countries, 1987.

A sportsman is like a soldier who is always ready to help the country.

General Zia of Pakistan, pressing Imran Khan to come out of retirement, 1988.

I am always ready to serve the nation and the game.

Imran's response, showing signs of a putative political career, 1988.

A WAVE OF GRIEF HAS SWEPT OUR COUNTRY – WE HAVE LOST OUR GLOBAL HONOUR.

Headline in **Al Akhbar**, Islamabad, following Pakistan's defeat against arch-rivals India in the World Cup quarter-finals, 1996.

Cricket? It civilizes people and creates good gentlemen. I want everyone to play cricket in Zimbabwe. I want ours to be a nation of gentlemen.

Robert Mugabe, Prime Minister of Zimbabwe, 1984.

The Apartheid Years

There can be no normal sport in an abnormal society.

The basic stance of the **South African Cricket Board**, who ran non-white competition during the apartheid years.

Fellow sportsmen say to me, 'I'm a sportsman, apartheid is nothing to do with me.' Does that mean they are sportsmen even before human beings? Well, I'm a sportsman second and a human being first.

John Abrahams, Lancashire's Cape Coloured batsman, 1988.

Dirty money earned by the dirty dozen.

Neil Kinnock, Labour leader, on the rebel England tour to South Africa, 1982.

By giving encouragement to those who have fought against apartheid, Graham Gooch and his team deserve, not blacklisting, but a medal for helping to create a more just and humane world.

The alternative view, as expressed by Conservative MP, **George Gardiner**, 1982.

Some of those who said I should have kept my mouth shut held that a parson should only speak about religion. Such men want to think of life as a series of watertight compartments ... Don't let religion affect the way you run the other parts of your life. But the whole point is that, if Christ is Lord, there are no other parts of life.

Rev David Sheppard, England batsman, justifying the need to oppose cricketing links with South Africa, in *Parson's Pitch*, 1964.

I'm ashamed I was so late in coming to the realization of the South African evil.

Rev David Sheppard, Bishop of Woolwich, 1970.

All our sportsmen have proved they are willing to meet players from any land providing it does not conflict with the policies over which they have no say.

Jack Cheetham, former South African captain, on the ICC decision to defer the question of his country's readmittance to the ICC after leaving the Commonwealth, 1960s.

Rod felt there were more things to life than playing for his country.

Donna McCurdy, wife of Rod McCurdy, Australian pace bowler, who joined the rebel South African tour, 1985.

I have been a member of the committee of the MCC and of the Conservative Cabinet and by comparison with the cricketers the Tories seemed like a bunch of commies.

Lord Monckton, at the MCC special meeting on South Africa, 1968.

We will never know the whole truth concerning the omission of D'Oliveira from the MCC touring party to South Africa. I come down on the side of honesty, a good honest piece of bungling by good honest men.

Ted Dexter's verdict as Cape Coloured Basil D'Oliveira was first omitted from, then selected for, MCC's party to tour South Africa in 1968.

Few of those within the world of first-class cricket are political animals. That, however, is no excuse for being politically unconscious.

John Arlott on the Basil D'Oliveira affair, 1968.

Thinking of you very much today. Love to you both, Penny Cowdrey.

Inscription on a bouquet of flowers after D'Oliveira was not chosen for the South Africa tour; her husband, Colin, was captain.

Guests who have ulterior motives usually find they are not invited.

Prime Minister **Vorster**, of South Africa, when hearing that Basil D'Oliveira, overlooked in the MCC party, intended to cover the tour as a journalist, 1968.

It is not the MCC team. It is the team of the anti-apartheid movement. We are not prepared to have a team thrust upon us.

Prime Minister **Vorster**, when D'Oliveira was drafted into the MCC tour party in place of the injured Tom Cartright, 1968.

I wanted to be a cricketer who had been chosen as a cricketer and not as a symbol.

Basil D'Oliveira, in *The D'Oliveira Affair*, 1968.

I can forgive, but I can't forget.

Basil D'Oliveira, weighing up whether to accept an invitation to the Lord's Test – England's first against South Africa for 29 years – in 1994. After much hoo-ha, he went.

What has been done is tantamount to punching a wife for the crimes of her husband.

Peter Pollock, South African pace bowler, on the cancellation of their England tour, 1970.

You do not cut yourself off from friends.

Raman Subba Row, pressing for the South Africa tour to England to go ahead, 1970.

The triumph of the campus bums.

The Conservative Party's **Monday Club** on the cancellation of South Africa's tour of England, 1970, in the wake of student demonstrations.

Why should we allow our boys to be insulted by these long-haired louts?

BJ Schoeman, South African Minister for Transport, supporting the cancellation of the South Africa tour to England, 1970.

I would always speak to a demonstrator, providing he was polite.

Ali Bacher, South African captain, prior to cancellation of the 1970 tour to England.

We cricketers feel that the time has come for an expression of our views. We fully support the South African Cricket Association's application to include non-whites on the tour to Australia if good enough and, furthermore, subscribe to merit being the only criterion on the cricket field.

Statement by South African players at Newlands, in a Transvaal vs Rest of South Africa match, after a walk-off protest against the government's refusal to allow integrated cricket, 1971.

That list is of no importance.

Robin Jackman, Surrey's South African-born bowler, on the United Nations' blacklist of players who had visited South Africa, 1981.

Every phone that I talk to you on is listened to.

Ian Botham, England captain, during the deportation of Robin Jackman from Guyana for South African links, England tour of West Indies, 1981.

All I know is there is a nice golf course there.

Alec Bedser, chairman of selectors, asked about the intricacies of the Gleneagles Agreement at the height of the Robin Jackman affair. Tour of West Indies, 1980/1.

Legally they're absolutely clean. And morally they're cleaner.

Mike Procter, former South African Test star, defending the rebels, 1982.

Wouldn't you go to Russia or China if it was a free trip with all expenses paid?

Geoffrey Boycott during England's tour of India, explaining that he would still visit South Africa, 1981.

When I toured South Africa with Oxbridge Jazzhats, I became physically ill for a week. We were being used for propaganda. I will never return there.

Derek Pringle, Essex and England all-rounder, 1982.

Isn't he the one who is a traitor?

Small boy about Graham Gooch at an Essex benefit match, in the wake of the South African rebel tour, 1982.

I was disgusted by the crowd's reaction. I am here to play cricket. Politics are nothing to do with me.

Alvin Kallicharran, West Indies batsman, after a hostile reception from the black section of the Cape Town crowd, 1982.

How can you play cricket with a bloke and then not be allowed to sit in a railway carriage with him?

Ken McEwan, Essex's South African batsman, on the ordering of West Indian Colin Croft from a 'whites-only' section of a South African train, 1983.

Being a Christian I cannot imagine a missionary saying: 'We won't go there until apartheid is finished.'

Alan Knott, justifying his place on the South Africa rebel tour, in *It's Knott Cricket*, 1985.

The question of South Africa has long been the nigger in the wood-pile.

Ken Turner, Northamptonshire secretary, bringing his intellect to bear on the England rebel tour of South Africa, 1982.

That man's got to appreciate it's a sensitive situation. He's a white man who has played in South Africa and he can't shout at a black man in the West Indies.

Lockhart Sebastien, of Windward Islands, after Greg Thomas challenged a batsman to walk, England tour, 1986.

It seems obvious they don't want to play in India.

Margaret Alva, India's Minister for Sport, after Graham Gooch withdrew from his South African commitment to accept the captaincy of the England touring team. The 1988/9 tour was cancelled.

Apartheid kept us back and restricted our opportunities. I watched white cricketers and stole from them with my eyes.

Omar Henry, the first coloured cricketer to represent South Africa, 1987.

If I'd known what was in store, I'd never have played the sport.

Omar Henry, discussing his rift with other coloured players, 1986.

Sorry, I can't say anything at the moment. My comment is in the car.

Anonymous rebel tourist replying to the press query about his reasons for going to South Africa, 1989.

A few days ago John Carlisle and Norris McWhirter were in court arguing about principles. They spoke in high-falutin' terms about freedom. It's a pity that they don't set equality of races as high as the freedom of 300 county cricketers.

Peter Roebuck, *Sunday Times*, 1989.

They can get £20,000 for having their heads knocked off in the West Indies or £60,000 for two tours of South Africa.

Jack Bannister, secretary of the Professional Cricketers' Association, on the financial choice likely to face English cricketers after ICC sanctions imposing bans on players touring South Africa, 1989. Bannister was also employed by South African TV.

The citizens of the United Kingdom have had a freedom curtailed at the insistence of the other countries.

Wisden editor, **Graeme Wright**, adding his weight to the 'freedom to play where you please' argument, 1989.

The price of blackmail is eternal ransom and they may live to regret it in future. Foreign Governments must be taught that whatever restrictions they place on their own citizens, we still live in a free country.

Norris McWhirter, chairman of the Freedom Association, opposing ICC's South Africa restrictions, 1989.

As far as I was concerned, there were a few people singing and dancing and that was it.

Mike Gatting, captain of the England rebel cricketers, after demonstrations at their arrival at Johannesburg Airport had been suppressed by dogs, tear gas and baton charges, 1990.

What happens in the townships is nothing to do with us.

Gatting, confronted by a black South African, who had been injured in anti-tour protests in Bloemfontein township, 1990.

He said he was shot on the way from a peaceful demonstration. That's bollocks.

Gatting's conclusion on same incident.

He's just helping out in the nets. He's nothing to do with the official party.

Peter Lush, England tour manager, defending Mike Gatting's presence in the nets following the defeat in the first Test against Australia in Brisbane, 1990. Gatting was still banned from international cricket for his South African connections.

Does my ban from international cricket mean I have to be treated like a leper?

Mike Gatting, on the same incident, 1990.

Gatting should not be allowed any creeping rehabilitation into English cricket.

Karen Talbot, British Anti-Apartheid Movement, sensing cricket's lack of resolve, 1990.

It was the most heroic sporting achievement off the field I have ever seen. You guys in the British press have vilified Mike. But he has come here with no knowledge of the country and has said nothing more stupid than a lot of white South Africans do every day.

Ali Bacher's opinion after Gatting crossed a line of demonstrators in Pietermaritzburg, 1990.

Nelson Mandela? He can't bowl, can he?

Bill Athey, with mind-numbing frivolity, asked about the implications of Nelson Mandela's release from jail, 1990.

'Have you been an innocent abroad?'
I've certainly been an innocent, a well-used innocent.'

Exchange between **Mike Gatting** and TV interviewer, 1990.

We did what we felt was right at the time to maintain our quality of cricket. But I would be man enough to say that, whilst I cannot have regrets, because I was part of the system, I am desperately sorry for any inconvenience we caused.

Geoff Dakin, president of the new multi-racial United Cricket Board, apologizes in the wake of South Africa's readmission to world cricket for the disruption caused by rebel tours to the Republic, 1991.

Dem dogs of apat-ide. Dey can run but dey can't hide.

Chant during Trinidad Test against England players banned for only three years for joining a rebel tour of South Africa.

Now I know how Neil Armstrong felt when he stood on the moon.

Clive Rice, captain of South Africa, on the tour of India which marked their return to Test cricket after a 21-year absence, 1991.

I feel like Christopher Columbus leading my team into the unknown.

Clive Rice, selecting a different historic figure, on the same India tour, 1991.

It will be a terrible thing if those who have benefited most from the unequal system in the past go charging off to international arenas, now that they have been allowed back in, without further thought for their less fortunate countrymen.

The Sowetan, Johannesburg's black newspaper, after the ban on South Africa's participation in Test cricket had been lifted during the ICC meeting at Lord's, 1991.

About now your foreign secretary, Douglas Hurd, is in Alexandra township with the boys of our development programme. Their progress must remain the most important thing. On this of all days, we must keep our priorities.

Dr Ali Bacher, whose development of multi-racial cricket had contributed to a change of mood both within and towards South Africa, minutes after the country's readmission, Lord's 1991.

Cricket saved my life. My mother made me play it because she didn't want me to rob white men's houses, wreck cars and do cannabis and cocaine.

Walter Masemola, black South African fast bowler, before facing England A in Alexandra township – the first match by an England side in the Republic for 29 years, 1993.

Cricket speaks in languages far beyond that of politicians.

Nelson Mandela, meeting the England team in Soweto, 1995.

There were 3000 Zulus killed in that one and only four Boers were injured!

Tony Greig, mindlessly chortling away on Channel 9 about a statue depicting the 1838 Battle of Blood River. Others present at Australia's one-day international against South Africa in Pretoria were aghast: South Africa's first multi-racial elections were only two months away and violence was escalating, 1994.

A cuddly little fellow.

Christopher Martin-Jenkins, on Archbishop Desmond Tutu, 1994.

At the end of this trip if you don't have a degree in United Nations relationships, you haven't learnt anything.

Hansie Cronje, South African captain, during the 1996 World Cup. (England's studies were less successful.)

9

The Great Controversies

Bodyline
Throwing
Ball-Tampering
Betting and Bribery
Umpiring
Drugs
Sledging
Yorkshire Rows

Bodyline

Bodyline bowling has assumed such proportions as to menace the best interests of the game, making protection of the body by the batsmen the main consideration. This is causing intensely bitter feeling between the players as well as injury. In our opinion it is unsportsmanlike. Unless stopped at once, it is likely to upset the friendly relationships existing between Australia and England.

Text of the cable from the **Australian Cricket Board** to the MCC, following the Adelaide Test, 1933.

We, Marylebone Cricket Club, deplore your cable. We deprecate your opinion that there has been unsportsmanlike play. We have fullest confidence in captain, team and managers and are convinced they would do nothing to infringe either the Laws of Cricket or the game. We have no evidence that our confidence has been misplaced. Much as we regret the accidents to Woodfull and Oldfield, we understand that in neither case was the bowler to blame. If the Australian Board of Control wish to propose a new Law or Rule, it shall receive our careful consideration in due course.

We hope the situation is now not as serious as your cable would seem to indicate, but if it is such as to jeopardize the good relations between England and Australian cricketers and you consider it desirable to cancel remainder of programme, we would consent, but with great reluctance.

MCC's cabled reply, 1933.

We have fought
We have won
And we have lost
But we have never squealed before.

Earl of Dartmouth, MCC elder statesman, putting his feelings into verse after the arrival of the Australian telegram.

Leg theory is generally a confession of impotence on the part of a bowler, and that should serve to cut it out of the game of any and every bowler claiming to be first class.

The Cricketer, opposing leg theory bowling seven years earlier, 1925.

If that little bugger can do that to him, what might I do.

Harold Larwood, England fast bowler, watching his team-mate Gubby Allen dismiss Don Bradman cheaply, England vs Australia, 1930.

Well, we shall win the Ashes – but we may lose a Dominion.

Rockley Wilson, Winchester cricket coach, upon hearing that Douglas Jardine would captain MCC in Australia, 1932/3.

Bowes should alter his tactics. He bowled with five men on the on-side, and sent down several very short-pitched balls which repeatedly bounced head high and more. This is not bowling, indeed it is not cricket, and if all the fast bowlers were to adopt his methods there would be trouble and plenty of it.

Editorial in **The Cricketer**, shortly before Bowes was drafted into the England squad for the Bodyline series, 1932/3.

If we don't beat you, we'll knock your bloody heads off.

Bill Voce, England pace bowler, to Australia's Viv Richardson at the start of the Bodyline series, 1932/3.

I don't want to see you Mr Warner. There are two teams out there; one is trying to play cricket and the other is not.

Bill Woodfull, Australian captain, to Pelham Warner, the England manager, during the Adelaide Test, 1932/3 series.

Well bowled, Harold!

Douglas Jardine to Harold Larwood after he hit Bill Woodfull over the heart in the Adelaide Test.

What about those fellows who marched to Kandahar with the fever on them?

Douglas Jardine's reply to Plum Warner when the manager informed him that Eddie Paynter, the Lancashire batsman, was in hospital and could miss the Test.

No politics ever introduced in the British Empire ever caused me so much trouble as this damn Bodyline bowling.

JH Thomas, Secretary of State for the Dominions, during a lunchtime speech at Claridges, 1933.

I would rather lose the rubber than win over the bruised body of my opponents.

Ranjitsinhji, condemning Bodyline tactics, 1933.

His Excellency is a conscientious objector.

Douglas Jardine's remark when the Nawab of Pataudi refused to join the leg-side field, Bodyline series, 1932/3.

Skipper, you seem to have forgotten your own instructions.

Nawab of Pataudi's undiplomatic jibe at his captain, Douglas Jardine, during the Bodyline series. Jardine had flinched in the leg-trap – after demanding courage from his close fielders, 1932/3.

It's a dangerous thing to score a century in our team – you might get dropped.

A rueful **Nawab of Pataudi**, dropped a few weeks later in Adelaide. His good form was deemed less important than his comments, which were 'bad form', 1932/3.

To take the most charitable view of the position, the behaviour of Australian crowds at its best, when judged by the standards accepted in the rest of the world, is not naturally good.

Douglas Jardine, after the Bodyline tour, 1933.

A dour remorseless Scot, 130 years after his time. He should have gone to Australia in charge of a convict hulk.

Jack Fingleton, Australian opening bat, passing judgment on Douglas Jardine.

He is a queer fellow. When he sees a cricket ground with an Australian on it, he goes mad.

Jardine as perceived by **Sir Pelham Warner**, in a letter to the governor of South Australia, in 1934, after the Bodyline rumpus.

He can be a powerful friend but a relentless enemy. He gives no quarter and asks none. He is a fighter, every inch of him. He will see a job through, no matter what the consequences, and will never admit defeat.

Bill Bowes, on Jardine, in *Express Deliveries*, 1949.

Leg-theory, even as bowled by Larwood, came as a natural evolution in the game. There was nothing sinister about it and nothing sinister was intended.

Bill Bowes, *Express Deliveries*, 1949.

The fact is that the Australians often used to stand in front of their stumps as a deliberate policy.

Percy Fender, Jardine's predecessor as Surrey captain, in defence of Bodyline. From *Fender* (1980), by Richard Streeton.

The Don had two views of bouncers – one when they were bowled against him and the other when bowled by his side with no fear of retaliation.

Jack Fingleton, on Sir Don Bradman's failure to limit Lindwall and Miller's use of bouncers in 1946. (From *Batting from Memory*, 1981.)

If I happen to get hit out there Dad, keep Mum from jumping the fence and laying into those Pommy bowlers.

Stan McCabe, resuming his innings of 187 in the Bodyline series, 1932/3.

The term is meaningless. What is bodyline?

Douglas Jardine.

Throwing

If they stop throwing, cricket in Australia will die.

Tommy Andrews, former Australian Test player, 1958/9 Test series.

It's like standing in the middle of a darts match.

Jim Laker, opining on the legality of the bowling actions of Ian Meckiff and Jimmy Burke, MCC tour of Australia, 1958/9 (*Over to Me*, 1960).

Bowl him one for a change Burkie, you'll surprise him.

Colleague's advice to Jimmy Burke, New South Wales.

Jimmy Burke had an action like a policeman applying a truncheon to a particularly short offender's head.

Ian Peebles.

To bowl fast is a gift given to very few; traditionally only to those with either a vast body or a long flexible arm. Now we see thin men, unco-ordinated men, ordinary men, qualifying as fast bowlers.

Robin Marlar, on the throwing era, *The Cricketer*, 1960.

Yes, I'm the last of the straight-arm bowlers.

Ray Lindwall, replying to Bill Bowes's congratulations on his selection for Australia vs England, 1958/9.

Throwing is unfair. It is insidious, infectious and a menace to the game. It must be stopped and the exchange of cables between countries will not do it. Unless it is stopped before the Australians arrive, a serious position is imminent.

Tom Smith, general secretary of the Association of Cricket Umpires, in *The Cricketer*, 1960.

One can readily appreciate Buller's predicament, and one cannot question his right to act as he did, but it was ironic that his action should be taken at a time when the players were engaged in a light-hearted knock about.

Editorial in *The Cricketer*, 1960, on Syd Buller's no-balling of South Africa's Geoff Griffin for throwing in the knock-up game at Lord's.

You must be the greatest thrower-out of all time, but I think your action is suspect.

A tongue-in-cheek **Ken 'Slasher' Mackay** to Joe Soloman after Soloman's run-out tied the Australia vs West Indies Test, 1960/1.

If his action is the same as it was, he will be no-balled walking down the gangplank at Tilbury.

England player on Ian Meckiff's illegal action, 1963.

Meckiff's selection represents one of the most fantastic somersaults in cricket policies in our time.

Bill O'Reilly on the recall of Ian Meckiff for the Australia vs South Africa Test of 1963/4.

I do not support the selection of men who do not play to the rules.

Clem Jones, Queensland representative on the Australian Cricket Board, opposing Ian Meckiff's selection for the 1963/4 series against South Africa.

I bowled Meckiff for hundreds of overs before umpires who approved his delivery and I have accepted their decision. Now that an umpire does not accept Meckiff's delivery, I accept that decision, too. I will not bowl him again.

Richie Benaud, Australia captain, after Ian Meckiff had been no-balled for throwing in the first Test, Australia vs South Africa at Brisbane, 1963/4.

I'm afraid this is the end, Dad.

Benaud's consoling remarks to Meckiff after he had been no-balled for throwing.

It defies description – the feeling that hits players when there is a no-ball called for throwing ... The game was carried on by instinct for a while, for the Australian players were not 'with it'.

Benaud again.

Was I bowled or run out?

Doug Insole, bowled by Tony Lock's quicker ball, The Rest vs Surrey, The Oval, 1955.

If they re-write the Laws and say that double-jointed people must not be allowed to play the first-class game, well, fair enough.

Harold Rhodes, Derbyshire pace bowler, during the throwing controversy, 1966.

I was filmed so much that I qualified for an Equity card.

Geoff Cope, the Yorkshire and England off-spinner, bemoaning his suspect action, 1970s.

The odd delivery used to be so quick I thought: 'I wonder if I chucked that?'

Graham Dilley, former England fast bowler, in *Declarations*, 1989. His action was questioned on the 1979/80 tour of Australia.

An out-and-out thrower.

The assessment of Manoj Prabhakar from his Indian colleague, **Dilip Vengsarkar**, during the Duleep Trophy final, 1991.

Open your ****ing eyes!

Aamir Sohail to umpire Goosen after his first sight of Henry Olonga, at the start of Pakistan's tour of Zimbabwe, 1995. Soon afterwards, Olonga became the first black man to play Test cricket for Zimbabwe – and the first Test bowler to be called for throwing since Ian Meckiff 32 years earlier.

Cricket has permitted the public humiliation of a player ... it is not a performance I'd care to witness again.

Peter Roebuck, on Darrell Hair's calling of Muttiah Muralitharan for throwing, Boxing Day in Melbourne, Australia vs Sri Lanka, 1995.

We should be celebrating his action, not trying to run him out of the game.

Bruce Yardley, former Australian off-spinner and Sri Lanka coach, after Muttiah Muralitharan had fallen foul of umpire Hair, 1995/6.

There are always going to be a lot of whispers and secret letters passed on to people. It's not quite as simple as an umpire putting his arm out.

Mark Taylor, Australia's captain, on the ramifications of calling a bowler for throwing, 1995. Muralitharan's action had been whispered as suspect for several years – but was later cleared.

He wasn't a first-class umpire. He normally umpires The Muppets vs Camberwick Green.

Ed Giddins, Warwickshire fast bowler, as his England chances were plagued by revelations that he had been called for throwing, by Minor Counties reserve-list umpire Bob Sutton, during a pre-season friendly for Sussex four years earlier, 1998.

That's a throw!

Giddins's response to Bob Sutton calling him for throwing was to deliberately fling the ball over the slips, Sussex vs Hampshire at Hove, 1994.

Thank-you sir, but I'm afraid if I play forward any more he'll tread on my foot.

Colin Cowdrey, advised by a well-wisher to play forward to Australian drag bowler, Gordon Rorke, 1968. The result was the introduction of the front-foot no-ball law.

It was an act of cowardice and I consider it appropriate that the Australian team were wearing yellow.

Robert Muldoon, New Zealand Prime Minister, on Trevor Chappell's underarm delivery for Australia in a one-day international against New Zealand, with six needed to win off the final ball, Melbourne, 1981.

Fair dinkum, Greg, how much pride do you sacrifice to win 35,000 dollars?

Ian Chappell, on the above incident. (His brother, Greg, was captain.)

Ball-Tampering

The Pariahs of Cricket.

The ***Sunday Telegraph***'s headline on a piece by Simon Heffer accusing the Pakistanis of 'degrading' the game by deliberately roughing up the ball to make it swing, 1992.

I shall never wear the insignia of the TCCB, its blazer or tie again.

Don Oslear, after his enforced retirement at the end of the 1993 season. The TCCB said he had reached 65; Oslear said he was a scapegoat for speaking out about ball-tampering.

The first genuine fast-bowling innovation since over-arm bowling was legalized in 1864.

Jack Bannister, journalist, broadcaster and former Warwickshire bowler, on reverse swing, 1992.

We can only guess at Allan Lamb's motives for his article in the *Daily Mirror*, but we hope that they are nothing to do with money or even worse our nationality.

Wasim Akram and **Waqar Younis**, as England batsman Allan Lamb led a belligerent campaign against alleged ball-tampering, 1992.

There is a lot of racism in this society. Where is that hatred coming from? I can show you millions of pictures of English players picking the seam. You see Australian cricketers with sun cream on their faces. They keep wiping sweat from their faces mixed with the cream and rubbing it on the ball. It is ball tampering. Scratching the ball is no bigger crime.

Imran Khan, former Pakistan captain, in *India Today*, 1994.

The people who have taken the rational side in this controversy – Tony Lewis, Christopher Martin-Jenkins, Derek Pringle – they are all educated Oxbridge types. Look at the others: Lamb, Botham, Trueman. The difference in class and upbringing makes a difference.

Imran, *India Today*, 1994. These remarks heralded another court case.

I've told him to be more discreet when he does it.

Imran Khan's remark about his fellow Pakistani fast bowler, Aqib Javed, who was persistently warned for ball-tampering when playing for Hampshire in 1991. (The remark, quoted in Allan Lamb's autobiography, was allegedly made to Lamb and Robin Smith in a wine bar in St John's Wood prior to the England vs West Indies Test of the same year.)

Why is it that you can moan about Australians, West Indians, South Africans, New Zealanders, Indians and all the others and never get accused of racist remarks?

Allan Lamb's response in his autobiography, 1996.

We came here wanting to play cricket in the right spirit but our players have been made to feel very uncomfortable.

Intikhab Alam, Pakistan tour manager, in England 1992.

Javed Miandad looks like a wild man with a face you might spot crouched behind rocks in ambush along the Khyber.

Mike Langley, reverting to depressing stereotypes in the *Daily Mirror* to describe Pakistan's batsman Javed Miandad at the height of the ball-tampering row, 1992.

The three H's: Hack, Hooligan and Hallucination must apply to the British media.

The *Asian Times*, angered by the ball-tampering accusations, 1992.

I buy my newspapers from them.

Trevor Bailey, former England all-rounder, seeking to illustrate on Channel 4's *Devil's Advocate* that he had no prejudice against Pakistanis, 1992.

Virtually all bowlers would have to say that they have tampered with the ball at some stage during their county career.

Angus Fraser, Middlesex and England fast bowler, 1992.

How can you make the ball swing with a bottletop? It was simply that the New Zealanders couldn't play the moving ball. On Pakistani wickets the ball gets rough automatically on the mud and the sand. All it needs is for the ball to be snicked for four early on over the rough outfield into the concrete of the stadium, or into some tin advertising hoardings, and it looks 30 overs old.

Case for the defence, provided by **Wasim Akram** and **Waqar Younis**, *Wasim and Waqar: Imran's Inheritors*, 1992.

The outlawed practice of roughing up one side of the ball to enhance swing must be eradicated in Pakistan. It's got to stop, it will be hard to enforce, but we will be firm.

Mudassar Nazar, Pakistan B team coach, during the 1992/3 New Zealand series.

The reason the Pakistanis get the ball to swing so much more than anyone else may in the end simply boil down to a racial characteristic. Perhaps their sweat has different properties to other people's which makes it ideal for shining the ball.

Gehan Mendis, Wasim Akram's Lancashire team-mate, in *Wasim and Waqar: Imran's Inheritors*, 1992.

The court didn't understand all this. There were nine young girls on the jury who didn't know the difference between a football and a cricket ball. We should have had a multi-racial jury, instead we had 11 English people. And most of those were women who kept looking and smiling at Lamby and Robin Smith and Botham. That's understandable, but it was not a serious court case – that's why we stopped it.

Sarfraz Nawaz, former Pakistan fast bowler, blaming the jury after his libel action collapsed against Allan Lamb in the High Court in 1993. Lamb had claimed that it was Sarfraz who had first explained to him how to obtain reverse-swing by deliberately roughing-up one side of the ball.

Yes, Lambie, I am the king.

The alleged admission by Pakistan bowler **Sarfraz Nawaz** that he had invented the art of reverse-swing by ball-doctoring.

Whatever I have done in my life, playing for Northampton and around the world, and inventing reverse-swing, was within the law.

Sarfraz Nawaz, after dropping his High Court action against Allan Lamb, 1993.

You know what'll happen if you do that again ... I'll sort you out.

Chris Adams' threat to Wasim Akram in the Lord's dining room, while holding a table knife, during the 1993 Benson & Hedges Cup final. Adams suspected ball-tampering at Derby earlier in the season after Wasim had reverse-swung the ball to devastating effect.

If the TCCB was to win a prize for anything it would be sweeping things under the carpet. As far as we know, nothing was done despite the clear evidence of the balls which looked as though a rottweiler had chewed them.

Former Derbyshire chairman, **Chris Middleton**, 1994. Derbyshire sent the ball with which Wasim Akram dismissed them at Derby in 1993 to Lord's for examination. The matter was not taken further.

The Soiled Skipper.

Daily Mirror headline during the Michael Atherton ball-tampering row. England's captain applied dirt from his pocket to the ball during the 1994 Lord's Test against South Africa ... and uproar ensued.

The action of having dirt in his pockets to dry the ball was foolish in the extreme and cannot be condoned, particularly when done by a Test captain.

Peter Burge, ICC match referee. (Burge deemed that Atherton's £2000 fine by the TCCB was sufficient punishment. Neither umpire, Dickie Bird nor Steve Randell, had submitted a critical report.)

We have to be whiter than white. I wouldn't really think Michael has done anything illegal but I didn't want him to have this round his neck for the rest of his life.

Raymond Illingworth, who levied the fine, and later claimed that he had 'saved Atherton's neck', 1994.

My mistake was using dust from my pocket to dry my sweaty hands, rather than rubbing my hands on the ground. But I did not attempt to change the condition of the ball and the umpires and referee accept that.

Michael Atherton, defending his actions, 1994.

I think the public will support Michael. There's a lot of pressure on a young man leading his country and I think most people realize that.

Bob Bennett, Lancashire chairman, 1994.

Get Out Now! 100 per cent in *Mirror* poll condemn him.

The *Daily Mirror*, promoting a different view from Bennett's, 1994. A similar public outcry was discovered by other tabloids.

It will go down as one of the most absurd pronouncements of all time – £1000 because he used dirt. He used dirt to dry his fingers. They are doing that every day of the week except that he chose to save time, for which he ought to be applauded, by putting the dirt into his pocket.

David Frith, editor of *Wisden Cricket Monthly*, 1994.

The referee asked me if I had resin in my pocket and I said 'no'. Then he asked me if I had any other substances and again I said 'no'. I was thinking of substances such as Vaseline, lip salve and iron filings. But I'm totally regretful I did it.

Atherton, in a clear-the-air press conference at Old Trafford, six days after the ball-tampering allegations began, on why he did not tell ICC match referee, Peter Burge, that he had soil in his pocket, 1994.

The fact that Atherton has misled an ICC referee by not giving a full and frank disclosure when given the opportunity to do so concerns me more than anything else because of the effect of the image of cricket.

Peter Burge again, 1994.

I have always taken pride in my own honesty and integrity, and while it is for others to judge, I would like to think that my cricket career has so far reflected those principles.

Michael Atherton, in the same clear-the-air press conference, 1994.

Following several days of anger, bewilderment and sadness at the furore following the dirt-in-pocket incident, I have been struck by its similarity to that of the woman taken in adultery (John ch. viii) ... in both cases the accusers are guilty of hypocrisy. The scribes and Pharisees of Jesus's time are now represented by the media hacks, and self-styled experts of today.

Jesus, after scribbling in the dirt (which it appears was on the ground rather than in his pocket), turns the focus back on the accusers, 'Which of you is without sin?' He then refuses to condemn the woman and urges her to 'go and sin no more.'

Rev Andrew Wingfield-Digby, former England chaplain, and co-director of Christians in Sport, in a letter in Atherton's defence, 1994.

I'm thinking of playing as an amateur.

Michael Atherton, England captain, totting up £4000 in fines after being found guilty of dissent later in the same series, 1994.

Enter the British media with all the subtlety of a Merv Hughes belch. 'ATHERTON MUST GO, SACK THE CHEAT. HANG THE SCOUNDREL. TRANSPORT HIM TO THE COLONIES.' (He could always get a game of club cricket in Port Arthur.) Blah, blah, blah.

Geoff Lawson, offering an Australian viewpoint, 1994.

This small, silly error was blown out of all proportion by the prying camera and by the hysterical clamouring for a man who has carried our beloved, if limping, cricket team through a blisteringly difficult year.

Mark Nicholas, *Daily Telegraph*, 1994.

Had he been reared by a couple of lesbians and graduated in car theft following some sporadic attendance at some terrorized secondary modern, he would have been lionized. Instead, Manchester Grammar and Cambridge did for him. Toff, see. Nearly a bleedin' aristocrat. So, predictably, they put the boot in.

Ian Wooldridge, offering the *Daily Mail* perspective, 1994.

Michael, if you sneeze at 11 a.m., you will have double pneumonia by 6 p.m.

Peter Burge, ICC match referee, to Atherton before the Headingley Test against South Africa, 1994. Burge was still seething at memories of the Lord's ball-tampering affair.

It's turning the game into a joke. You could take pictures like this 100 times a day. It's paranoid, laughable.

Mike Procter, shown photographs allegedly revealing ball-tampering by South Africa's fast bowlers, 1994.

I don't understand about all this tampering and reverse-swing. In my day you bowled inswing or outswing.

Denis Compton, at the height of the Atherton ball-tampering allegations, after the South Africa Test at Lord's, 1994.

I thought that was the day I had to resign when Jimmy Tarbuck told me to go!

Michael Atherton, reflecting on the dirt-in-the pocket affair, 1996.

Although it was against the law, I must break down and confess that I always carried powdered resin in my pocket and when the umpire wasn't looking lifted the seam for Jack Gregory and Ted McDonald.

Arthur Mailey, *10 for 66 and All That*, about illegal practices in the 1920s.

It was the most beautifully-smelling ball I'd ever come across.

Harold Gimblett, Somerset batsman, discovering that Surrey's Alf Gover had been illegally shining the ball with hair oil, 1930s.

True, with Vaseline ball keeps its shine,

Lever, bowl true, if you have spine.

Indian banner, Madras Test, 1977. John Lever had been accused of illegally shining the ball with the help of Vaseline on his eyebrows.

Nobody is strong enough to live up to their ideals ... there are many temptations to sin.

Kepler Wessels, South Africa captain, in his biography, 1994.

Betting and Bribery

'It's big.'
'Is it drugs?'
'It's much bigger than that.'

Australia's **Deep Throat**, breaking the Pakistan bribes allegations to Phil Wilkins, of the *Sydney Morning Herald*, 1995.

Cricket's biggest crisis for 20 years.

Graham Halbish, chief executive of the Australian Cricket Board, 1995. Three Australian players accused Pakistan's captain, Salim Malik, of trying to bribe them to throw the 1994 Karachi Test.

Do they think we are all crooks?

Javed Burki, chairman of the Pakistan Cricket Board, questioning why Australia's allegations of attempted bribes during their tour of Pakistan had not been reported for five months, 1995.

Quite a few players' living standards had improved so quickly that their involvement in gambling seems closer to fact.

Khalid Mahmood, the Pakistan team manager on their 1993 tour of England, considering allegations of bribes and betting scams involving the Pakistan team, 1995.

We just wanted to make sure because there were so many ugly rumours.

Intikhab Alam, Pakistan's manager-coach in Zimbabwe, explaining why his players had been asked to swear on the Koran following the three-Test series against Australia that they were not involved in betting, 1995.

The mountain doesn't come to Moses.

Arif Abassi, chief executive of Pakistan's cricket board. Australia had agreed that their players could be cross-examined over their bribery allegations against Salim Malik ... but only in Australia, 1995.

The inquiry needs more than four little letters.

Arif Abassi again, on the Salim Malik inquiry. The 'four little letters' made up the written allegations supplied by the Australian Cricket Board, 1995. Pakistan's official enquiry found the allegations 'unfounded' but a government investigation into corruption was launched.

It showed there is justice in the game.

Shane Warne's one-liner after he dismissed Salim Malik in the Brisbane Test between Australia and Pakistan, 1995. Warne's bribery allegations against Salim had also been ignored by the ICC.

I live and die for cricket but to go on a tour where there is a chance of maybe not coming back, that's a big thing to do.

Shane Warne, Australia's leg-spinner, fearing recriminations from Pakistan fans in the 1996 World Cup after his allegations against Salim Malik, 1996.

When Salim Malik was captain he would bowl himself at crucial stages in the match. He would set an offside field and bowl on the legside. While batting, he would run out his colleagues.

Rashid Latif, as quoted by *Outlook* magazine, alleging Salim Malik's involvement in the bookmakers' match-rigging scam, 1997. Latif quickly claimed he had made no such comments. He became Pakistan captain.

Umpiring

What worries me is his tolerance level.

John Woodcock, *The Times*, upon Mike Gatting's appointment as England captain, 1986.

If you get one or two bonus decisions, then it can make up for some bad luck which goes against you. If Saleem Yousuf picks up a half-volley, all right, it is called cheating. It has now become absolutely necessary in professional cricket today. Every team is working out strategies in the dressing room on how to pressurize an umpire.

Haseeb Ahsan, Pakistan manager in England in 1987, excusing Saleem Yousuf's blatant attempt to cheat out Ian Botham during the Headingley Test.

That one man's vindictiveness could ruin the game of cricket should not surprise anyone ... The two smallest minds, in collusion with the umpires, set out to thrash England and the aim of the establishment is not only to win at all costs, but to frustrate the opposition by blatant cheating.

Nazir Mirza, former Pakistan Test cricketer, condemning the political manoeuvrings of Haseeb Ahsan and Javed Miandad, manager and captain respectively, during England's 1987 tour.

The history of Pakistani cricket is one of nepotism, inefficiency, corruption and constant bickering.

Imran Khan, *All Round View*, 1988.

The weather was far from pleasant, so were the opposition, so were the media.

Confidential report by the **England selectors** to the TCCB after the Pakistan tour of England, 1987.

Constant has behaved badly and we will leave it to the British public to judge his integrity.

Haseeb Ahsan, Pakistan tour manager in England, attacking David Constant's umpiring.

I will not be making any comment about the pitch or the umpiring, and I want that to be known.

Mike Gatting, England captain, after his side were dismissed for 175 in the Lahore Test vs Pakistan, 1987/8.

F****** cheating c***.

Shakoor Rana's outburst to Mike Gatting in Faisalabad, which started the rumpus on England's 1987/8 tour of Pakistan. Gatting had annoyed Shakoor by moving a fielder.

Mike Gatting used some filthy language to the umpire, and let me tell you, some of the less filthy words are 'bastard' and 'son of a bitch' and so on. No one has a right to abuse umpires.

General **Safdar Butt**, president of the Pakistan board, after the row between Mike Gatting and Shakoor Rana in the Faisalabad Test, 1987/8 tour.

I think he is not the son of man. That is why his face is from a white monkey.

Letter from the **Lahore Railways depot chief** to Shakoor Rana, insulting Mike Gatting, after the Faisalabad Test, 1987/8 tour.

I didn't hit it. You can like it or lump it. I'm not going. I didn't hit it and I'm not out.

Chris Broad, refusing to walk in the Lahore Test after Shakeel Khan adjudged him caught at the wicket. Broad took a minute to leave the field. Peter Lush, the tour manager, settled for a 'stern reprimand', 1987/8.

We want players to continue to tour here and enjoy their cricket, whoever wins, but if they feel they are competing on unequal terms they won't want to come again and the game will suffer.

Peter Lush, England tour manager, on why he allowed Chris Broad to escape with a token reprimand, 1987/8 tour.

What happened between Gatting and me does not seem so ugly after Broad hitting his stumps. Now Dilley has sworn and everybody in the ground has heard his words. Maybe the cricket public will now agree with me that Gatting has some bad boys in his team.

Shakoor Rana, highlighting further outbreaks of dissent in Gatting's England side, 1987/8 tour.

I will find it very hard to get the motivation to play another match in Pakistan.

Mike Gatting after receiving instructions from the TCCB to send a written apology to Shakoor Rana, 1987/8.

Dear Shakoor Rana,
I apologize for the bad language used during the 2nd day of the Test match at Fisalabad [sic].

Mike Gatting

11 Dec 1987.

Gatting's handwritten apology in Faisalabad after his on-field row with Shakoor Rana had caused the suspension of the Test, 1987/8.

I am not surprised that the whole of Pakistan is proud of Shakoor. In the history of Pakistan cricket, he will rank along with Hanif, Zaheer, Imran and others for his 'contributions' to Pakistan cricket.

Sunil Gavaskar, Indian captain, on umpire Shakoor Rana, 1988.

Pakistan have been cheating us for 37 years and it is getting worse. It was bad enough when I toured in 1951.

Tom Graveney, 1988.

They've been cheating us for 37 years. Not just us, but other teams as well. In a way, I'm glad it came out into the open, because something might be done about it now.

Mike Gatting, implacable, after England's 1987/8 tour of Pakistan.

Perhaps other people hadn't seen the anguish out there. I'd never seen such an unhappy bunch of blokes in my life. In view of the exceptional circumstances of the tour, I thought the payment was warranted.

Raman Subba Row, TCCB chairman, defends his controversial hardship bonus of £1000 to the 1987/8 England touring team in Pakistan. The TCCB executive committee had subsequently condemned it.

Both team manager Micky Stewart and Mike Gatting have given us assurances this week that dissent will not occur again. Players cannot behave as they did in Pakistan even if the provocation was immense.

Raman Subba Row, prior to England's tour of New Zealand, 1988.

We want Mike to play for England again don't we? What we would like is for you to write 2000 words that are very bland.

Donald Carr, at Lord's, heavily censoring Mike Gatting's book *Leading from the Front*, which sought to give his version of the Shakoor Rana affair (his on-field argument with a Pakistani umpire). Carr's 'advice' was given to Gatting's ghost writer, Angela Patmore, 1988.

One of the absolutely unbreakable rules of cricket is that no one, but no one, disputes anything with the umpire, least of all the captain of England. There are no excuses.

Ossie Wheatley, chairman of the TCCB cricket committee, justifying his use of the veto over the reappointment of Mike Gatting as England captain. Wheatley objected to Gatting's row with the Pakistan umpire, Shakoor Rana, 1989.

We started the game. We have the moral right to lead it. If we let our standards slip, the others will slip too. It's up to us to impose draconian measures to make sure that doesn't happen.

Ossie Wheatley again, 1989.

Professional sportsmen are hard people. Once you allow a chink to appear in the rules, they will drive a wedge through it.

Ossie Wheatley, 1989.

I've got a feeling Australia will feel a positive backlash.

Australia's captain, Allan Border, optimistic before his side's 1988 tour that Pakistan's umpires would be eager to show their integrity in the wake of the Gatting-Shakoor Rana affair.

We were never going to be allowed to win by fair means. The team have voted in favour of stopping the tour right now.

Allan Border, after Karachi, 1988. The tour continued.

What are you going to do if you feel you don't have a chance? It is a conspiracy from the word go. The team will do some rethinking and decide about the future of the tour. If the management insist on completing the tour then we will play under protest.

Allan Border on Pakistani umpiring after Australia had lost the first Test in Karachi by an innings, 1988.

We have outclassed the Australians. It would be cruel to suggest that victory was due to any other reason than our good performances.

Intikhab Alam, Pakistan manager, rejecting Australian protests about the umpiring, Karachi, 1988.

The modern umpire is caught between two opposing forces – the domestic pressures which encourage error and the technology which reveals them.

Imran Khan, advocating neutral umpires, *All Round View*, 1988.

We don't know anything about the two guys appointed, but we believe they will be better than having two Pakistani umpires.

Martin Crowe, New Zealand captain, approving of the Pakistan Board's plan to appoint neutral umpires. The Board were offended by Crowe's comments, so changed their mind, 1990.

I would defend the English umpires against charges of international bias; but I would not be completely sure that there was no trace of subliminal prejudice.

Mike Brearley, former England captain, during ill-tempered Pakistan tour, 1992.

I don't think umpiring can decide the fate of a match.

Mark Taylor, Australia's captain, determined to avoid excuses during a losing tour of India, 1998.

Drugs

Too ridiculous for words.

Ian Botham's response to claims from Lindy Field, a former Miss Barbados, that she snorted cocaine with Botham and made love so passionately that the bed broke. All part of a disastrous England tour of the West Indies, 1985.

I'm aware he smokes dope, but doesn't everyone?'

Tim Hudson, on Ian Botham, 1986. That comment hastened his sacking as Botham's agent.

I have been to many great functions where some of the great cricketers of the past have been present ... to see them sink their drink is to witness performances as awe-inspiring as ever any of them displayed on the cricket field.

Ian Botham, excusing his use of marijuana, 1986.

Certainly I am told that you can play cricket better after a marijuana cigarette than after a couple of pints of beer.

Lord Wigoder, Old Bailey judge and cricket follower.

The hardest drug anyone would have taken would have been Valium, and that would have been on sleepless nights.

Ian Botham, as allegations of drug-taking started to appear, 1984.

0.19 grams. I remember it well.

Ian Botham, reflecting on the cannabis raid on his house, during the Imran Khan libel trial, 1996.

The fact is that I have, at various times in the past, smoked pot. I had been with a group of people who had been doing it and I went along with it. On other occasions I have smoked simply in order to relax – to get off the sometimes fearful treadmill of being an international celebrity.

Ian Botham's admission, in *The Mail on Sunday*, finally brings the dope saga to an end, 1986.

He should be paid for bringing the game into repute.

Frank Keating, *Guardian* sportswriter, responding to Botham's admission on BBC's *Newsnight*, 1986.

Pakistan brought in two legal beavers, one from Trinidad and one from London, who played on the players' sense of grievance, even to the extent of claiming that a cut on Wasim's forehead had been incurred when he 'fainted with shock' on the beach.

John Woodcock, in *The Cricketer*, describing events following the arrest of four Pakistani players, including Wasim Akram, on suspicion of being in 'constructive possession' of marijuana on a Grenada beach. All charges were dropped after Pakistan threatened to abandon their West Indies tour, 1993.

I'm not into drugs. I'm high spirited enough without them.

Yorkshire's left-arm spinner, **Richard Stemp**, the first county cricketer to fail a drugs test (with Worcestershire in 1992), and on the brink of England selection, 1994.

I wouldn't like to go into which colours are best, but they're not on the banned drugs list.

Philip Bell, England team doctor, prior to the tour of South Africa, on the efficacy of jelly babies, 1995.

I was batting against Surrey when a bowler called out, 'Can I have a snort leg for this guy please.' At Sussex I heard cracks like, 'keep a tight line, Ed', and 'that's a snorting delivery'. But probably the best one was when I was taking a bit of stick in one match and someone called out, 'Don't let them get up your nose, Giddo.'

Ed Giddins, after the TCCB upheld their two-year ban for his testing positive for cocaine, 1996.

I don't want to creep back into the game. I'm going to take up martial arts and get even fitter.

Ed Giddins, contemplating 18 months' inactivity after his cocaine ban, 1996.

The next thing you know they will be saying I wear stockings and suspenders under my flannels.

Phil Tufnell, rubbishing pot-smoking allegations on England's tour of New Zealand, 1997.

I feel a bit sorry for him but he was being a prat.

Bar manager, **Janelle Rossiter**, who reported Phil Tufnell for allegedly smoking dope in a disabled toilet in Christchurch, during England's tour of New Zealand, 1997.

Wine (or more likely beer), women and all that came with the territory. After a game it was into the bar with the lads for a booze-up. I met so many famous people, sports stars and celebrities. I was amazed at how many were on the same disastrous roundabout. None of us could get off.

Paul Smith, Warwickshire, on the drinking and drug taking that shortened his career, 1997.

I've played many games under the influence. I was on cocaine on and off during my 12 years playing for Warwickshire. There are drug tests in the sport, but they never really concerned me. Anyone in sport on drugs can take blockers, aspirin-like pills you can get from the States at 225 dollars per hundred. Every morning I took a blocker and a painkiller.

Paul Smith, 1997.

A cricketer's life involves a lot of travel. I always had a room to myself. Behind closed doors I could do what I wanted. Drugs would fire me up or chill me out or boost my sex drive. My whole life was regulated by drugs. It got so bad I would leave the field during a first-class match, pretending I was going to the toilet. I needed a lift.

Paul Smith, 1997.

I saw my friends' faces in the crowd and realized I'd rather be watching than playing. I walked up to Dermot Reeve, the captain, and told him I was going in. I didn't have to explain. He knew.

Paul Smith, Warwickshire, on the day at Headingley that he decided to retire from county cricket, 1997.

For most of the last 10 years of my career I popped pain-killing anti-inflammatory drugs like they were polo mints.

Ian Botham, perhaps identifying a more serious problem in *The Botham Report*, 1997.

Sledging

You don't get good players out by sledging.

Imran Khan, *All Round View*, 1988.

The one who really got up my nose was Steve Waugh, who spent the entire series giving out verbals – a bit of a joke really when he was the one bloke wetting himself against the quick bowlers.

Michael Atherton, prior to the Australia vs England series, 1994.

He has virtually accused me of being a coward. You just have to leave the figures to speak for themselves. I averaged 80 last year so I don't mind wetting myself every time I average 80.

Steve Waugh's reply, 1994.

I can't think of any player who has been put off his game by verbal abuse.

Australia's captain, **Mark Taylor** (in his 1995 autobiography, *Taylor Made*). His predecessor, **Allan Border**, couldn't think of anyone who hadn't.

A Warning: 'Unacceptable behaviour on the cricket field involving violent language to batsmen, unseemly theatrics designed to unnerve umpires, a melodramatic defiance of the conventions of cricket.

Sydney Morning Herald, appalled by the dissent shown by Shane Warne during the first Test in Johannesburg, South Africa vs Australia, 1994.

I don't really sledge batsmen. If I beat his outside edge and say 'You're a shit batsman' and then the next ball he hits me for six, who's the prat?

Phil Tufnell, 1994.

If you play against the Australians you can bash one another out on the field and have a beer afterwards. The English are a little different. If you give them a go they think you're the biggest so-and-so under the sun and they won't have a beer with you. You can abuse the Indians all day long, they just nod their heads and carry on.

Brian MacMillan, South African all-rounder, prior to their tour of England, 1998.

I bet he knows more about the Melbourne Cup than the Epsom Derby.

New Zealand captain, **Ken Rutherford**, after England's selection of Craig White (Yorkshire born, but Australian educated), for the Trent Bridge Test, 1994.

They are traitors. They are still Australians. They only did it because they were never going to be good enough to play for Australia.

Shane Warne, Australian bowler, on Martin McCague and Craig White, 1994.

I learned all my cricket over here. Why should you want to give another country credit for what England has done for me?

Adam Hollioake, answering questions about his Australian background, 1997.

It's just like big business. If the local man isn't up to it, a company might appoint someone else from abroad to do his job. It's as simple as that.

Andy Caddick, New Zealand born, expounding his theory about his right to play for England, back in his native country for England's 1997 tour.

No, I'm no Pom mate. I'm a fair dinkum Aussie. I couldn't be persuaded to become English. When you're a baby, you don't know where you're born, do you?

Andrew Symonds's pro-Australian commitment after scoring his maiden first-class hundred against the England tourists in Toowomba, Ashes tour 1994/5. Symonds then played for Gloucestershire in 1995, signed a declaration making himself available for England, but refused a place on the A tour to Pakistan.

I'm an Aussie and always have been. It wasn't a very tough decision, mate. I know in my heart that I've always been an Aussie. I love living here, and the cricket and the lifestyle. I don't think England was a temptation for me. It would have been too much of a soft option.

Symonds, reiterating his view late in 1996. In the interim, being Birmingham born, he had played for Gloucestershire as English-qualified, and had kept his own counsel.

Yorkshire

In an England cricket eleven, the flesh may be of the South, but the bone is of the North, and the backbone is Yorkshire.

Sir Len Hutton.

Just tell them that a strong Yorkshire is a strong England.

Raymond Illingworth, England's chairman of selectors, after the choice of two Yorkshire players (Craig White and Richard Stemp) and one Yorkshire-born player (Worcestershire wicketkeeper Steve Rhodes) in the first Test squad under his jurisdiction, Trent Bridge, 1994.

Don't tell me his average or his top score at Trent Bridge. How many runs, how many wickets, did he get against Yorkshire?

Douglas Jardine's standard in the 1930s for judging potential Test cricketers.

They play the most miserable game and set the most miserable example for the whole country on how games should be played.

Dr Cyril Norwood, headmaster of Harrow School, on Roses matches, 1929.

We shake hands on t'first morning and say, 'How do'. Then we say nowt for three days but, 'Howzat'.

Roy Kilner on Roses matches in the 1920s. (Also ascribed to Emmott Robinson.)

Gerrup, tha's makin' an exhibition o' thissen.

Arthur 'Ticker' Mitchell to his Yorkshire colleague Ellis Robinson after a spectacular catch.

Yorkshire cricket is soulless. Bowl six good-length balls and they're all pushed safely back. Decide to toss one higher and slower and, crash, it goes for four. After that, the same remorseless push, push, push until you make another mistake.

Middlesex's **'Tubby' Owen-Smith**, quoted by Bill Bowes in *Express Deliveries*, 1949.

The trouble with you damn Yorkshiremen is that you are only interested in playing this game to win.

Former England captain to Fred Trueman during a tour of Australia.

My conscience is clear. Yorkshire had no chance of winning and my job was to stop the other side from winning.

Brian Close, sacked as England captain because of time-wasting allegations during the Warwickshire vs Yorkshire championship match, 1967.

Scarborough at Festival time is first-class cricket on holiday.

JM Kilburn, *Yorkshire Post*.

What's tha think it is – bloody Scarborough Festival?

Disgruntled **Park Avenue spectator** to John Hampshire after his rapid 42 for Yorkshire against the Australians, 1964.

I'd like to build a row of houses across this wicket. Any more tricks like this and I'll be finished in 12 months.

Fred Trueman after Warwickshire had scored 269 (yes, that's all), against Yorkshire in 1963.

Fred Trueman's forever moaning about this wicket, but it's only an 'abit. 'E knows that Wilfred's tekken five wickets on 'ere and scored 60-odd, same day.

Tom Parkin, Bramall Lane groundsman, 1950s. (Wilfred was Wilfred Rhodes, the Yorkshire and England all-rounder.)

Someone born within the sound of Bill Bowes.

Mike Carey's definition of a Yorkshireman, in the *Daily Telegraph*.

He may be good enough for England, but not for Yorkshire.

Brian Sellers, defending Yorkshire's decision to sack Johnny Wardle, four days after his selection for the MCC tour of Australia, 1957/8.

Maybe I swore with justification. Often they were the sort of catches that could have been taken comfortably had the offender been in bed at the same time as I was.

Johnny Wardle, accused by Clifford Hesketh, chairman of Yorkshire's selection committee, of foul-mouthing team-mates, 1958.

Yorkshire sacked me because I refused to accept the authority of the quite hopeless old man appointed captain.

Johnny Wardle, 1958. Ronnie Burnet, the 'quite hopeless old man', led Yorkshire to the championship the following year.

For years I have said that Yorkshire is run by a lot of people who think their old-fashioned methods are good enough to cope with modern cricket. A rot has set in with Yorkshire. And it's eating away the greatest county club in the world.

Johnny Wardle, sacked by Yorkshire, 1958.

Let him go then, and he can take any other bugger who feels t'same way.

Brian Sellers after Ray Illingworth's 'contract or I'll leave' ultimatum to Yorkshire, 1968. Illingworth joined Leicestershire.

Tha'll 'ave trouble wi' t'bugger.

Brian Sellers, chairman of the Yorkshire cricket committee, to Mike
Turner, Leicestershire secretary, the day that Leicestershire signed Ray
Illingworth, 1969.

Well, Brian, you've had a good innings. I'm going to give you the
option of resigning or getting the sack.

Brian Sellers, Yorkshire's cricket chairman, to Brian Close, 1970.

His removal will have to be handled as delicately as a military
operation.

Yorkshire committee-man, planning the removal of Geoffrey Boycott from
the captaincy, 1971.

It's unbelievable, but it's the old bowler hat and the umbrella and
the 'Morning Illingworth' – they're still back in the thirties, they
really are.

Ray Illingworth, then at Leicestershire, on the Yorkshire committee, 1973.

It is the bugbear of Yorkshiremen that they always feel that they
have to behave like Yorkshiremen, or like their fixed belief in what
a Yorkshireman should be: tough, ruthless, brave, mean.

Alan Gibson in *The Cricketer*, 1978.

I could not time the ball. I did what others have done often enough
in the past.

John Hampshire, after his infamous go-slow vs Northamptonshire, 1978.

They are small-minded people – people who think they are always
right. The whole thing was a set-up. They knew they were going to
sack me, but at least they could have postponed the meeting. They
could have allowed my mother to be buried in peace, but they could
not wait.

Geoffrey Boycott, to Michael Parkinson, BBC TV, after his sacking as
Yorkshire captain, 1978.

It is not for what you have done, but because of what you are.

Arthur Connell, Yorkshire's chairman, informing Geoffrey Boycott why he had lost the captaincy, 1978.

He is so dedicated to the perfection of his own batting technique that he is sometimes oblivious to the feelings and aspirations of his team-mates.

Arthur Connell, chairman of the Yorkshire committee, which replaced Boycott as captain, 1978.

Geoffrey Boycott is a giant playing among pygmies.

Peter Briggs, leader of the Yorkshire Reform Group, 1981.

It's about time they buried the hatchet – and not in each other's backs.

Michael Crawford, Yorkshire chairman, announcing that Boycott, Illingworth and Old would stay with the club, 1982.

The situation is a smaller version of the United States and Russia. They have their differences, but they still have to live on the same planet.

Michael Crawford, on the interminable civil war at Yorkshire, 1982.

I've been swamped by letters from ordinary Yorkshire members who can't contain their outrage. I've heard from others whose children won't stop crying because they'll never see Geoff bat again at Headingley.

Sid Fielden, policeman, lay preacher and pro-Boycott organizer on the Yorkshire committee, after the Yorkshire batsman's sacking, 1983.

My lasting memory will be of the greatest of all counties reduced to a squabbling rabble, a squalid, petty argument, of supporters, once the most loyal and sane of all memberships, torn apart by a cult which regarded one man as greater than the club.

John Hampshire, describing his feelings as he abandoned Yorkshire for Derbyshire, in *Family Argument*, 1983.

I don't know of any other club in history which finished bottom of the league, sacked its star player and left the manager in the job. The Yorkshire committee are guilty of the biggest whitewash I can ever recall.

Brian Clough, football manager, suggesting that Ray Illingworth should have been sacked at Yorkshire, not Geoffrey Boycott, 1983.

When anyone tells me that so-and-so's indispensable, I always reply, 'I know, the churchyard's full of 'em.'

Fred Trueman, defending Boycott's sacking, 1983.

The Yorkshire County Cricket Club has behaved like the Labour Party in its worst periods. Every time there's a little dispute, everybody attacks each other in public.

Roy Hattersley, Labour Party politician and Yorkshire supporter, 1983.

We are a magnificent and united club and no one is going to say any different.

Reg Kirk, Yorkshire chairman and Boycott loyalist, on the day Brian Close resigned as cricket chairman, 1984.

It is not likely to be able to pass judgment on the cricketers of Yorkshire, qua cricketers, until the club has undergone radical heart surgery.

John Arlott, 1984.

I am happy and relieved at the outcome. I accept the members' offer to me with joy and humility and will do my best to be worthy of the confidence and affection shown to me.

Geoffrey Boycott, reinstated as a player following the vote of 'no confidence' in the Yorkshire committee, 1984.

The decision is a triumph for non-cricketers over cricketers.

Sir Len Hutton, after the overthrow of the Yorkshire committee which sought to sack Geoffrey Boycott, 1984.

Ray will find it rather strange joining us after all he has been through in recent years. He's joining a team where the players actually talk to and like each other.

Fred Trueman, welcoming the sacked Yorkshire manager, Ray Illingworth, to the Old England charity cricket team, 1984.

Geoff has only two points of view. You are either for him or against him. There is no middle ground.

Brian Close, resigning as Yorkshire's cricket chairman because he claimed the committee was dominated by Geoffrey Boycott and his acolytes, 1984.

Geoffrey Boycott is a very good batsman. I wish I had never met him.

Sid Fielden, switching camps in the Boycott row, 1985.

I would like him to resign, but I don't think there is an earthly chance of him doing so.

Sid Fielden, on Geoffrey Boycott's dual role as player and committee-man, 1984.

One of Yorkshire's faults is that some of the older players live in the past and give the impression that things are no longer as good. Some of the younger players can't stand talking to them. The game is as good as ever. It's just played under different conditions.

Johnny Wardle, ex-Yorkshire and England left-arm spinner, during a tragically short return to the county as assistant bowling coach, 1985.

We are a cricket club, not a debating society.

David Bairstow, Yorkshire captain, 1985.

A dark thundercloud seems to have descended upon this club, clouding the thoughts of those running the club in the day-to-day affairs and affecting the players' team spirit. There are those who have been grabbed by an overriding passion to proliferate their own desires. This situation cannot be allowed to continue. It is destroying what used to be a great cricket club.

Viscount Mountgarret, maiden speech as Yorkshire president at the 1985 annual meeting in Leeds.

I never thought it would come to this – just think, waiting for a result at Pontypridd.

Yorkshire committee-man. Yorkshire would have finished bottom of the championship in 1989 if Glamorgan had taken seven points from their last match against Worcestershire. They didn't.

It was a huff-and-puff meeting. Nothing ever gets done. They want to make me the whipping boy, and it won't work.

Geoffrey Boycott, after flouncing out of a Yorkshire committee meeting, called in response to the county's second-from-bottom finish in 1989.

There are too many old fogeys up there ever to sign an overseas player.

Doorman of the Holiday Inn in Leeds, as Yorkshire's general committee debated whether to sign Dean Jones, the Australian Test batsman. The doorman was right up to a point – overseas players were again rejected, by 15-5, in 1990, but only for a year.

Anyone who, while not born in Yorkshire, has grown up and lived in the county from an early age, so that by home, school, local team, and so forth, he is to all intents and purposes no different from his friends and colleagues who are Yorkshire-born.

Brian Walsh, Yorkshire chairman, on the county's new definition of 'Yorkshireness,' following relaxation of the birthright tradition, 1990.

It's a bloody disgrace. Anybody not born in this great county – no matter who he is – shouldn't be allowed to take the field for Yorkshire. When I was playing we beat everybody in sight and there's no reason why we can't do it again. All we have to do is get rid of half the committee and replace them with people who actually know something about cricket.

Fred Trueman's angry response to Yorkshire's decision, by 18-1, to allow a form of residential qualification, 1990.

Yorkshire cricket is still living in the dark ages.

The opposite view from Yorkshire's next generation of fast bowler, **Paul Jarvis**. He was disgusted that the county had not gone a step further, and signed an overseas player, 1990.

The biggest community in this area is the Asian community, the poorer people that hadn't got jobs over there came over to come into the textile trade, low wages. Did you know that over in Pakistan and India the poorer people didn't know cricket even existed? There's a hundred years of bloody tradition on Yorkshire lads. As soon as a male's born, bloody hell, the fellow says, good, I'm glad he was born in Yorkshire. By the time he's toddling, he's got a bat in his hand. Bloody Pakistanis – they don't know the damn thing.

Brian Close, Yorkshire cricket chairman, explaining the club's inability to produce an Asian cricketer in the county side, 1990.

If they want younger members then why don't they sign a giant Ninja turtle?

Irate Yorkshire member, reacting to pressure within the county to reverse the membership decline by signing an overseas player. (Reported by Derek Hodgson, in *The Independent*, 1990.)

It doesn't take a mathematician to work out that if present trends continue we could be bankrupt within four years.

Sir Lawrence Byford, only four months into his presidency, justifying Yorkshire's abandonment of their birthright tradition, 1991.

Do you expect me to let this great club go to the wall?

Sir Lawrence Byford, after the same meeting, 1991.

I was the prophet – it's all in my book.

Geoffrey Boycott's perspective on the need for Yorkshire to abandon their birthright tradition. It was Boycott's resolution that Yorkshire should compete on the same terms as the other first-class counties which was accepted at Headingley, 1991.

If he needs me, I'm not far away, but I don't think he will. His mother wouldn't have let him come if she'd been worried about him.

Geoffrey Boycott, extending Yorkshire's hand of friendship (cautiously) to the county's first overseas player, Sachin Tendulkar.

If he gets 3000 runs I don't care if he wears a dress.

Yorkshire member at the 1993 AGM, upon hearing assurances that the West Indian captain, Richie Richardson, would have to replace his maroon sunhat with a Yorkshire cap.

Unhappy? I'm not unhappy. It's the only ground I've ever had trouble getting into ... and after playing there for 20 years!

Fred Trueman, asked if he was unhappy about Yorkshire's plans to leave Headingley for an envisaged £50m sports complex off the M1 near Wakefield, 1996.

It can be absurd, cantankerous, self-destructive and pompous, but it is never crass.

Peter Roebuck, on Yorkshire cricket, 1995.

What we are about is to make England great internationally.

Sir Lawrence Byford, Yorkshire president, at the county's AGM in 1995, overlooking the fact that Yorkshire last won the championship in 1968.

10

Changing World

Generation Gaps
Fitness, Diet and Equipment
Commercialism
Pacing the Game
The Packer Circus

Generation Gaps

It's a different game now but people won't accept it ... Trueman would still be a good bowler but he wouldn't be called Fiery Fred.

Ian Botham in *It Sort of Clicks*, Botham and Peter Roebuck, 1986.

I'd have looked even faster in colour.

Fred Trueman, who reckoned that black-and-white film made him look slower than in real life. BBC radio, 1990s.

Fast bowlers wearing earrings? I don't know what the game's coming to.

Fred Trueman, on Derek Pringle's Test debut, 1982.

It's truly impossible for those balls to get through a modern defence.

Ben Hollioake, observing TV footage of Jim Laker's 19 wickets for England against Australia at Old Trafford, 1998.

Hobbs, Hammond and Broad: it doesn't quite ring true, does it?

Chris Broad, following Hobbs and Hammond as the third Englishman to score centuries in three successive Tests in an Ashes series, 1986.

These days you pick a team of workers and you would beat the teams of the past that had five stars who did it all.

Jack Bond, Lancashire team manager, 1985.

The gap in application between the earlier greats and their lesser contemporaries was far greater than the one between today's Test and county cricketers. It is not that modern top-line cricketers are inferior to their predecessors, it is that the average post-war county cricketer has raised his game.

Peter Walker, Glamorgan all-rounder in *The Cricketer*, 1963.

You don't know anything about it – it's a different game today.

Yorkshire player to retired seam bowler Tony Nicholson, 1981.

If I came into the game now, I'd probably end up as a medium-paced dobber.

Fred Titmus, former England off-spinner, 1982.

A straight ball has a certain lethal quality about it. If you miss it, you've 'ad it.

Jim Sims, Middlesex bowler, quoted by Mike Brearley in *The Art of Captaincy*, 1985.

I was never coached; I was never told how to hold a bat.

Sir Don Bradman.

A coach who suppresses natural instincts may find that he has lifted a poor player to a mediocre one but has reduced a potential genius to the rank and file.

Sir Don Bradman, 1967.

Old ladies of 80 are wishing me well. I can't let them down can I. Anyone got a coaching book?

John Edrich, called up as England's batting coach at 58, for 1995 series against West Indies.

English cricket, for as long as I can remember, has been bedevilled by the cult of the left elbow.

Lord Cobham, former MCC president, 1967.

If style counts for anything (and who really would attempt to deny it?), it simply must be insisted upon; in which case, in nine instances out of ten – bang goes individualism.

Major GA Faulkner, South African player and cricket coach, *The Cricketer*, 1925.

When you see a cricket coach, run off as fast as you can.

Bill O'Reilly, Australian spin bowler and journalist.

Fitness, Diet and Equipment

It is very important for a man who wishes to have a good season to take regular exercise.

Prince Ranjitsinhji.

If ever there was a larger-than-life guy it was Greeny; extremely intelligent and witty, he had an old-fashioned attitude to new-fangled things such as training and fitness programmes. He didn't believe in them. For him, cricket was a way of making a lot of friends, knocking the cover off the ball if possible and making regular attempts to boost the profits of certain breweries.

Mike Procter on David Green (Lancashire, Gloucestershire), in *Mike Procter and Cricket*, 1981.

We had different ideas of fitness. To me the best preparation for batting, bowling and fielding was batting, bowling and fielding.

Peter May, chairman of the Test selectors, on the clashing generations, in *A Game Enjoyed*, 1985.

I'm banning forthwith all early morning jogging. It's making you tired in the evenings. I've noticed a few times lately that you've been nodding off after supper.

Ian Botham's assault on Graham Gooch's training habits, West Indies tour, 1980/1, during an extraordinary team meeting in Barbados. Gooch retorted that Botham only knew about the dawn runs because he was just coming back from a party.

There's a big difference between being fit and being strong. Sebastian Coe is fit, but he couldn't bowl all day.

Alec Bedser, who kept fit in his day by working on farms, or digging up trees, dismissing modern training techniques, 1993.

When you tell a footballer to jump, he asks, 'How high?' When you tell a cricketer to jump, he asks, 'Why?'

Laurie Brown, England and former Manchester United physiotherapist, assessing David Gower's England party in India, 1984/5.

Good players don't need 'em. Bad players aren't worth it.

'Tonker' Taylor, Essex captain, on physios, 1960s.

I reckon you can't pull a muscle if you haven't got any.

John Emburey, England and Middlesex off-spinner, 1989.

Fit? I don't know the meaning of the word, old boy.

Phil Edmonds, coming out of retirement to play for Middlesex at the age of 41 against Notts at Trent Bridge, 1992.

If there's someone with a big stick standing over you, you never do your two times table.

Phil Tufnell, on why he objects to long training runs, 1994.

We could just wire his mouth up.

Keith Fletcher, England's team manager, dwelling on John Crawley's finish at the bottom of England's Lard League (a measure of body fat), 1994.

I never mind flying into Sydney because it's got a McDonalds.

John Crawley, England batsman, on the 1994/5 Ashes tour.

Please don't print it, I haven't told my parents yet.

John Crawley, caught smoking a cigarette (in an attempt to lose weight) by journalists during England's home Test series against the West Indies, 1995. They didn't print it … not for a while, anyway.

During the winter I train on 20 fags and a couple of pints of lager and an unrelieved diet of cricket talk.

Brian Brain, Gloucestershire seamer, *Another Day, Another Match*, 1981.

Wickets are more important than waistline.

Merv Hughes, Australian quickie, 1994.

When you walk off the field you have a gallon of beer.

Allan Lamb (in cabaret with Ian Botham), opposing Graham Gooch's work-ethic regime as England captain, 1995.

The wheels of the social bandwagon have come off. The five cans of ale that the old-timers might have enjoyed before a civilized dinner each night have turned into prolonged, boredom drinking in public.

Bob Willis, *Lasting the Pace*, 1985.

The fat boys are taking all the wickets.

Robert Croft, contemplating the success of himself and Darren Gough in New Zealand, 1997.

I'm really craving for some canned spaghetti on toast.

A slimmer **Shane Warne**, existing on a diet of cereal, vegemite on toast or naan bread, and toasted cheese sandwiches, during Australia's tour of India, 1998.

Shane Warne's idea of a balanced diet is a cheeseburger in each hand.

Ian Healy, Australian wicketkeeper, 1996.

I was eating too much junk food. I was overweight. I was never a porker, but I was known as 'guzzler'. I ate and drank too much.

Darren Gough, Yorkshire fast bowler, called up by England in 1994, on life as a single lad.

We used to eat so many salads there was a danger of contracting myxomatosis.

Ray East, describing lunchtime fare on the county circuit, in *A Funny Turn*, 1983.

You can't consider yourself a county cricketer until you've eaten half a ton of lettuce.

Gary Sobers, welcoming a West Indian newcomer to the county circuit.

I always have my lunch at 1.30.

George Gunn, of Nottinghamshire, getting out deliberately when informed that the lunch interval was later than usual.

Too many English county cricketers live on junk food like fish and chips and hamburgers.

Michael Holding, in *Declarations*, 1989.

I expected to find a special high-fibre lunch, the sort of thing Alan Knott apparently eats, but the only choice was stodgy steak and kidney.

Simon Hughes, on his first day in county cricket. (From *A Lot of Hard Yakka*, 1997.)

Massive bats, helmets, big gloves ... it's rather like sending Nureyev onto the stage at Covent Garden to dance the *Nutcracker Suite* in sea-fisherman's waders.

Denis Compton on modern batting techniques, *Cricket and All That*, 1978.

How much simpler it is to swat a fly with a rolled-up newspaper than with a telephone directory.

Denis Compton, advocating a return to lighter bats, *Cricket and All That*, 1978.

I hate the helmets, the visors and the chest protectors. I would dearly love the boys to go out there like playboys, with a box, some gloves and a bat, play off the back foot and enjoy it.

Denis Compton, former Middlesex and England batsman, 1995.

If Mohammed Ali can sway inside a straight left from three feet, I'm sure that Brearley can avoid a bouncer from 22 yards.

Denis Compton, opposing the advent of batting helmets. (From *Cricket and All That*, Denis Compton and Bill Edrich, 1978.)

If someone had produced a batting helmet during the Bodyline series, I would certainly have worn it.

Sir Donald Bradman.

I don't know what the game's coming to. You wouldn't get me wearing one of those plastic things.

Brian Close, on Tony Cordle's use of a fielding helmet for Glamorgan, following the near-fatal injury to his team-mate Roger Davis, 1971.

I'm going to make them wear their caps this season. After all, you don't get awarded your county floppy hat, do you?

Jack Bond, Lancashire manager, 1985.

I only wish some of the players' trousers fitted better.

The Duke of Edinburgh, asked if he had any complaints about modern cricket, 1987.

Commercialism

Cricket has become no more than a car, a beer or a washing-up liquid when it can be marketed by someone who needs no interest in the game, its history and traditions, the emotions it arouses and its place in national life. If that is so, it has not only ceased to be more than a game. More seriously, it has ceased to be an institution.

Graeme Wright, *Betrayal: The Struggle for Cricket's Soul*, 1993.

Sponsors are sponsors and if they become too powerful we could finish up in a situation where the sponsors are making all the decisions.

Chris Peaker, Lancashire CCC treasurer, recommending an increase in members' subscriptions as a way of safeguarding control of the club, 1988. The proposal was rejected.

I know of no other sport which would secretly negotiate such a deal without bothering to inform its sponsor.

The TCCB awarded rights for the 1990 Benson and Hedges Cup to British Satellite Broadcasting – but failed to tell B&H until 24 hours before the announcement. This was the response of **Len Owen**, B&H's special events manager.

When you come as a sponsor, you are treated like royalty. I'd recommend it to anyone. When you come as a member on Test-match Saturday, you are shunted around as some species of sub-human.

Douglas Lever, Lancashire member and sponsor, on how money talked at Old Trafford, 1988.

By the way, do you still have sixes in cricket?

Hospitality-box spectator to Simon Hughes, journalist, B&H final at Lord's, 1988.

I proved that I do possess the dedication and determination to build a big innings. I've always got out after about 160 for Northants before. This time I wanted to see if I was able to hold on. I must admit the financial incentives also played a part.

Allan Lamb on his 294 for Orange Free State, a South African record. Sponsors awards amounted to £26,500.

The star player is making so much money from the game that created him, that unless Auntie Clara and the two poodles are allowed to tour with him, he is not disposed to represent England overseas.

Wilf Wooller, infuriated by Tony Lock's statement that he would not tour Australia in 1962/3 unless his wife could join him.

I don't care what money I get man – it's the buzz of playing for Australia that's got me.

Greg Matthews, making his Test début, 1983.

It should surprise no one that cricket is not self-supporting. It never has been.

Colin Cowdrey, in *MCC*, 1976.

Cricket must be the only business where you can make more money in one day than you can in three.

Pat Gibson, *Daily Express*, 1975.

The modern cricketer will do a lot for money. He will hawk autographed miniature cricket bats in Calcutta, one of the world's most impoverished cities, to children in the crowd at £15 a time.

John Woodcock, *The Times*, 1977.

We must expand, and a tournament in Disneyland will help us achieve that.

Still selling – with the optimistic outlook of an **ICC spokesman** – in 1996.

We're looking to monopolize the cricket world. We can get you any player you want.

Luke Brill, from Gareth James' agency, Jasmin Public Relations. Adam and Ben Hollioake later stood down as James's clients, 1997.

Pacing the Game

Arguments are put forward in favour of transforming the great game into a thing of immense rapidity – a sort of Bolshevist cricket devoted to hurricane yorkers and 'swipes'. This, of course, would make quite impossible the science, the law and beauty which are the charm of cricket – to cricketers.

Manchester Guardian editorial, 1918. The end of the First World War had brought calls to liven up cricket.

First-class cricket is a subtle as well as a strenuous game. It is a thing of leisure, albeit of leisure today not easily found or arranged; a three-act play, not a slapstick turn.

RC Robertson-Glasgow, *Wisden*, 1945.

There is nothing wrong with the game but only the players' approach to it; unless this is remedied soon, most players will have lost the ability, through lack of practice, to play strokes, and the game will face an age of strokeless batsmen opposed by throwers and draggers – a complete prostitution of the art.

Warwickshire committee report, after attendances fell by more than half a million in a single year, 1959.

I'm told that it was not until the first week of June 1946 that the public was told that county cricket was dying and it's been on its last legs ever since.

Doug Insole, *Cricket from the Middle*, 1960.

As for an 'amateur approach', a careful study will reveal that this is a modern myth. Today's alleged leaders in brighter cricket are often the dullest and most cautious members of their sides.

Peter Walker, Glamorgan and England, 1961.

In real cricket, the player who has developed imagination and skill makes the game, but in the one-day match it is the other way round. The match dictates to the player.

Brian Close, prior to his sacking by Yorkshire, 1970.

Throw down some sawdust, everybody put on top hats and red noses and you've got the John Player League.

Brian Close, deriding Sunday 40-overs cricket, 1969.

For six days, thou shalt push up and down the line but on the seventh day thou shalt swipe.

Doug Padgett, Yorkshire batsman, offering an 11th commandment on the advent of the Sunday League, 1969.

To a man of my age the introduction of the Sunday League has been nothing less than an act of cruelty.

Tom Graveney, England and Worcestershire batsman, 1970. (Graveney was 41 when the first season of Sunday cricket began.)

The game is injecting a dementia into the souls of those who play it.

Bill O'Reilly, *Sydney Morning Herald*, on the effects of one-day cricket, 1981.

I suppose he got it for winning the toss.

Bob Willis, losing Warwickshire captain, after Lancashire's John Abrahams, who scored nought and did not bowl, won the man-of-the-match award in the 1984 Benson and Hedges Cup final.

I can hardly remember an innings I have played in one-day cricket.

Greg Chappell, Australian batsman, 1984.

There is a possibility that your ability as a player may well be analysed by future generations on your one-day statistics. That's the day I dread most.

Allan Border, Australian captain, 1985.

If there is a threat to the game of cricket, that threat lies in the first-class arena. One-day cricket, especially day-night cricket, is here to stay.

Sir Donald Bradman, *Wisden*, 1986.

I don't think we're going to get these runs. We'd better go for the draw.

Sadiq Mohammad to Tony Greig, at the crease for a World XI against Australia in the early days of one-day internationals.

You can see the moon. How far do you want to see?

Arthur Jepson, umpire, refusing an appeal for bad light by Jack Bond in the Gillette Cup tie, Lancashire vs Gloucestershire, at Old Trafford, 1971. (Lancashire, the batting side, won at 8.50 p.m.)

If I can see 'em, I can hit 'em.'

David Hughes, Lancashire, before scoring 24 off one over by John Mortimore to settle the above tie.

You don't expect to be beaten by a tail-ender – not at midnight anyway.

Roger Knight, defeated Gloucestershire captain, after their late-night defeat in the Gillette Cup tie vs Lancashire, Old Trafford, 1971.

A Test match is like a painting. A one-day match is like a Rolf Harris painting.

Ian Chappell, Australian captain.

One-day cricket is like fast food. Nobody wants to cook.

Viv Richards, West Indies captain, after their tour of India, 1988.

Sixteen needed from two overs. If we win, jubilation; if not, despair. It matters not how we played the game, but whether we won or lost.

Vic Marks, with regrets, on Sunday League cricket, 1988.

We came to play cricket but lost at skittles.

Kent seamer, **Alan Igglesden**. His side had lost to Warwickshire in the Benson and Hedges quarter-final in an indoor bowling shoot-out, 1994.

It looked more like baseball than cricket.

Spectator's summation of Shahid Afridi's fastest one-day century (37 balls) against Sri Lanka in Nairobi, 1996.

Lancashire are boring us to death. They're blocking absolutely everything now.

Tony Murphy, of the Minor Counties, on a mobile phone at fine leg, broadcast live on Radio Merseyside. Lancashire were 41 for five at the time, but recovered to win, 1997.

One-day cricket is entertaining all right, but not entirely a sport. Once sport consciously tries to be entertaining, it sets off on the short but dangerous road that leads to the Worldwide Wrestling Federation.

Simon Barnes, *The Times*, 1997.

I always thought that the best way to contain a batsman was to get him back into the pavilion.

Alec Bedser, former England bowler, deriding negative one-day tactics.

There is no way we will allow Test cricket to die. Test cricket is like classical music; limited-overs cricket is like modern commercial music.

ICC president **Jagmohan Dalmiya**, of India, before the start of the World Youth Cup in South Africa, 1997.

Why aren't all the fielders back on the boundary then?

Frank Woolley, great pre-war Kent batsman, told during his first visit to a Sunday League match that the game was only 40 overs.

The dot ball has become the Holy Grail.

Colin Cowdrey, on containment, 1982.

This was combustible strokeplay that challenged our assumptions. Steady starts, playing yourself in, wickets in hand – such tenets had been adapted, for sure, to the demands of one-day cricket, but never so freely abandoned. Jayasuriya's method of playing himself in seemed to consist of taking three steps down the pitch and carving the ball high over cover.

Wisden on Sanath Jayasuriya (Sir Lanka), 1997.

We have far too much to do in the game these days. You need one eye up your backside.

Arthur Jepson, umpire, bemoaning the arrival of fielding circles in one-day cricket, 1981.

At times you can run up and bowl an orange and it will do something.

Chris Cowdrey, Kent captain, in 1988, on the sporting state of county pitches. The TCCB responded by demanding pitches more in favour of the batsman, and a switch from three-day to four-day championship cricket.

It was easier to get past a Lord's gateman than an outside edge.

A bowler's life on the flat pitches of 1990, as directed by the TCCB, and described by **Martin Johnson** in *The Independent*.

Cricketers do not expect anyone to watch three-day games.

Peter Roebuck, Somerset batsman, 1985.

Everyone, without exception, approved the cricketing argument.

AC Smith, TCCB chief executive, supporting a switch to four-day championship cricket in 1989.

There is massive opposition to this scheme among those who pay to watch the game. Championship cricket is more than just a breeding ground for Test players.

Tony Vann, Yorkshire committee-man, seeking to rally grassroots opposition to four-day cricket, 1989.

Four-day cricket is boring. I wish I was playing it – I'd think all my birthdays had come at once.

Geoffrey Boycott, 1992, as the TCCB were set to consider a four-day championship.

Don't think it will be more entertaining than three-day cricket.

Graham Gooch, on the four-day game. Nevertheless, he approved of its introduction, 1992.

Undoubtedly four-day cricket is better than three-day cricket *had become* on the dead wickets of modern England. There is no evidence yet that it is any better than three-day cricket once was. The orthodoxy of the moment is that players have to be allowed to build innings to Test-match length. One is now terrified to shout 'Get on with it' to a boring blocker in case this inhibits the development of the poor darling.

Matthew Engel, 1994.

The Packer Circus

There is a little bit of the whore in all of us, gentlemen, don't you think?

Kerry Packer, meeting the Australian Cricket Board to discuss TV rights, prior to the threatened breakaway from established Test cricket by offering lucrative TV contracts to the world's best players.

In affectionate remembrance of International Cricket, which died at Hove, 9th May, 1977, deeply lamented by a large circle of friends and acquaintances. RIP. NB – The body will be cremated and the Ashes taken to Australia and scattered around the studio of TCN9 in Sydney – NTJCBM.

Notice placed by **three Australian journalists** in *The Times*, 1977.

What has to be remembered of course is that he is not an Englishman by birth or upbringing, but only by adoption. It is not the same thing as being English through and through.

John Woodcock, *The Times*, on Tony Greig's defection to the Kerry Packer Circus when England captain.

I am not my brother's wicketkeeper.

Clyde Packer, brother of Kerry, 1977.

I have sacrificed cricket's most coveted job for a cause which I believe could be in the interests of cricket the world over.

Tony Greig, switching to Kerry Packer Circus, 1977.

Cricket is the easiest sport in the world to take over. Nobody bothered to pay the players what they were worth.

Kerry Packer, Australian TV executive, 1977.

The whole basis of this is an ideal – but nobody is going to do it for peanuts.

Tony Greig, England captain, revealing plans for a Packer Circus at a press conference, Hove, 1977.

The plight of the modern cricketer is certainly not the best. Many who've been playing eight years or more are living on the breadline. In the winter they go abroad coaching, leaving their families behind. Test cricketers are also not paid what they are worth. As a result of this action, cricket may in five or six years time come into line with tennis and golf. Then, if a young man is faced with a decision which to play, he can choose cricket with confidence. People who give up their lives to a game should be rewarded accordingly.

Tony Greig, at the same Hove press conference, 1977.

The administrators have had 100 years to improve pay and conditions for the players and they haven't made any progress.

Mushtaq Mohammed, Pakistan all-rounder, in Peter McFarline's *A Game Divided*, 1977.

His action has invariably impaired the trust which existed between the cricket authorities and the captain of the England side.

TCCB cricket council, sacking Tony Greig as England captain after the announcement of the Packer Circus, 1977.

From now on, it's every man for himself and let the devil take the hindmost.

Kerry Packer, angrily leaving the ICC meeting at Lord's, 1977.

I've read a lot about Genghis Khan. He wasn't very lovable, but he was bloody efficient.

Kerry Packer, 1977.

It's unfortunate that we Australians inherited the English mentality rather than the American.

Kerry Packer, *The Guardian*, 1977.

I've heard the only way to get out of a Packer contract is to become pregnant.

Ray Steele, Australian Cricket Board treasurer, during the High Court hearing, 1977.

They are dedicated lovers of the game who nevertheless found it hard fully to understand the feelings and aspirations of those who seek to make their livings out of it.

Justice Slade, describing the cricket establishment, during the High Court ruling that the ban on Packer players was illegal, 1977.

A professional cricketer needs to make his living as much as any other man. I think it is straining the concept of loyalty too far for the authorities ... to expect him to enter into a self-denying ordinance not to play cricket for a private promoter during the winter months, merely because the matches promoted could detract from the future profits made by the authorities, who are not themselves willing or in a position to offer him employment over the winter or to guarantee him employment for the future.

Justice Slade, in the High Court, ruling for the plaintiffs. The TCCB and ICC became liable for £250,000 costs and damages.

Tests are not built in a day.

Mutthian Chidambaran, Indian representative, High Court, 1977.

They want the penny and the bun.

Geoffrey Boycott, High Court, on Packer players, 1977.

I have no desire to be a hack bowler up the bush with Packer.

Rodney Hogg, Australian quickie, 1978.

You British reckon everything can be solved by compromise and diplomacy. We Australians fight to the very last ditch.

Kerry Packer, 1978.

Wake up, you lazy lot! You've got to get used to this daytime cricket.

Mushtaq Mohammed to his World XI colleagues on a bus taking them to a rare morning start in Packer's World Series, 1978.

I do not know that Test cricket can be saved. I hope so but I am not convinced. People will no longer sit through five days of a match. Those days are long gone. People don't go to watch beautiful defensive shots or the battle of tactics any more. Unless something is done to change the rules and the manner in which it is played, then officials will have a hard time to make it attractive.

Lynton Taylor, Channel 9 executive, 1978.

He had everything: courage, variety, high morale, arrogance, supreme fitness and aggression ... but I am afraid I will also remember him as the bloke who stopped playing for love of the game and his country and started playing for money and to please the TV producers.

Bob Willis, on Australian fast bowler Dennis Lillee, in *The Cricket Revolution*, 1981.

It makes me laugh when I hear the anti-Packer lobby telling me how I should spend my winter. When I was a teenager, the same sort of people didn't give a damn what I did between September and April.

Gordon Greenidge, West Indian batsman, 1980.

I wish they'd appeal.

Lord Denning, Master of the Rolls, after the TCCB lost its High Court case against Kerry Packer, 1979.

The next thing you know, they'll be wanting to play with a ball with a bell in it.

Alec Bedser's response to Packer's introduction of floodlit matches.

It was always 'Kerry says this' and 'Kerry says that' like a speak-your-weight machine.

Bob Taylor, England wicketkeeper, on the aspirations of Packer players, in *Standing Up, Standing Back*, 1985.

Realize what you have got and don't give it away. Don't let a media organization run your game.

Kerry Packer's advice to Australian Rugby League clubs, considering a Super League which would have been broadcast on a rival channel, 1995.

11
Domestic Ills

Our cricket is too gentle – all of it.

Alec Stewart, England vice-captain, 1994.

Cricket (in England) is widely perceived as elitist, exclusionist and dull.

Matthew Engel, *Wisden Cricketers' Almanack*, 1997.

The most famous cricketers are too big to play county cricket.

Ian Botham, 1980s.

County cricket is not a good competition. They would be facing bowlers who are no more than pie-throwers. They would not learn anything about the game.

Rodney Marsh, former Australian 'keeper, and Academy coach, explaining why he would not recommend an Australian batsman to sample county cricket.

Sometimes I'm standing in the slips and start day dreaming. I think, what the hell am I doing here? What a waste of time. There must be more important things to do for a living. And sitting in the pavilion after I've been in, that's the worst of the lot. I can't stand watching cricket.

Barry Richards, South African, banned from Test cricket and making do with Hampshire instead, 1974.

No disrespect, but playing for Surrey Seconds against Sussex this week in front of a few dogs and coffin-dodgers is quite a different experience to playing before packed houses at The Oval, Headingley and Old Trafford.

Alistair Brown, Surrey, after the announcement of England's Texaco Trophy squad, 1997.

I make the crowd 24 – 23 really, because one of 'em's died there overnight.

Tom Young to RC Robertson-Glasgow during a Somerset match at Taunton in the 1920s.

About two grand a game.

Graham Thorpe, Surrey and England, on the difference between county and Test cricket, 1994.

The rush of sponsorship in the early 70s did for English cricket, because it propped up the knackered counties and the weak players who should have been consigned to the history of the game.

Greg Chappell, explaining England's failure to regain the Ashes in Australia, 1994/5.

As preparation for a Test match, the domestic game is the equivalent of training for the Olympic marathon by taking the dog for a walk.

Martin Johnson, *The Independent*, 1995.

Most of us were technically better at 14 than we are now.

Peter Roebuck, bemoaning the lack of quality practice in county cricket, 1984.

This softness comes from playing county cricket, which is all very matey and lovey-dovey. We're all mates out there and it's about a few cups of tea and maybe a Pimm's or two afterwards. The gap between that cosy little world and Test cricket is immense. The Aussies, even in their grade cricket, are abusing you and rucking you. Our club cricket, in comparison, is like a social gathering.

Nasser Hussain, England's vice-captain, advancing reasons for the Ashes defeat, 1997.

I'm not condoning sledging or fighting. I'm talking about inner strength, inner toughness.

Hussain, forced to clarify his remarks two days later after a highly publicized spat between Mark Ilott and Robert Croft in the Benson and Hedges Cup semi-final between Essex and Glamorgan, 1997.

It was hardly a heavyweight contest featuring the two hardest blokes on the county circuit. More like Spice Boy versus Spice Girl. I've already had my mum on the phone. She thinks I've committed some sort of crime against the state.

Ilott's conclusion on the dust-up, 1997.

And I suppose if anyone's bowled it's just a nasty accident?

Nottinghamshire's **George Gunn**, unimpressed by the news that the umpires would be generous with lbws during a festival match in the 1920s.

We can have a cosy game among ourselves but that will do us no good in international cricket.

Dennis Silk, chairman of the TCCB, recognizing flaws in England's domestic structure during a disastrous World Cup campaign, 1996.

The nets will be up, but don't expect our fellows to use them too much. They will be afraid of being jeered at by the men in the tramcars.

W Findlay, Surrey secretary, 1915. (Source: *Wisden* 1917.)

I've lost more good players through interfering parents than for any other reason.

Colin Page, Kent coach, in *From the Nursery End*, 1985.

County bowlers are nothing if not philosophical. I'll be there in midsummer, running up to Sir Geoffrey, convincing myself he's going to pad up to a straight one.

Brian Brain, workaday county seamer, on the joys of bowling to Geoffrey Boycott, in *Another Day, Another Match*, 1980.

There are 250 players in county cricket. All are on first-name terms, all know the other 249's strengths and faults in the techniques of the game, and play on those failings, thus resulting in low totals more slowly accumulated.

Peter Walker, Glamorgan and England, 1961.

There is an accent upon sameness in approach, sameness in method, none of which helps to make the game more eye-catching. This uniformity has extended itself into wearing apparel – a coloured cap is looked upon as definitely 'Non-U' among professionals – and in batting styles. Numbers one to eight are carbon copies of each other both in technique and tactical approach.

Peter Walker, Glamorgan and England, bemoaning the dull county circuit of the early Sixties, *The Cricketer*, 1963.

All cricketers have large egos. That is why there are so many below-average players still in the game. Each player secretly believes that he is a better cricketer than his results show.

Peter Walker, Glamorgan and England.

County cricketers are a cautious lot. Though they've scored runs throughout their careers they do not trust to luck. They construct a technique in which imagination plays no part. Everything is tight, everything is predictable.

Peter Roebuck, *It Sort of Clicks*, Roebuck and Ian Botham, 1986.

It would have been a paltry and unworthy bribe to deprive Australia, by means of a money bribe, of her finest batsman.

Wisden, on efforts to attract Victor Trumper into county cricket, 1908.

Without overseas players, the English county game would be dead.

Richard Hadlee, New Zealand fast bowler, *At the Double*, 1985.

In the ten years I was at Notts, only a couple of young players ever approached me for advice. I find that amazing, and it's an insight into the modern attitude. Maybe some guy has learned a bit from watching me, but as far as talking to me about technique and attitude, forget it. Nobody ever wanted to know.

Richard Hadlee, 1988.

I saw them all around me on the county circuit – guys who are just playing for next year's contract. The batsmen do just enough to creep to 1000 runs in the season. The bowlers will sneak to the fifty-wicket mark. Then they feel safe. But it's not enough.

Richard Hadlee, 1988.

We used to celebrate like this just for beating Derbyshire.

Ken Taylor, Nottinghamshire's 70-year-old cricket manager, overcome by their revival under Rice and Hadlee in the 1980s.

They should stop whining about overseas players. There are too many old men in English cricket. Look at Ray Illingworth, at the age of 50, Geoff Boycott and so many others like them – these are the men who are stopping the young players coming through.

Asif Iqbal, Kent and Pakistan, on moves to reduce the number of overseas players in county cricket, 1983.

Cricket is a job and they have played so long that they are basically fairly bored by it all. Most of them go through the seasons complaining that it's too hot, or too cold, or too wet, or that the wicket is too slow, or too fast, or never in their favour, and so on and so forth. Anything new is deeply disliked – one-day cricket, for example, or team stretching exercises before the match, or overseas cricketers. Coloured overseas cricketers are particularly disliked since the 'old pros' are usually slightly racist.

Imran Khan, *All Round View*, 1988, on cricket's 'old pros'.

They tended to enjoy horse racing, and the suspension of play due to rain. Without any doubt the best hours of the day for them were spent in the pub after the day's play.

Imran Khan, expanding on the 'old pros', 1988.

I once got an unplayable ball from Ambrose that exploded on a wet wicket in Trinidad, and before I could do anything it was in third slip's hands. Otherwise, all my dismissals have been avoidable – either bad footwork or judgment or loss of concentration.

Australia's batsman **David Boon**, hoping to spread the same theories of self-determination as captain of English cricket's perennial strugglers, Durham, 1997.

Most county cricketers play the game for the life rather than the living. For them it's the motorways of England rather than the jet lanes of the world. It's sausage, egg and chips at Watford Gap rather than vol-au-vents and small talk on the Governor-General's lawn in Barbados.

Michael Carey, journalist.

A whole generation of professional cricketers has emerged who don't know the sheer pleasure of lazing around on a free Sunday ... the Saturday nights when you didn't have to climb into the car and drive 150 miles after a long day in the field. You could have a few pints with the opposition, a night on the town and then relax next morning in bed with the Sunday papers, contemplating nothing more strenuous than a game of golf in the afternoon.

Brian Brain, *Another Day, Another Match*, 1981.

Where we went to play, there we dined. Not like the present club cricket: 'When is the next train home?'

Sammy Woods, Somerset and England, comparing cricket in 1923 with habits at the turn of the century.

You're in charge from the moment you wake up until you buy a pint in the bar for the other players after the game. At times there are so many demands before play starts that I suddenly realize I've had no time for a knock-up myself.

Mark Nicholas, on his first season as county captain, at Hampshire, 1985.

They can all resign themselves to the fact that none of them will ever be quite as good as the talkative gentleman with the packet of ham sandwiches who sits square with the wicket on every county ground in the land.

Doug Insole, on the fate awaiting cricket's new county captains, 1963.

The vast majority of county cricketers have two topics of conversation: 'Me And My Cricket', or, as a high day and holiday variant, 'My Cricket And Me'.

Frances Edmonds, 1994.

The typical 1990s cricketer was a decent, regular middlebrow man who read the *Daily Mail* and Wilbur Smith novels and (except in Lancashire) dressed at C&A.

Simon Hughes, former Middlesex and Durham seamer, in *A Lot of Hard Yakka*, 1997.

Scratch the surface of the average county cricketer and a nasty little racist appears.

Frances Edmonds, 1994.

Many of the more prominent players daub the slogan 'Form is temporary. Class is permanent' on the lids of their bulging coffins. It isn't class they lack, but charisma.

Simon Hughes, *A Lot of Hard Yakka*, 1997.

Mastering boredom is the chief requirement of the cricketer.

David Oldam, Somerset scorer, during the rain break at the Bath Festival, 1991.

I absolutely insist that all my boys should be in bed before breakfast.

Colin Ingleby-Mackenzie, explaining Hampshire's success under his captaincy, on BBC Radio, 1961.

I think I could write a sort of Egon Ronay guide to casualty departments – a kind of *Good Hospital Guide*.

Grahame Clinton, Surrey opener, injured in 15 of the 17 first-class counties, 1986.

Simon Hughes thanks everyone who donated to today's benefit collection, which raised 1230 pounds, 30 pence, 70 Canadian cents, 50 pesetas, 1 Kenyan shilling and 2 Iranian shekels.

Benefit announcement over the Lord's tannoy, 1991.

Clinching the championship is a strange sensation. It's the culmination of five months' team-work, of map-reading and exhausting drives, of sharing rooms in tasteless motorway hotels, of cramming shut bags full of dirty gear, of practice on damp, patchy nets, of knee niggles and scraped elbows and rowdy arguments over silly card games, of ecstasy and agony and sometimes apathy, all compressed into a few smiles and handshakes and the presentation of a great cardboard cheque in front of a few pensioners sitting in stripey deckchairs and shrouded in blankets. There's more atmosphere in a doctor's waiting room.

Simon Hughes, *A Lot of Hard Yakka*, 1997.

The captains and the committees of the Sixties will have a lot to answer for in the course of time. They are making a drudgery of a beautiful game.

John Woodcock, *The Times*, 1966.

Bloody Derby! What a way to go!

Jon Agnew, Leicestershire bowler, contemplating his last match before retirement, 1990.

More reported cases of frostbite than any other first-class venue.

Agnew on Derby again.

Derbyshire batsmen always labour under certain difficulties both psychological and technical. They have no tradition to inherit, no heroes to emulate. They are regarded as subordinates, an inferior race with a secondary role; not much is expected of them and therefore not much is forthcoming. They know that 250 is enough in most games and therefore are incapable of aiming at higher totals. They bat just as well – or badly – on a bad wicket as a good one. Their aim is, by playing within their limitations, to scrape together enough runs to win matches.

Guy Willatt, former Derbyshire player and committee-man, 1970.

It was like getting out of jail.

Chris Adams, upon leaving Derbyshire, 1998.

I can only hope the conditions at The Oval are exactly to Chris's liking – a nice flat pitch with nothing moving about off the seam – because he never stopped crybabying about the wickets at Derbyshire.

Kim Barnett.

When it comes to moaning, he is world-class.

Kim Barnett, Chris Adams's former Derbyshire captain, attacking Adams's attitude in the *Daily Mail* on the morning of his England one-day debut, 1998.

That load of madmen will never win anything until they learn some self-discipline.

A **Raymond Illingworth** chunter about 1970s Essex, shortly before they won everything. (Quoted by Ray East in *A Funny Turn*, 1983.)

You plan your cricket like a war, but play it like a party game.

Tony Lewis, Glamorgan captain, extolling Essex's virtues to their captain, Keith Fletcher.

Pringle goes out looking like Worzel Gummidge with a borrowed untucked shirt, half-mast trousers six inches too short and no socks to cover up his hairy shins because he can't get the shoes on as well as socks; and anyway his toes are all crunched up inside them, it's a damp field, and he'd slip all over the place so he doesn't bowl anyway.

Derek Pringle in borrowed kit, in a Sunday League match between Yorkshire and Essex at Scarborough. (Told by Graham Gooch in *Gooch: My Autobiography*, 1995.)

Barrie, old boy, sorry, but you're not going to like this at all.

Neil Foster's apology to umpire Barrie Meyer before kicking the stumps over at Old Trafford in pique at Essex's fielding performance against Lancashire. He was fined £250, and reported that it was worth every penny. (As related in *Gooch: My Autobiography*, 1995.)

Steady boys, put down a canary first!

JB Evans, Glamorgan fast bowler, about to descend into the visitors' basement dressing room at Taunton.

When I tap the pitch with my bat, someone else taps back.

Peter Walker, Glamorgan and England, on playing in mining country at Ebbw Vale, 1967.

I maintain I can contribute more in one telephone discussion with the chairman, Ossie Wheatley, than all the amateurs in a hundred meetings on the subject of cricket.

Tony Lewis, sacked from Glamorgan's cricket committee for non-attendance, 1980.

What number is Snow White batting?

John Emburey to Mike Gatting, after experiencing Glamorgan's miniscule batting line-up of Cottey, Dalton and Phelps, none of them much over 5ft 5in, 1994.

Only two problems with our team – brewer's droop and financial cramp. Apart from that we ain't bloody good enough.

Charlie Parker, England slow bowler, on life at Gloucestershire in the 1920s. Quoted by David Foot in *Cricket's Unholy Trinity*, 1985.

Dear Simon,

Just clearing up a few letters before going to India tomorrow. I can't remember if I told you you'd got your county cap. Did I? I hope so. And hearty congratulations. Best wishes.

Yours, Mike.

Mike Brearley's letter with which Simon Hughes discovered he had been capped by Middlesex, 1981.

What benefit is there to anyone, Middlesex or me, to stay here in that capacity?

Phil Edmonds, made 12th man by Middlesex two days after he had helped England to win the Ashes. He went home instead, 1985.

His bowling performances and more especially his fielding have been so lacking in effort that the selection committee have no alternative.

Sussex's selectors dropping John Snow, an England fast bowler, after he became bored with championship cricket, 1971.

It was often soul destroying. On wet wickets or slow ones, I was expected to charge up and down and let it go when I knew I had no earthly chance of getting anything out of the wicket.

John Snow, on the downside of bowling for Sussex, *Cricket Rebel*, 1976.

The chairman of the cricket committee would come into the dressing room just before we were going out to play an important Gillette Cup match and start telling us how the Sussex Martlets had got on on Sunday. And he expected us to be interested.

John Snow, England fast bowler, 1960s.

Sussex have always been regarded as the amateur gin-and-tonic men of English cricket – well, I'm going to change all that.

Tony Greig, Sussex captain, 1974.

Hove is a genial mixture of the raffish and run-down, like the numerous blazers in the pavilion bar, most sporting military buttons and yet many with frayed cuffs.

George Plumptre, *Homes of Cricket*, 1988.

A terrace with deck chairs would not do. It would be considered a health hazard.

Nigel Bett, Sussex secretary, considering how Hove could be renovated in light of modern safety regulations, 1994.

This is the last thing we need. He should not be entering nude pictures in magazine competitions. He is supposed to be an ambassador for Sussex County Cricket Club.

Sussex member, quoted in *The Times*, condemning the photographs of club secretary, Nigel Bett, in the pages of *British Naturism*. It was a chill wind for Bett; after the overthrow of the old committee, he left his job, 1997.

We just need David Icke's predictions to speed up and the world to flood now.

Adrian Jones, back at Sussex, and surprised to find them leading the championship, May 1991.

As far as I'm concerned, you are part of the buildings and the furniture at Somerset and so are Vic and Ian ... I hope that you'll be able to play with us until those legs turn to jelly, because I think that you and I and Ian and Vic are Somerset players right down to our bootstraps.

Peter Roebuck's letter to Viv Richards on Roebuck's appointment as Somerset captain for the 1986 season. Roebuck later said that he didn't regret his words; his feelings had just changed.

When you have two workhorses and shoot them in the back, I think it's evil. You don't treat animals in this way. I was blindfolded, led up an alley and assassinated.

Viv Richards, upon hearing in August 1986 that Somerset were not renewing his contract.

We had great difficulty this season in getting Richards to play in our evening pub games. He declined to play at Clevedon, Truro and Braunton, and the only reason he played at Ottery St Mary was that we reminded him that they had staged a benefit match for him the year before.

Michael Hill, Somerset chairman, defending the committee's decision, 1986.

Judas

The sign hung on Peter Roebuck's locker by **Ian Botham**, during the Somerset civil war over the sacking of Viv Richards and Joel Garner.

It's hard to cut down a huge tree, let alone three.

Martin Crowe in 1986. The three trees were Viv Richards, Joel Garner and Ian Botham. The first two were cut down, the third, Botham, uprooted himself and joined Worcestershire.

I could see why they were lost. They had no sense of direction, no sense of purpose, no pride. They were drifting. The club had no leadership.

Martin Crowe, on the state of Somerset's young players prior to the sacking of Viv Richards and Joel Garner, 1986.

This committee has done for fair play what Colonel Gaddafi has done for air safety.

Jan Foley, Bristol barrister, putting the Somerset rebels' case at the county's special meeting, 1986.

I'm told that Peter Roebuck is flying out to have a man-to-man talk with me. I suggest he stays in London. He'll be a whole lot safer there.

Ian Botham's response, while in Australia, to confirmation of Somerset's sacking of Viv Richards and Joel Garner.

Richards may look great, but there's no point if all the others are getting noughts.

Martin Crowe, caught up in the Somerset civil war, 1987.

Surrey is run as a regime of fear and secrecy. It is not a members' club. It is more influenced by the Meet John Major syndrome.

Paul Ames, Surrey Action Group, 1995.

Don't catch it!

John Carr, Middlesex's stand-in captain, to his team-mate Desmond Haynes in a contrived championship finish against Somerset at Lord's. Haynes did catch it, Somerset were dismissed more cheaply than agreed, and Middlesex went on to an embarrassing victory, 1993.

One sees more pretty cricket in Kent in a three-day match than can be seen anywhere else in England in a fortnight.

Learie Constantine, *Cricket in the Sun*.

I suppose if you don't play in gloom up here, you never play at all.

Alan Knott, on the joys of Old Trafford, 1981.

I couldn't stand the Birmingham accent.

John Emburey, explaining why he had once turned down an approach to captain Warwickshire, 1995.

It's just like a zoo out here!

Tim Curtis, Worcestershire batsman, regretting the lack of decorum in Dermot Reeve's all-conquering, and not very popular, Warwickshire side, 1995.

How many companies of 43 employees have a board of 20?

Bob Evans, sacked in his absence as chairman of Warwickshire for his proposals to reduce the size of the committee, 1990.

They are status seekers who would as quickly get themselves on the tiddleywinks committee if that game should suddenly acquire prestige.

'Bomber' Wells, Gloucestershire spinner, on the majority of committee-men, 1970.

They've done the hat-trick on us, uncle.

David Graveney, to Tom Graveney after David had been deposed as Gloucestershire captain in 1988. Tom had been replaced by an Old Etonian, Tom Pugh, in 1960; his brother Ken had been deposed as county chairman.

Perhaps I don't have enough initials – it's a handicap only having two.

Trevor Jesty, leaving Hampshire for Surrey after being passed over for the captaincy in favour of MCJ Nicholas, 1985.

He makes Michael Atherton look positively cheerful.

Hampshire member, **Tony Perks**, part of a group trying to remove John Stephenson as Hampshire captain, 1997.

The visit to the dressing-room of a senior committee-man, watch chain dangling, smacked of a Dickensian mill-owner's visit to a shop-floor. The players would stiffen into attitudes of modest respect.

Mike Brearley, on the Middlesex committees of the 1960s, in *The Art of Captaincy*, 1985.

This is the Lancashire League, an historic league. We don't need a Premier League. In the Lancashire League, we're planning for the year 200.

Peter Westwell, chairman of the Lancashire League, resisting ECB pleas for the restructuring of club cricket, 1997.

It's like starting Tesco all over again. We had a great vision of changing this cheap and cheerful company into something great, and we did.

Lord MacLaurin, considering the challenges as chairman of the England and Wales Cricket Board, 1997.

He will see that trying to shake up English cricket is like stirring dead sheep.

Raymond Illingworth, doubting MacLaurin's chances of success.

We have a great opportunity for the rebirth of English cricket ... the creation of one happy and successful family from the village green to the Test arena.

AC Smith, retiring chief executive of the TCCB, as it gave way to the English Cricket Board, 1996.

12
The Media

If anyone had told me I was one day destined to make a reputation as a writer upon cricket I should have felt hurt.

Neville Cardus, *Autobiography*, 1947.

Robinson seemed to be made out of the stuff of Yorkshire county. I imagine that the Lord one day gathered together a heap of Yorkshire clay and breathed into it and said, 'Emmott Robinson, go and bowl at the pavilion end for Yorkshire.'

Neville Cardus, *Good Days*. (The amended version in Cardus's autobiography gave God a Yorkshire accent instead of Yorkshire clay.)

Ah reckon, Mr Cardus, tha's invented me.

Emmott Robinson, Yorkshire. (There again, Cardus recorded this too...)

It is doubtful whether anyone, unwittingly, has done more harm to the game than Cardus. No doubt unconsciously, Cardus condescended to cricket, encapsulating social attitudes that were unreal even when he started watching it. Cricket writers deal in stereotypes with regional and social overtones – Ranji, the wily Oriental, Tyldesley, the honest yeoman, MacLaren the lordly aristo. On the one hand, the gents, on the other, lovable but inarticulate, full of character and simple humour, possessed of a God-given gift they did not rightly understand – the professionals.

Nicholas Richardson, *New Society*, 1975.

But my dear chap, it's the spirit of the thing that counts. Often when I quoted a player he may not have literally said those things. But he'd have liked to.

Neville Cardus.

'We don't have any semi-colons in this paper, Mr Cardus.'
'What do you want me to do, send you some?'

Neville Cardus, while filing a report to a copy-taker on the *Sydney Morning Herald*.

Yorkshire were 232 all out, Hutton ill. No! I'm sorry, Hutton 111.

John Snagge, radio commentator.

A unique occasion really – a repeat of Melbourne 1987.

Jim Laker in the 1980 Centenary Test at Lord's, BBC TV.

Halfway between the 10 Commandments and Enid Blyton.

JJ Warr's assessment of EW Swanton's cricket broadcasting.

If you don't go away, I'll throw you off the top of the pavilion.

An early meeting between **John Arlott** and EW Swanton just after the Second World War, in the Trent Bridge commentary box.

Exact, enthusiastic, prejudiced, amazingly visual, authoritative and friendly ... he sounds like Uncle Tom Cobleigh reading Neville Cardus to the Indians.

Dylan Thomas's view of John Arlott's early commentary style, from letters written in 1947.

My word, I know what the problems are. I've failed at everything.

John Arlott, asked whether playing first-class cricket would have assisted his role as cricket writer and broadcaster, farewell broadcast, BBC Radio, 1980.

It's one thing to do commentary and then go and write your news-paper report, but then it's altogether a different thing when at ten to seven you go out with 250 miles to drive home.

John Arlott, explaining the reasons behind his retirement, BBC Radio, 1980.

The commentary lost more than just Arlott's unassuming gravitas. When he retired, the commentary team lost much of its humanity.

Simon Barnes, *The Times*, upon the effect on Test Match Special of John Arlott's death in 1991.

Probably the most celebrated British voice after Churchill's.

Frank Keating, on John Arlott in the *Guardian*, 1991.

He absorbed and distilled everything. He was in no sense verbose. The words were always spare and rationed. But they created the sense of a game and a ground and a cast and a drama unfolding with such deft accuracy that cricket itself somehow grew in significance.

The *Guardian*, in an editorial upon John Arlott's death, 1981.

If Test Match Special does pass away, it won't be from starvation.

Scyld Berry, 1980.

In Arlott's day the radio team had a centre of gravity; in the age of Johnston a centre of levity.

Russell Davies, *Sunday Telegraph*, upon Brian Johnston's death, 1994.

Players enjoyed their company. You can't say that about many commentators.

Ian Botham, on the popularity of Brian Johnston and John Arlott, 1994.

A man with a music-hall imagination.

John Arlott, on Brian Johnston.

A man of simple tastes, instinctively generous, ungovernably corny, quite without artifice, totally loyal, utterly unaffected, unfailingly enthusiastic, highly principled, endearingly old-fashioned, immensely stubborn and seemingly ageless ... an institution.

John Woodcock, *The Times*, upon Brian Johnston's death, 1994.

His was the last great voice of radio cricket commentary.

David Lloyd, on Brian Johnston, 1994.

Batsmen wear so much protection these days that I mostly identify them from their posteriors.

Brian Johnston, studying Derbyshire's players through a pair of old binoculars, in preparation for commentating on the 1988 Benson and Hedges Cup final. From *A Lot of Hard Yakka*, **Simon Hughes**, 1997.

He had, over half a century, perfected and personified that hardly definable English sound, the burble.

Johnston seen by **Godfrey Smith**, *Sunday Times*, 1994.

Cricket would be a better game if the papers didn't publish the averages.

Jack Hobbs, who could normally be found at the top of them. From John Arlott's *Jack Hobbs: Profile of The Master*, 1981.

It is a policy to receive them even with a bath towel, because if you don't they will report you just the same, only it would be their idea of things, not mine.

EJ Metcalfe, describing Colonel Greenway's tour of Philadelphia, 1913. (From *The Cricketer*, 1932.)

We sincerely hope that in future ... no one will be chosen to represent England except on the understanding that when he becomes a Test match player he lays aside his pen.

Editorial in ***The Times***, 1922.

If you've signed the c***, you can sack the c***.

The *Sun*'s editor, **Kelvin McKenzie**, dispensing with Ian Botham's services as a columnist after he lost the England captaincy, 1981.

My ghost is writing rubbish.

England player on West Indies tour, 1986.

No cricketer I have known has ever been able to write well.

Alex Bannister, *Daily Mail*, 1970s.

One would suppose that the invasion of publicity and the general mateyness of radio and press would have tended to produce something like swollen-headedness in the prominent players. But one would be in error. The tendency, so far as one can see, is for publicity to produce more and more modesty of demeanour.

CB Fry, *The Cricketer*, 1955.

His public relations and relaxed, imperturbable style were ideal qualifications for the rigours imposed by a long overseas tour.

Denis Compton (in *Cricket and All That*, 1978), assessing MJK Smith's style of captaincy on the 1964/5 Ashes tour.

We're here to play cricket, not to talk about it.

Smith's soured approach as England's tour manager in Australia 30 years later.

By 2000 the TV cameras will be everywhere: dressing room, hotel and bathroom. I visualize the newsman's mania for live human action and reaction breaking all bounds of privacy and decency.

Tony Lewis, 1969.

One gets used to the abysmal ignorance of some colleagues, to whom any slip catch has resulted from 'an outswinger' and any shot which ends in the third man area is 'a cut'.

Michael Stevenson, returning to teaching, with a sideswipe at his erstwhile colleagues in the press box.

One old drunk once accused me of not getting into line against Patrick Patterson or Malcolm Marshall in Jamaica. He couldn't have even got into a straight line to walk out to the wicket!

Graham Gooch, on the gentlemen of the press. (From *Gooch: My Autobiography*, 1995.)

I will never be accepted by the snob press.

Raymond Illingworth, 1973.

It's plastic-cupped can-I-borrow-your-phone press boxes. When we talk, it's talk of mortgages. 'Whose turn old boy?' means 'Get out your Thermos.' You can never borrow a Biro, they've only got fountain pens. When play gets going, it's eyes down into *Wisden*.

Frank Keating on life in cricket press boxes, 1974.

What exactly is the Internet anyway?

Gerald Mortimer, Derby press box sage, informed of cricket columns on the Internet, 1998.

I have grown to trust and like several of the cricket writers. Equally, there are some I trust, but don't like, others I like but don't trust and the occasional individual I neither like nor trust.

Bob Willis, *The Captain's Diary*, 1983.

I wouldn't enjoy making my living by criticizing my former colleagues.

Bob Willis, 1983. Willis went on to be a Sky TV commentator all the same.

British airways steward: 'Would you like me to take anything home for you?'
Bob Willis, England captain: 'Yes, 34 journalists and two camera crews.'

England's tour of the West Indies, 1986.

One viewer told me the other day that listening to my old mate Jim Laker and his new sidekick Bob Willis was better than taking two Mogadon.

Fred Trueman, on TV commentators, 1985.

Bloody Botham Bastard Bugger Mother Evil Satanist KGB.

Rupert Murdoch, naming another *Sun* exclusive on Ian Botham, Spitting-Image style, ITV, 1987.

The selectors emphasized that they did not believe the allegations in the newspapers and accepted Gatting's account of what happened. The selectors were concerned, however, that Gatting behaved irresponsibly by inviting female company to his room for a drink in the late evening.

The England committee's statement upon removing Mike Gatting from the captaincy in the sake of the 'barmaid affair', 1988. *The Sun*'s front-page headline had been 'Test Stars in Sex Orgy'.

The selectors asked me for an explanation, which I gave. They tell me they believe my version of the events, even issuing a statement saying so – and then sack me. I couldn't believe it.

Mike Gatting, pointing out the curious logic behind his sacking, 1988.

If chairman of selectors Peter May et al are genuinely concerned about Gatting bringing the game into disrepute, then surely the image flashed across the world of an England captain poking a Pakistani umpire in the chest might have been a far better reason to sack him. But oh no! For that disgraceful tour the TCCB not only failed to axe the captain, they even voted the lads an extra £1000 bonus into the bargain. On the basis of that sort of lunacy, the average cricketer might be forgiven for expecting a couple of hundred quid for bonking the odd barmaid.

Frances Edmonds on Gatting's dismissal, *Mail on Sunday*, 1988.

There will be an extremely strict code. Rule number one: that they are extremely good-looking ladies.

Ted Dexter's philosophy on a Test cricketer's social behaviour, expressed shortly before taking up his position as chairman of the England committee, 1989.

If a young bachelor player spends some time with a smart lady, returns to the hotel in good time and then ends up in the tabloid press, I'm likely to commiserate, and even congratulate. But good clean fun and late-night revelry are two different things. Nothing that is illegal, immoral or offensive can be condoned.

Ted Dexter's more considered view on the same, 1989.

What goes on in the middle is our business, nothing to do with anyone else.

Mervyn Kitchen, English umpire, refusing to respond to press enquiries about his no-balling of Australia's fast bowler Jeff Thomson, 1985.

Yesterday, a very good umpire cracked under pressure ... it wasn't his mistake that was so sad, it was the fact that Lloyd Barker was pressurized into changing his initial decision. If that is gamesmanship or professionalism, I am not quite sure what cheating is.

Christopher Martin-Jenkins, BBC Radio, commentating during Barbados Test on Richards's jig, 1990.

When I do my little jig, it is ceremonial, just a celebration.

Viv Richards's defence, 1990.

Viv appeals that way all the time and no one coerces me.

Lloyd Barker, echoing Richards's sentiments, 1990.

You write anything bad about me and I'll come and whack you. It is time someone was sorted out. I'll start with you. I'll be checking this out. Be careful.

Viv Richards to *Daily Express* columnist James Lawton in the Antigua press box, 1990. Richards missed the start of play to berate Lawton, who recalled the conversation in those words.

I knew I could never be a 'real' newspaper journalist – it was such a difficult job to be hail-fellow-well-met-what's-yours-old-boy in private life and the next day have to scalpel-slash a reputation in public print.

Frank Keating, *Another Bloody Day in Paradise*, 1981.

They smile and then they stab – and they think the next time they come along for a comment you are going to forget the wounding things they write and obligingly talk to them.

Geoffrey Boycott, on press behaviour after he was sacked as Yorkshire captain, *Put To The Test*, 1979.

So much of modern sport is spiteful that there is little room for the wry, reflective smile: aggression is the thing, on and off the field, as players glare and gesticulate and the media make mountains from molehills to satisfy producers and editors alike.

Mark Nicholas, Hampshire captain, 1994.

When you have to spend the tour in your hotel room so you're not stitched up, there's something wrong.

Ian Botham, England tour of the West Indies, 1986.

Judgments by commentators should be made on probability not on outcome. So when Jim Laker writes in *The Express* on Friday that it was a mistake to put Australia in to bat at The Oval, one should know that his opinion (given to Paul Parker's father) an hour before the start on Thursday was that we should field.

Mike Brearley, on the advantages of hindsight, 1981.

Among those who have seen most of Gooch as a captain, I have found no one who regards him as at all a natural leader, either in terms of personality or tactics.

EW Swanton, in *The Cricketer*, 1988. Graham Gooch's appointment as captain for the tour of India (eventually cancelled because of his South African connections) had annoyed cricket's media establishment.

English first-class cricket has been played for the benefit of the cricket writers and the newspapers ... most writers knew the parlous state of county cricket, yet they had to support it, to ensure it survived to support them. They had a vested interest in the system which existed.

Andrew Caro, former World Series Cricket managing director, on the hostile reaction to the Packer Circus, 1980.

I am not talking to anyone in the British media – they are all pricks.

Allan Border, Australian captain, to Meridian TV's Geoff Clark, before the tourists' match against Sussex at Hove, 1993.

Newspapers are only good enough for wrapping up fish and chips. They are the pits.

Martin Crowe, New Zealand batsman, in *The Cricketer*, 1993.

I thought you needed designer stubble to get into the England team these days.

Mike Gatting, explaining his new beardless look at the start of the India tour, 1993.

We weren't at all impressed by their World Cup coverage. They failed to appreciate the significance of the World Cup, and then when we went to play a Test series in Pakistan afterwards the only coverage was in the news bulletins.

Peter Lush, England tour manager, as the special relationship with the BBC began to break down, 1988.

Why should I buy cricket? Nobody watches it.

Greg Dyke, chairman of ITV Network Sports Committee, 1988.

The whole of our national sport is not doing very well. We may be in the wrong sign or something. Venus may be in the wrong juxtaposition to somewhere else.

Ted Dexter's response after England, beaten by an innings by Australia at Lord's in the summer of 1993, suffered their seventh successive Test defeat.

You buggers have been lampooning and harpooning me.

Ted Dexter, to assembled media, 1993.

It is possible that some of Dexter's visions might one day become a little more solid. However, he also talked a good deal of tosh in an arrogant tone of voice. For a professional PR man he was extraordinarily unaware of the impression he made.

Matthew Engel, *The Guardian*, upon Dexter's resignation as chairman of the England committee, 1993.

When I've made off-the-cuff remarks it's been as much as anything because the atmosphere at press conferences has been so poisonous, so thoroughly unpleasant, that I've tried to lighten it a bit.

Ted Dexter, upon his resignation, 1993.

The 1000cc motorbike rider who came in like Lawrence of Arabia and went out like Mr Magoo.

Martin Johnson, on the public's perception of Ted Dexter, 1993.

For those of you wondering what that round of applause was, it was to mark the resignation of Ted Dexter.

Jon Agnew, on BBC radio, explaining the response of the Edgbaston crowd, 1993.

No one has ever called me Future England Captain. That was a media invention.

Michael Atherton, 1993.

Quite obviously, there does exist a gang in the media which is going to be very difficult to deal with. How can I hope to get on reasonably with people who get their kicks from hiding surreptitious cameras in ceilings or who nick the Queen's Speech before Christmas Day? I cannot see myself doing reasonable business with that sort.

MJK Smith, wary of cricket's tabloid press, before he undertook the manager's role on England's 1993 tour of the West Indies. (*The Sun* had published the Queen's Christmas message in advance in 1992; the following year, the *Daily Mirror* had caused an outcry by publishing photographs of Princess Diana working out in a London gym.)

I thought he might have given me a tinkle, but he hasn't so I assume everything is OK.

Raymond Illingworth, England's chairman of selectors, feeling ignored and awaiting a phone call from the captain, Michael Atherton, before the first Ashes Test in Brisbane, 1994. Illingworth's remark was characterized as 'a tirade'.

Each word in a bar, each whisper in a lift, each phrase in a Press conference, each indiscreet stroke on the pitch, is whacked on the back page, replayed on the TV screens and tut-tutted on the radio.

Mark Nicholas, Hampshire captain, in the *Daily Telegraph*, about the pressures of playing for England, West Indies tour, 1994.

My back is my problem. It is not a cause for national concern.

Michael Atherton, 1996, as England's captain was beset by problems in Zimbabwe.

Doom and gloom merchants.

Michael Atherton on the English press in Zimbabwe, 1996.

If this England lot were put up against Rutland Thirds they would lose. They would lose heavily. It is the only thing they are good at. But Messrs Bumble, Fumble and Crumble have achieved one thing. A lifetime's disdain and despair for every remaining English cricket supporter. The poor sod.

The Sun, unimpressed, 1997.

We have the worst press in the cricketing world. Hardly any of them could write a proper cricket report, even if their editors wanted that ... which they don't.

Allan Lamb, in his autobiography of the same name, 1996.

Posing with no clothes on doesn't do the game any good and there is far too much of that thing going on.

Lt Col **John Stephenson**, secretary of MCC, responding to revelations that Chris Lewis was appearing in a semi-nude photo set for *For Women*, 1993.

Chris has a marvellously fit and muscular body at the peak of physical fitness which deserves to be displayed in all its glory.

Spokeswoman for *For Women* magazine, 1993.

If he's standing with his wedding tackle out we'd certainly take action. But I've spoken to Chris and he was in the showers at the time. I think I saw far more than he's revealed in the photos.

TCCB spokesman, **Ken Lawrence**, 1993.

Gosh, it's difficult to identify these chaps. Sometimes they turn out to be brothers or cousins, and sometimes not to be related at all.

Henry Blofeld, coming to terms with the Pakistan tourists, 1987.

Allowing the bowlers to swig away at the edge of the field cannot be conducive to the public good.

Pakistan were beating England in 1992, and the nation was debating whether their fast bowlers achieved reverse-swing by illegal means. *The Cricketer*, meanwhile, found other ways to berate them.

Cricket's Colonel Gaddafi.

The *Daily Mirror*, stuck in the timewarp of racial stereotyping, Pakistan tour of England, 1992.

What are you doing on the field? You should know better.

Richie Richardson, West Indies captain, incredulous to see Greg Richie, former Australian batsman and Channel 9 commentator, joining a pitch invasion in the 1995 Jamaica Test to celebrate Steve Waugh's 200.

Get stuffed, Richie. It's a great 200!

Greg Richie's response.

I'm glad they hadn't invented Spinvision in my day. It would have shown the ball coming out straight. I'd have been carted.

Vic Marks, former England off-spinner, musing on Sky TV's new camera close-up for spin bowlers, 1995.

They find a ghost in everything – the air, the food, the hotels – and also mock our culture. I will not even wrap a fish in these tabloids.

Shakoor Rana, Pakistani umpire, describing the English tabloids, during the 1996 World Cup.

Will someone remove this buffoon?

Michael Atherton, losing patience with the broken English of Asghar Ali, of the Pakistani Press Association, following England's World Cup defeat against South Africa in Rawalpindi, 1996.

I'm on a personal mission to clear my name. My personal life has been ruined. My fiancée has broken off her engagement, my friends and family taunt me. I want to tell the English they cannot get away with insulting a respected person, especially an Asian.

Atherton's 'buffoon', **Asghar Ali**, seeking out the England team in Lahore the following year. Atherton himself was not present, 1997.

You have to try to reply to criticism with your intellect, not your ego.

Mike Brearley, 1995, on handling the media.

13
England's Woes

I find it mystifying that England produces any cricketers at all.

Colin McCool, Australian, on English coaching soon after the Second World War.

There's no way at all we should lose. If we do, then a few heads will roll. You could bat for 10 days on this pitch and not get a result.

Ian Botham, England's captain, during the first Test against the West Indies in 1981. (They lost by an innings and Botham said the media had taken his remark out of context by expecting changes.)

Even today with those artificial hips and at the age of 70, wouldn't he be still more of a success in the West Indies than some of the snivelling, long-haired, money-conscious yobbos that now represent England?

John Junor, columnist, on Bill Edrich, Middlesex and England, in the *Sunday Express*, 1976.

One is always a little nervous when watching England bat.

Peter May, chairman of selectors, 1984.

England won't improve in world terms until the younger players rediscover some professional pride.

Bob Taylor, England wicketkeeper, in *Standing Up, Standing Back*, 1985.

The modern cricketer is not an ogre, nor is he deliberately obstructive. Although in most cases it would be unfair to dismiss him as a spoilt brat, he is too often lazy, ill-disciplined and reluctant to put in the effort and dedication commensurate with the wages he is earning. He has a very low boredom threshold with a constant need to be told what to do with his time.

Bob Willis, England fast bowler, in *Lasting the Pace*, 1985.

Another day another dolour.

Matthew Engel, *The Guardian*, on life with England in the West Indies in 1985/6.

If we had shown the kind of attitude and guts during the war that our cricketers have in the West Indies, Hitler would have walked all over us.

Brian Close, former England captain, 1986.

If you want cosmetics, go to Boots.

England's captain, **David Gower**, responding to press criticism for not holding net practice in sub-standard conditions, West Indies tour, 1986.

What do they expect me to do? Walk round with a T-shirt with 'I'm in Charge' on it?

David Gower, responding to the selectors' doubts about his laid-back captaincy style, 1986. He printed one up anyway, and handed it to his successor, Mike Gatting, later that year.

He is too laid-back, perhaps too self-centred. Gower lacks the authority to impose his will when senior players are questioning his tactics. And he cannot whip his men into renewed efforts when their spirits are flagging. That was only too evident when England were in the West Indies in 1986. They just gave up.

Clive Lloyd, on David Gower's leadership, 1988.

England have only three major problems – they can't bat, they can't bowl and they can't field.

Martin Johnson's famed assessment in *The Independent* at the start of England's tour of Australia 1986/7. England's recovery to win the Ashes later led Johnson to remark: 'Right quote; wrong team.'

Too much cricket will kill cricketers before they are ready to be killed.

Mike Gatting, a victorious England captain in Australia, 1987.

I may not be a good enough player, or have the right leadership qualities, but at least I deserve an explanation of where I went wrong.

Chris Cowdrey, Kent batsman, dropped as captain after only one Test, England vs West Indies, 1988.

It's about time some big, big men started being honest with themselves.

Viv Richards, West Indies captain, pointing the finger at England's cricket management, after Cowdrey's Test had continued a chop-and-change summer, 1988.

He bowls too many wicket-taking balls.

Micky Stewart, England team manager, analysing Phil DeFreitas's bowling in 1988. Test statistics hardly bore out Stewart's theory.

I can remember some good Saturdays against the West Indies before – the only trouble is that the Thursdays, Fridays, Mondays and Tuesdays were a bit of a disaster.

John Emburey, refusing to become carried away after a successful first day under his leadership, second Test vs West Indies, 1988. He was a good judge.

You should play every game as if it's your last, but perform well enough to make sure it's not.

John Emburey's reflections upon replacing Mike Gatting, albeit briefly, as England captain, 1988.

Hell's teeth, I was a bloody greyhound next to this lot.

Geoffrey Boycott, on England's pedestrian batting display vs New Zealand, 1988.

I am not necessarily forecasting success for England. There is no reason why, in a country where it is often impossible to have building work done or a motor car serviced properly, its sporting tradesmen should perform any better.

Graeme Wright, *Wisden* editor, previewing the 1989 season.

I told the fellas we had to get a little angry in our cricket. I told them this was not a tea party.

Peter Roebuck, captain of the England eleven beaten in Holland, 1989, in a one-day game. They won the second match, but the initial defeat discouraged speculation that Roebuck might become the next England captain.

You bowled everyone at the wrong end, didn't you.

The remark, from **Phil Edmonds**, in the Lord's press conference that encouraged David Gower, on the end of another thrashing from Australia, to leave early for the theatre, 1989.

It would be unkind to David Gower to say that he was second best or that the results would have been any different. While the England bowlers bowled as they did, it didn't matter who was the captain. The result would have been the same four-nil stuffing.

Ossie Wheatley, at the end of the summer, as the veto of Mike Gatting as England captain was followed by a 4-0 defeat against Australia under Gower's leadership.

This TCCB veto is ridiculous. There was so much stick flying around when England lost the Ashes that at least Ted Dexter and Micky Stewart should have been able to defend their own decisions. Things don't change very quickly. I remember going along to Lord's 20 years ago as captain, with four selectors, to choose the side to tour Australia. When we sat down there must have been 15 people around the table, all having their say.

Raymond Illingworth on the Wheatley veto of Mike Gatting's captaincy in the wake of the row with the Pakistani umpire, Shakoor Rana, and allegations of late-night high-jinks, 1989.

England's 17th choice.

Micky Stewart, England team manager, did not exactly inspire confidence with this description of the Kent seamer, Alan Igglesden, selected for an injury-stricken side at The Oval, England vs Australia, 1989.

We had to go out and field late in the day. I set no sort of example to the side, but I think they understood. I was miles away, wondering what on earth I had done to deserve suddenly being judged incapable.

David Gower, discovering that he had lost his England touring place as well as the captaincy, 1989.

We were going to sack him anyhow.

Alec Bedser, England's chairman of selectors, discussing David Gower's resignation as England captain, Ashes series, 1989.

I sense a lower level of satisfaction than I would want among many English players at Test and county level. Players settle for just enough to get another contract.

Bobby Simpson, Australian coach, 1989.

We try to maintain the intensity of practice. You still rely on the willingness of the individual.

English faults, as perceived by Australia's coach, **Bobby Simpson**, 1989.

In 1964 I was allowed to turn up late for a tour because I was canvassing in a by-election in Cardiff.

Ted Dexter (Conservative, lost deposit), justifying Ian Botham's late arrival on the New Zealand tour so that he could fulfil a pantomime season in *Jack and the Beanstalk*.

Who can forget Malcolm Devon?

Ted Dexter, chairman of the England committee, 1989. Derbyshire supporters responded to his renaming of Devon Malcolm by calling him Ted Lord.

I'm convinced that what the public want are heroic performances and chivalrous conduct. and like most of them, I don't believe winning is everything.

Ted Dexter, upon his appointment as chairman of the England committee, 1989.

Onward Gower's cricketers
Striving for a score,
With our bats uplifted,
We want more and more,
Alderman the master,
Represents the foe,
Forward into battle,
Down the pitch we go.

First verse of 'Onward Gower's Soldiers', which **Ted Dexter**, chairman of selectors, penned before the third Test against Australia at Edgbaston in an attempt to raise spirits, and advised players to sing in the bath at the top of their voices, 1989.

What chance do we have of producing a new pace talent when a county like Derbyshire go into a match with an attack comprising a West Indian, a South African and a Dutchman?

The question, from **Ted Dexter**, chairman of the England committee, that so infuriated Derbyshire in 1989. The 'West Indian', Alan Warner, was born in Birmingham; Simon Base, allegedly a South African, was from Kent. Even Ole Mortensen was not Dutch – he was a Dane.

I'm not aware of any mistakes I've made this summer.

Ted Dexter, after a disastrous England Ashes summer, 1989.

There is a modern fashion for designer stubble and some people believe it to be very attractive. But it is aggravating to others and we shall be looking at the whole question of people's facial hair.

Ted Dexter, responding to TCCB accusations of 'scruffy England' following defeat in India, 1993.

He crossed the line between eccentricity and idiocy far too often for someone who was supposed to be running English cricket.

Ian Botham on Ted Dexter, *My Autobiography*, 1995.

I wouldn't say I have reached the stage where I am going to tell the selectors to stuff it, but ... I have got as far as saying sod 'em.

David Gower, denied an England recall until he had shown consistent form for Hampshire, 1990.

The Phil Tufnell Fielding Academy.

Our fielding has been the worst I have ever seen in all forms of cricket.

The verdict of **Graham Gooch**, their captain, on England's efforts in the 1990/1 Ashes series.

It was perhaps fortunate that Gower – who had attended the team's Christmas Day fancy-dress parade as Biggles – and Morris abandoned their original idea of dropping a water bomb on the ground.

Mike Selvey, *The Guardian*, on the joy ride in two Tiger Moths during England's match against Queensland in Carrara which cost David Gower and John Morris a fine of £1000.

While it is appreciated that the incident was intended to be no more than a prank, the management and captain considered it to be immature, ill-judged and ill-timed.

Peter Lush, England's tour manager, levying a £1000 fine for their Tiger Moth escapade.

For all their dereliction of duty in leaving without permission a game in which they were playing, it was a harsh penalty for an essentially light-hearted prank, reflecting all too accurately the joyless nature of the tour.

Wisden's verdict on the Tiger Moth jaunt by David Gower and John Morris, to greet Robin Smith's century at Carrara, Queensland vs England, 1990/1.

I just thought they were a couple of joy-riders.

Micky Stewart's response when informed of the players' identities.

Some players found it a shock – the type of cricket played here, the standard, the approach, the attitude.

Micky Stewart, England team manager, explaining the Ashes flop in 1990/1.

A fart competing with thunder.

England in Australia in 1990/1, as assessed by their captain **Graham Gooch**.

I'm probably best out of touring. Nobody seems to smile any more.

Ian Botham, after England's heavy defeat in Australia in 1991.

My biggest failure of man-management since I became England captain.

David Gower, as perceived by **Graham Gooch** in *Captaincy*, 1992.

In some quarters my approach is described as a joyless regime. Well, I can think of many a joyless day with England when we were being soundly thrashed because it was felt that flair and big-match experience would suffice.

Graham Gooch, in defence of his work-ethic regime, in *Captaincy*, 1992.

I've picked my team for the wedding and you could say that Graham Gooch is not in it. He wasn't selected – he's too old.

David Gower, omitted from the India tour, before his wedding at Winchester Cathedral, 1992.

In the old days men were sometimes omitted because they did not buy their round at the bar; these days they are more likely to be left out because they do.

Matthew Engel, in his notes to the 1993 *Wisden*, on the omission of David Gower from Graham Gooch's England party in India, 1992/3.

How have I survived in 117 Tests without this wretched commitment?

David Gower, in his final Hampshire season, 1993.

Is not David Gower the romantic gentleman of countless romantic novels, the young lord into whose arms every self-respecting house-maid – when there were housemaids – dreamed of casting herself? 'Oh, young master, Sir, you are a one,' she said, laughing softly.

William Rees-Mogg, in *The Times*, upon the differences between David Gower and Graham Gooch, after Gooch had omitted Gower from England's 1993 tour of India.

Is not Gooch his romantic opposite, the strong, silent, surly game-keeper ... he will express himself in profound but brief sentences of unintelligible dialect ... he would weave daisy chains for delicate purposes in his big hands.

William Rees-Mogg, in *The Times*, warming to his theme, 1993.

I've not had much of a postbag on the matter. This is just a knee-jerk reaction.

Ted Dexter, chairman of the England committee, dismissing protest by MCC members over David Gower's omission from the Indian tour party, 1992/3.

We were treated like recalcitrant fifth-formers.

Dennis Oliver, MCC rebel, after a meeting in the Long Room with the MCC president, Dennis Silk. Silk, who had spent a lifetime in the public schools, failed to persuade the rebels not to force a special meeting over Gower's omission.

Everyone thinks they can do a better job than the selectors, but I think the MCC people are now carrying things a bit far. There must be better ways of spending £17,000.

Ted Dexter, chairman of the England committee, 1993.

They are either incompetent, inert or inept, or all three. They have made a mockery of their responsibilities.

Dennis Oliver's verdict on the selectors, 1993.

Forty-year-old John Emburey is in India because he is a friend of Graham Gooch. Thirty-five-year-old David Gower is not because he isn't.

Dennis Oliver, speaking in favour of his motion of no confidence in the England selectors at an MCC special meeting. Age had been given as one reason for Gower's omission from the India party, 1993.

Try telling Montgomery that he could not pick the side he wanted.

Field Marshal Lord Bramall, opposing the MCC no confidence motion, 1993.

Forty-three per cent – enough to win a general election.

David Gower, musing on the defeat of the no confidence motion at the MCC special meeting, following his omission from the India tour, 1993.

The other day it took me 45 minutes between waking up and thinking 'I have got to go and play cricket today' and actually doing something about it.

David Gower, considering retirement after the loss of his England place, 1993.

This is one of the worst things to happen in cricket history.

Dennis Oliver, MCC pro-Gower campaigner, on the batsman's premature retirement, 1993.

We didn't read the mat conditions at all.

Keith Fletcher after England's defeat against Holland on a matting wicket, 1993.

I've no objections to Holland joining our one-day competitions – but they can't play on these mats!

Keith Fletcher, team manager of the England XI beaten, for the second time in four years, by Holland, Haarlem, 1993.

I'm just carrying out TCCB regulations – a hard dry pitch which will last for five days. The last time I prepared a four-day pitch they weren't slow to let me know that it had cost them £150,000 in lost revenue.

Andy Atkinson, Warwickshire's groundsman, in a parting shot to English cricket authorities before the Ashes Test at Edgbaston, 1993. Atkinson was about to take up a new post in South Africa. England expected a seaming pitch; instead they had to make an emergency call-up of John Emburey.

They need to stop choosing players by the colour of their eyes.

Maureen Beagley, pest controller, canvassed on the state of the England team, 2-0 down in the Ashes series, 1993.

It is to be assumed that Mr Trevor Bailey was unavailable for selection.

Byron Denning, Glamorgan scorer, announcing England's 13 for the Trent Bridge Test over the PA at Cardiff, 1993. Nasser Hussain had become the sixth Essex player to be picked that summer, bringing charges of regional bias. Glamorgan, second in the championship, had no representatives.

And once again Essex are now in deep trouble.

Trevor Bailey, ex Essex and England all-rounder, watching Graham Gooch's dismissal in the Trent Bridge Test quicken an England collapse. Bailey could be forgiven for his momentary confusion, 1993.

I can't bat, can't bowl and can't field these days. I've every chance of being picked for England.

Ray East, former Essex spinner, before leading Minor Counties side Suffolk against his old county in the NatWest Trophy, Bury St Edmunds, 1993.

Meekness is a nice word. Wimpish is the one I would use. The England side recently has had no spunk about it.

Ian Botham, asked if the England side was 'too meek', Ashes series, 1993.

All the never-say-die qualities of a kamikaze pilot.

England's cricketers, as seen by an **Australian journalist**.

Dad had plenty to say, but he was loyal to the boy as we would expect him to be.

Ted Dexter's comments about Micky Stewart's advocacy of his son, Alec, as England captain, after Graham Gooch resigned midway through the 1993 Ashes series. Michael Atherton was appointed instead and Stewart was livid that he might be left open to charges of nepotism.

I thought suggestions of a father and son business were in the past. For six years as England manager I avoided the words 'dad' and 'son', much to the merriment of the media. The only thing I have ever been concerned about is English cricket.

Micky Stewart's reply, 1993.

Our most important task is to identify the talent to win games. Then we must stick with them.

Michael Atherton, three days into his first Test as England captain, 1993.

It's nice to go into the rest day as favourites. I might get some sleep.

Keith Fletcher, in Trinidad, 1994. England were bowled out for 46 in their second innings.

We were the better side for three days. Then we got blown away inside an hour.

England's captain, **Michael Atherton**, considering defeat in the Trinidad Test. England, needing 194 to win, were dismissed for 46 (their lowest Test score this century) as Curtly Ambrose took six for 22, 1993/4 tour.

I'm not going to tolerate a situation where we get some hang-up about Warne. We must play him emphatically, positively, and not develop a mentality that says 'where are we going to score runs?' when he comes on to bowl.

Michael Atherton. Warne then took 20 wickets at an average of 9.5 runs each in the first two Ashes Tests, 1994.

As good a cricketing mind as there has ever been.

Sir Colin Cowdrey on Ray Illingworth, appointed as chairman of selectors, 1994.

I did once try to become a selector, but the application seemed to get blocked along the way.

Ray Illingworth, freshly appointed as England's chairman of selectors, at a youthful 62, explaining why his involvement with the national side had taken so long.

We have been running scared.

England's new chairman of selectors, **Ray Illingworth**, in his first day in the job, on the policy of playing six specialist batsmen, 1994.

He is one of our best batsmen. But I'm not going to tolerate part-time players who want to pick and choose which series they play in.

Ray Illingworth, assessing the likelihood of a Graham Gooch comeback, 1994.

Current players admired?
'None.'

Raymond Illingworth's response in a questionnaire in *The Cricketer* upon becoming chairman of England's selectors, 1994.

I fear he will be too keen to run the train-set all by himself.

Mike Brearley, in *The Observer*, upon Ray Illingworth's appointment as chairman of England selectors, 1994. (Brearley regarded Illingworth, nevertheless, as the shrewdest captain he had ever played against.)

I don't want players who need a shoulder to cry on.

Raymond Illingworth, justifying his decision to dispense with the England chaplain, Andrew Wingfield-Digby, 1994.

Providing a shoulder to cry on has never been a definition of my work. I agree with Mr Illingworth that our players should be tough. I know of no tougher person to walk the face of the earth than my boss – Jesus Christ.

Andrew Wingfield-Digby, who was still to be allowed occasional dressing-room visits on an unofficial basis, 1994.

I see it as a kind of spiritual battleground, a spiritual test.

Wingfield-Digby again, 1994.

If they're not going to work hard, they're not going to play.

Gospel according to **Ray Illingworth**, newly appointed as chairman of selectors, 1994.

Why are people too old to play Test cricket at 37, but too young to select the team until they are collecting their pension?

Ian Botham, 1994, objecting to an England selection trio (Illingworth, Titmus, Bolus) all over 60.

You are not too old to play cricket at 35-plus. But you've got to be about 60-plus if you want to administer the game or administer the team at international level. So you walk around a field for about 20 years and forget everything you've learned. It doesn't make any sense.

Ian Botham, 1995.

Questions have been asked at Lord's these past few days to which it is hard to find reassuring answers. Such as 'Why is DeFreitas not told it is out of order to wear a watch?' 'Why do England wear their beach clothes on the balcony?' And 'Why don't England captains shave in the morning?'

John Woodcock, in *The Times*, finding much to annoy him in England's standards of dress against South Africa at Lord's, 1994. The appointment of Raymond Illingworth as chairman of selectors was held by some to be at the root of it.

He has a good cricket brain and I want to give him every opportunity to use it.

Raymond Illingworth, England's new chairman of selectors, explaining why he would insist that his captain, Michael Atherton, took a balanced attack of five bowlers into the next Test, 1994.

If I had my way I would take him to Traitor's Gate and personally hang, draw and quarter him.

Ian Botham on Ray Illingworth, 1994.

If I were being polite, I'd say that Gatt is a little long in the tooth, somewhat immobile and carries too much weight. But I prefer straight talking, so I'm saying what I really think. Gatt, is too old, too slow, and too fat.

Geoffrey Boycott, in *The Sun*, after Mike Gatting's selection for the Ashes tour, 1994/5.

Fraser never looks over-lively and once or twice in the West Indies we thought he might not make it back to the end of his run.

Raymond Illingworth, chairman of selectors, defending Angus Fraser's omission from the 1994/5 Ashes tour. Martin McCague's return home with shin splints soon brought Fraser a call-up.

Fraser did bugger all last summer. I can't believe there is serious talk from the captain about drafting him in. If he's suggesting that Fraser plays in the first Test, I'll be on the phone to him like a rocket.

Raymond Illingworth, grouching in England at a sportswriters' lunch at suggestions that Michael Atherton might draft Fraser, a replacement on the 1994/5 tour of Australia, straight into the Test side. Fraser made a nonsense of Illingworth's assessment that he was over the hill by taking a record-equalling 27 wickets in the West Indies three years later.

He's team manager isn't he? He nicks a few catches in practice.

Raymond Illingworth, chairman of selectors, deriding Keith Fletcher at a sportswriters' lunch in England, while Fletcher, the team manager in Australia, prepared the side for the first Test in Brisbane, 1994/5.

England trained and grass grew at the MCG yesterday, two activities virtually indistinguishable from each other in tempo, but each with its own fascination.

Greg Baum, *Melbourne Age*, unimpressed by England's practice sessions on the 1994/5 tour of Australia.

I tried so hard to dig deep, but in the end I just couldn't do it. I'm completely knackered.

England's captain, **Michael Atherton**, reaching the end of the 1994/5 Ashes series, in which all his efforts could not prevent a 3-1 Test defeat.

The place for gnomes is in my back garden.

Geoffrey Boycott, TV pundit, as England struggled under the management of Keith Fletcher, nicknamed 'The Gnome', in Australia, 1994/5.

I don't think he could motivate a stuffed mullet at the moment.

Allan Lamb (in cabaret with Ian Botham), after England's 3-1 Ashes defeat under Fletcher's team managership, 1995.

There's some good red wine, good white wine, the food and the sunshine ...

Mike Gatting, fresh from his first Test century for nearly eight years (vs Australia in Adelaide, 1995), explaining why only he and Graham Gooch, the tour's elder statesmen, had stayed fit in the Ashes series. Seven Englishmen returned home early.

We have made no progress here at all. This tour has proved that we have to invest more in younger players and I implore the selectors to do so.

Michael Atherton, irritating as well as imploring the selectors, after the series defeat on the 1994/5 Australian tour.

It's not a captain's job to go around criticizing selectors.

Raymond Illingworth, chairman of those selectors, dragging his heels over Atherton's reappointment, 1995.

A youth policy should be the preserve of the England A team.

Test selector **Fred Titmus**, finding fault with Michael Atherton's call for England to turn to youth, following another Ashes defeat, 1995.

Contrary to what you may have read elsewhere, Ray Illingworth, Keith Fletcher and Mike Atherton are united in their efforts to build a successful England team.

TCCB news update to county members. It arrived in mid-April 1995, after Fletcher had been sacked, and as Illingworth delayed Atherton's reappointment.

Michael Atherton had a rotten job taking over the captaincy from Graham Gooch and he was treated like a child by long-range criticism in the winter.

Patrick Whittingdale, withdrawing his city investment company's sponsorship of English cricket in protest at Raymond Illingworth's 'sniping from afar' at his captain, 1995.

One began to feel that the right adjective was the one never attached to him in his playing days: amateurish.

Matthew Engel, editor of *Wisden*, on Raymond Illingworth's outspoken first year as chairman of the England selectors, 1995.

Ray and his panel did a brilliant job as far as I'm concerned. It was a privilege for me to captain such a good side.

Allan Wells, England A captain in India, learning the correct public tone to England's chairman of selectors, Raymond Illingworth, 1995.

He's frightened of his own shadow.

Denis Compton, on Ray Illingworth's style as chairman of selectors, 1995.

He's not a motivator – he's just a whinger.

Allan Lamb on Raymond Illingworth – in *Beef and Lamb in a Stew* video, 1995.

In any walk of life, you cannot create a winning team if you make the captain grovel.

Patrick Whittingdale again, upon Illingworth's delayed reappointment of his captain until 'a few matters had been cleared up', 1995.

I don't care what is said within the four walls of a dressing room or a selection meeting. But that's where it must begin and end. It should not finish up on the back pages of newspapers.

Michael Atherton, in David Norrie's biography, *Athers*, confirming his irritation with Raymond Illingworth's media-friendly reign as chairman of selectors, 1997.

If I were chairman of selectors, I wouldn't pick anyone over 25.

Denis Compton, at 76, proving that old selectors do not have to mean an old team, 1995. He then advocated Allan Wells, well into his 30s, as captain.

I suppose you've got to start with Pontius Pilate Illingworth ... the man who covers his backside ... he's a whinger not a motivator.

Ian Botham, asked what was wrong with English cricket, 1995.

I'm not against the cut ... I'm not against the hook.

Raymond Illingworth, chairman of England's selectors, as England's batsmen fast ran out of safe shots during a heavy defeat against the West Indies, Headingley Test, 1995.

We'll have to get the Bowie knife out now. We're becoming blood brothers.

Raymond Illingworth, England chairman of selectors, about his blossoming relationship with skipper Michael Atherton, in the wake of a 2-2 series against the West Indies, 1995.

ILLINGWORTH (n) A measure of rich humbug, prob originating in Yorkshire. Used figuratively of person who claims credit for success but blames others for failure. Examples: any interview with the chairman of England's cricket selectors.

Private Eye, 1995.

What we require are selectors who are more in touch with the dynamics of the modern game, ideally Test players of the recent past who are able to communicate more effectively because they have played the same game.

Michael Atherton, during England's Ashes defeat in 1995. His fellow selectors – Raymond Illingworth, Fred Titmus and Brian Bolus – were all the wrong side of 60.

If Illy picked all his friends we'd never win a game.

Vic Isaacs, secretary of the Association of County Cricket Scorers, enraged by Raymond Illingworth's appointment of Malcolm Ashton, an old BBC buddy, to score on England's tour of South Africa, 1995.

The original British Bulldog.

Bob Woolmer (South Africa's coach) on himself, 1995.

I really don't know how we let him escape.

Dennis Silk, chairman of the TCCB, upon South Africa's England-born coach, Bob Woolmer, 1996. (Silk had a short memory: they chose Illingworth instead.)

He has just one asset – pace. That apart, he is a nonentity in cricketing terms.

Devon Malcolm, in the view of England's bowling coach, **Peter Lever**, after an abortive attempt to change Malcolm's run-up and bowling action, tour of South Africa, 1995.

He tried to bowl the way they wanted him to bowl and hit the side of the net. At gnat's pace. Then he went back to bowling his old style and he bowled fast and swung it.

Graham Thorpe's assessment on Malcolm. Thorpe was facing Malcolm in the nets when attempts were made to change his style, 1995/6 tour of South Africa.

There was an urgent need to be cheery and upbeat on that tour, but from the moment he got on the team bus every morning, our Raymond was moaning – about the traffic, the weather, the hotel, the breakfast – it was all so negative.

Dermot Reeve, in *Winning Ways*, 1996, about Raymond Illingworth's attitude to touring Pakistan during the 1996 World Cup.

By the end of the World Cup, nobody among the England players could take him seriously and we all wanted him out of the job. He was too negative, far too dogmatic and he lacked any awareness of how much the game had changed.

Dermot Reeve, expanding upon Raymond Illingworth, *Winning Ways*, 1996.

At the 1996 World Cup, the England squad resembled a bad-tempered grandmother attending a teenage rave. Unable to comprehend what was happening – on the field or off it – the players just lingered, looking sullen and incompetent.

Matthew Engel, *Wisden*, 1997.

His captaincy lacked drive, purpose and flair. Add to that his passive body language and you're struggling when the team is up against it.

Dermot Reeve's assessment of Michael Atherton's captaincy in the 1996 World Cup.

If our team keeps going the way it has been doing then our game will die. All you will have left will be village and club cricket.

Dennis Silk, chairman of the TCCB, dismayed by England's defeat against Sri Lanka in the World Cup quarter-final, 1996.

Atherton lacks that one vital ingredient an England captain needs to survive. Miracles.

Graham Gooch, who as a former England captain ought to know, after England's dismal performance in the 1996 World Cup.

He wants everyone's job.

Raymond Illingworth, sensing a rival in David Graveney, 1996.

Whoever takes over my job as chairman of selectors, the one thing he must not do is be a yes man to Michael Atherton.

Raymond Illingworth, who tended to be a 'no' man, 1996.

Captaining a Test side these days is an anxious, wearing, unending business, made all the more so by the hype and scrutiny and bally-hoo and, in England's case, the criticism and condescension that accompanies it.

John Woodcock, *The Times*, 1996.

You feel you're not having an influence. You go from thinking you're making progress to realizing you're going nowhere. Then you get frustrated and dejected ... and rejected. I was criticized for my body language. It was too negative. Now Athers is getting the same stick.

Graham Gooch, on the task facing an England captain, 1996.

I intend to maintain my good form of this season at county level and fully intend to justify my swift recall to the England fold for the winter tour.

Chris Lewis pleads his case in a letter to *The Times* after England dropped him in the wake of the 'punctured tyre' incident. He wasn't picked, 1996.

Lewis turned up substantially late for a Test match. His explanation is that he had a puncture – it is irrelevant if we believe him. Chris did not try and ring or contact us.

David Lloyd, England's coach, on the dropping of Lewis from the one-day squad, 1996.

Doug, the problem with English cricket is you.

Mark Nicholas's chances of becoming the first chief executive of the England and Wales Cricket Board were fairly slim. After this outburst against Doug Insole, one of the most influential men in English cricket, and one of his interviewers to boot, they were zero, 1996.

I can't wait to leave this place. Whenever you order room service, you are told to repeat your order.

England player summing up the tourists' unhappiness with life in Zimbabwe, 1996.

December 19: Zim score 376 today. Bulawayo is like the film *Groundhog Day*. Absolutely nothing to do. I go to my room and work out Take That's 'Back for Good' on the guitar and after realizing I'm getting sad I go to bed at 10.15.

John Crawley, diary of Zimbabwe, *Sunday Telegraph*, 1996.

A document of such melancholy and despair that he confessed to being homesick before he'd even left London.

Ian Wooldridge, in the *Daily Mail*, lambasting the tone of John Crawley's 1996 Zimbabwe tour diary, as featured in the *Sunday Telegraph*, 1997.

Professional sport has to be seen in the context of a person's whole life. There has to be a balance in their lives, taking into account their physical, mental and spiritual health.

Andrew Wingfield-Digby, England chaplain, unsettled by England's siege mentality in Zimbabwe, 1996.

I'm getting dangerously close to ordering a full bottle of wine with my dinner.

Jack Russell, virtually a teetotaller, out of favour during England's tour of Zimbabwe, 1996.

Soft cricket and soft cricketers.

Raymond Illingworth, ex-chairman of selectors, sniping at England from his retirement flat in Spain after the Zimbabwe debacle, 1996.

I need to know where I stand. I am not prepared to let my name and reputation be dragged down by this team if I have no real input. I would be guilty by association.

The *News of the World* outburst that **Ian Botham**, technical advisor to England's bowlers, sought to deny in Zimbabwe, 1996.

Forget the White Rhino. Save the Poms!

Banner in Harare as England's tour of Zimbabwe collapsed into chaos, 1996.

He's a friend of mine and I'd never have appointed him.

Tony Lewis, 1996, on David Lloyd, the England coach during the side's failings in Zimbabwe.

They should not be let into the sun in New Zealand, but brought home in disgrace.

Terry Dicks, Tory MP, after England lost the one-day series against Zimbabwe 3-0, 1997.

It is a defining moment. I just ask England's fans to bear with us because we are determined to get things right.

Tim Lamb, the England and Wales Cricket Board's chief executive, after England's 3-0 defeat in the one-day series against Zimbabwe had ensured that the new board, in existence for a matter of hours, started 1997 at the bottom of the pile.

You wouldn't last long in my business if you just said everything is cyclical.

Lord MacLaurin, considering the stock excuse for English cricket, during the unsuccessful tour of Zimbabwe, 1996.

I want to warn you that the world is going to end by the year 2000.

An 88-year-old **Roman Catholic priest**, bearing an 8ft high cross, to Michael Atherton (who had enough problems after England's tour of Zimbabwe). By then, England had moved on to Palmerston North, and the early stages of a more productive New Zealand tour, 1997.

I was very proud and pleased with the way we approached this game, and that we stuck at it.

David Lloyd, England's coach. The match? England's 90-run defeat by New Zealand A, 1997.

I tugged at my England shirt and shouted at my team-mates 'remember the three lions'. I didn't know what else to do.

Jack Russell, dismayed by a feeble-minded defeat against New Zealand A between the first and second Tests, 1997.

My batting is a bit of a joke and has deteriorated since I left high school, and I became known as a little prick who could run in and bowl fast. But I did bat for 4 hours and 10 minutes to score 25 and bore the tits off Pakistan in Faisalabad a few years ago.

Danny Morrison, the world-record holder for ducks in Test cricket, after holding out against England for nearly three hours in the Auckland Test, 1997. Morrison's unbroken last wicket stand with century-maker Nathan Astle was worth 106 and ensured a New Zealand draw.

It was a terrific effort from their last batsmen and a terrific effort from our lads.

David Lloyd, England coach, putting on a brave face after Morrison's resistance, 1997.

English cricket is an irrelevance on and off the ground. And that is not the ramblings of an Anglophobe. It is a statement of fact.

Mike Coward, Australian cricket writer, 1997.

I look at the team on paper and think they are good players, but they aren't tough enough or hungry enough on the field. They don't play as a team, they worry about themselves. When you're out there, you don't feel that you've got 11 guys against you.

Mark Waugh, considering the Ashes tour in *ABC Cricket*, 1997.

The refuse tip has been overflowing with talented but complex characters – Lewis, Ramprakash, Tufnell, Hick – who, with sensitive, imaginative handling could all have produced so much more. But no, we go on blindly stating that 'If three lions on your chest doesn't motivate you, nothing will' and dismiss people with, 'He's just a show pony', without ever comprehending why they fail to deliver. I'll tell you why. Because they're all wracked with self doubt.

Simon Hughes, *A Lot of Hard Yakka*, 1997.

When the pressure point comes, English cricketers crumble.

Shane Warne, Australian, 1997.

One of the worst captains we've had since the war. For him to get Peter May's record is a travesty, but there is only one man he should thank and that's Illingworth.

Fred Titmus, former England selector, in bitter mood as Michael Atherton surpassed Peter May's record number of Tests as England captain, 1997.

We've thought about bowling underarm in practice so he can knock hell out of every ball.

David Lloyd, England's coach, on Michael Atherton's batting problems, 1997.

I didn't see Peter May, but even Ray Illingworth said he was tremendous. For him to say that about somebody with three initials who had a southern background and went to public school, he must have been good.

Michael Atherton on Peter May, 1997.

Cricket is our national summer game, but it is run selfishly as if it is a private recreation. It's such a shame.

Mark Nicholas, quoted in *The Botham Report*, 1997.

Do we really need more gimmickry and exhibitionism to make the game 'relevant' to youngsters who might otherwise be sniffing glue and nicking video recorders?

Michael Henderson, *The Times*, 1997.

It's Saturday, it's eight o'clock, it's the lottery.

Alec Stewart, in wise-cracking mood, greeting Nasser Hussain to the crease before the abandonment of the 1998 Jamaica Test on the first morning because of a dangerous pitch.

If I had stayed out there much longer, I would have looked like the lady in the French court.

Alec Stewart, for once far from politically correct, after the Jamaican Test had been abandoned because of a dangerous pitch. The bruised lady in the French court had made accusations of violence against Geoffrey Boycott, 1998.

Never sacrifice a strength to a compromise.

Alec Stewart, explaining why he would rather open England's batting with
Michael Atherton than keep wicket, West Indies tour, 1998.

It can therefore be laid down as an absolute principle in team selection that the best wicketkeeper, irrespective of all other
considerations, should always be chosen.

MCC Coaching Manual – which, as Alec Stewart was in better form than
Jack Russell, offered an alternative view.

A 'keeper should be captain only on the rarest of occasions in first-
class cricket. The mental strains of keeping wicket are just too
much.

Bob Taylor's view, expressed in *Standing Up, Standing Back*, 1985, only
highlighted England's dilemma.

I've seen so many players come in with the attitude of enjoying it
while it lasts. I've always wanted to be there long-term.

Angus Fraser, one of England's 'survivors', in *Fraser's Tour Diaries*, 1998.

I don't want to think at the end of my career that I didn't captain
England simply because I was misunderstood.

Nasser Hussain, passed over for the England captaincy in favour of Alec
Stewart amid innuendo about selfishness and hot temper, 1998.

Because I'm not the sort who can breeze up to someone I barely
know, some people say, 'oh, Nasser Hussain, he's a bit up himself'.
But often I'm surrounded by people who have done a hell of a lot
more than me.

Nasser Hussain, England batsman, 1998.

People say I'm still angry with the world. I'm not angry with the
world at all. I'm doing exactly what I want to do: contributing Test
hundreds to the England cause. All I'm trying to do is get every
ounce out of my ability.

Nasser Hussain, on his 'bad boy' reputation, 1998.

I just wish that most of 'em weren't so bloody arrogant.

Experienced county player on the England Test side, 1998.

They seem to be making all the same mistakes ... all these 40-year-olds in charge who reckon they know everything about the game.

Raymond Illingworth, back in chuntering form at Headingley, with England 2-0 down in the three-match Texaco Trophy series against South Africa, 1998.

... And here's to a successful
new century ...

14

The End of the Century

No longer should we allow international cricketers to appear on our television sets to be interviewed unshaven, chewing gum and altogether looking slovenly. These habits are to be deplored and should be eliminated.

Lord MacLaurin, chairman of the ECB, in an open letter to Jagmohan Dalmiya, the ICC chairman. Lord MacLaurin had been apalled by on-field behaviour during the West Indies vs England series, 1998.

You have to hand it to Lord MacLaurin. He may not have improved English cricket at all, or have the faintest idea how to do it, but at least he understands the basics of gents' tailoring. No international team in the world has shinier buttons.

Marcus Berkmann, Wisden Cricket Monthly, on the chairman of the ECB, 1999.

He just emanates joy, the kind of joy that comes from somebody who is filled with the Holy Spirit.

The religious conviction of Jonty Rhodes did not please everyone; some wondered how it fitted with his perceived gamesmanship. His South African captain, **Hansie Cronje**, was impressed, though, 1999.

I really believe that Brian needs psychiatric help. He needs to learn the part he has to play in real life, not in the world he has in his head.

West Indies captain Brian Lara, judged by the former West Indian quick, **Michael Holding**, 1999.

I'm in charge of this game. You'll stand where I want you to. If you don't stand there, there won't be a game.

Arjuna Ranatunga to the Australian umpire, Ross Emerson, in Adelaide, 1999. Ranatunga was insisting that Emerson stood up to the stumps, in an effort to protect his leg-spinner, Muttiah Muralitharan, who had just been called for throwing, 1999.

Your bahviour today has been appalling for a country captain.

Alec Stewart's admonishment (picked up by the stump mic) to Sri Lankan captain Arjuna Ranatunga during the notorious one-day international in Adelaide, 1999. Sri Lankan protests at the calling for Muttiah Muralitharan for throwing had caused play to be suspended.

He must think he has the best eyes in the whole world.

Arjuna Rantunga's condemnation of Ross Emerson, Australian umpire, after he called Muttiah Muralitharan for throwing in Adelaide, 1999.

Murali is being tormented because somebody else decided to play God.

Ranjit Fernando, Sri Lankan manager, offering his criticism of the same incident, 1999.

You are my favourite player. Please take it as a token of my appreciation for you taking the time to meet me. There are no strings attached.

Shane Warne's version of his meting with 'John,' the Indian bookmaker, who offered money to Warne and Shane Warne in a Sri Lanka casino in 1994. Evidence of Warne to Pakistan match-rigging enquiry in Melbourne, 1999.

I lost the World Cup. Nobody died.

Lance Klusener, whose run out in a tied semi-final ended his heroic tournament disastrously, and sent Australia, not South Africa, into the World Cup final, 1999.

You've just dropped the World Cup.

Australia's **Steve Waugh**, batting against South Africa at Headingley. Waugh was as good as his word: Gibbs' dropping of Waugh, as he tried to throw up the catch in celebration, enabled Australia to qualify for the semi-finals, and go on to win the tournament, 1999.

I've never seen a bit of grass in Amsterdam.

Simon O'Donnell, Australian commentator and ex-international, during 1999 World Cup. O'Donnell was referring to Holland's widespread use of matting wickets, not their legal use of cannabis.

I no more want to be a European than I do an Eskimo.

Ian Botham, resisting England's pro-European political moves, 1999.

Buttock-clenchingly grim.

Michael Henderson, in the *Daily Telegraph*, on Graeme Hick's seventh England comeback, against New Zealand, 1999.

He has a cruciate problem, a left kneecap problem, left knee joint, feet obviously, and his Achilles tendons always develop huge blisters.

The state of Ian Botham, as seen by his physio **Dave Roberts**, on his last Botham Leukaemia Walk, 1999.

Why is Tufnell the most popular man in the team? Is it the Manuel factor, in which the most helpless member of the cast is most affectionately identified with?

Mike Brearley, a more cerebral type of England player, wrestling with the rapscallion popularity of Phil Tufnell among Test crowds, 1999. The Fawlty Towers imagery was apt – England were about to slip to the bottom of the Test rankings.

I don't mind seeing blood on the pitch.

Jason Gillespie, Australian fast bowler. Shortly afterwards, he did see blood – on the outfield – the result of a fielding collision with his captain, Steve Waugh, which put them both in hospital. Sri Lanka vs Australia, Kandy, 1999.

I love you Sachin. I was really sad on going through reports that you would never be able to play again and hence I am taking this extreme step.

Part of the suicide note from **Deepa Vasanthalaxmi**, an 18-year-old Indian orphan, who set fire to herself in the mistaken belief that Sachin Tendulkar's back injury would end his career, 1999.

It's not going to be old farts talking about cakes.

Talk Radio spokesman on their approach to cricket after winning the South Africa tour contract ahead of Test Match Special, 1999.

It is only ever against the Asian cricketers. Why not the others? Why not plan against Brett Lee when he bowls the faster one?

Shafqat Rana, secretary of Pakistan Cricket Board, angered by ICC's month-long ban on Shoaib Akhtar, Pakistan fast bowler, because of a suspect action, 2000.

And so the conflict and contradictions continued into a new century . . .

Index